普通高等学校规划教材

看看再说

Read Before You Speak

当代非英语专业口语教程

Oral English for Non-English Majors

张周易　曹顺发　主　编

人民交通出版社股份有限公司
China Communications Press Co.,Ltd.

内 容 提 要

本书讲述了14条迅速进入话语状态的有效途径，共分14章。本书所有语料均来自真实的生活语言环境，如电影、电视、广播、讲座以及交流等，各章先透彻地讲清该思路的来龙去脉，并用轻松幽默的语言进行案例分析，辅之相关的练习，这种“一条龙”式的精心设计有助于读者达到“看”了能“说”的目的。

本书可作为非英语专业研究生和本科生选修教材使用，也可供普通的英语爱好者使用。

图书在版编目（CIP）数据

看看再说：当代非英语专业口语教程/张周易，曹顺发主编．—北京：人民交通出版社股份有限公司，2014.8

ISBN 978-7-114-11587-5

Ⅰ.①看… Ⅱ.①张… ②曹… Ⅲ.①英语—口语—教材 Ⅳ.①H319.9

中国版本图书馆CIP数据核字（2012）第179924号

书　　名：看看再说：当代非英语专业口语教程
著 作 者：张周易　曹顺发
责任编辑：刘永芬　潘艳霞
出版发行：人民交通出版社股份有限公司
地　　址：（100011）北京市朝阳区安定门外外馆斜街3号
网　　址：http://www.ccpress.com.cn
销售电话：（010）59757973
总 经 销：人民交通出版社股份有限公司发行部
经　　销：各地新华书店
印　　刷：北京市密东印刷有限公司
开　　本：787×1092　1/16
印　　张：15
字　　数：345千
版　　次：2014年8月　第1版
印　　次：2014年8月　第1次印刷
书　　号：ISBN 978-7-114-11587-5
定　　价：34.00元
（有印刷、装订质量问题的图书由本公司负责调换）

前　言

在全民学英语的中国，其教学的各个环节（即：听说读写[译]）可谓耳熟能详，但其中的“说”，即口语大概人人都能说上几句，但十有八九并不流利。出现这一“短板”现象的原因不少，主要有如下三方面：

第一，同经济发达的国家和地区相比，我们缺乏更为真实的语言环境，另外，社会对学生口语技能方面的要求大都停留在证书上（如英语专业的四、八级，非英语专业的四、六级），而非其实际运用能力上（当然近年兴起的翻译资格证书似乎有所改变，但口译仍滞后于笔译）。

第二，尽管国内优秀的口语教材不断推出，但绝大多数仍将其重心放在语料的提供和语境的设置上，对学生真正需要“如何开口”的思路和方法介绍相对较少。

第三，从英语学习过程来看，学生主要是通过书本语料进行学习，导致其口语交流大量涌现书本上的“大词”或“大结构”，让人觉得不像是在“说话”或“交流”，时感“丈二和尚摸不着头脑”，甚至常有交流困难的囧状，对口语产生乐趣的学生似乎“凤毛麟角”。

正因为上述原因，多数学习者虽然学了多年英语（从小学到大学，甚至硕士、博士阶段），仍不能开口，也不敢开口。鉴于此，本书的编写目的便是着力解决以上问题。

首先，尽量使得本书的语料来源于真实的生活语言环境，如电影、电视、广播、讲座以及交流等“源头活水”。

其次，本书着重强调“如何开口”的思路和方法。学生在口语交流中出现的“失语症”或“不知所措”感有两方面因素，一是对别汉语文字文化的英语文化背景较为生疏，二是对英语（语言）能力的把握不够到位。本书从不同的角度和途径启动“说话机制”，尽量让学习者重拾信心，从交流中获得一定的乐趣，希望能收到“条条大路通罗马”之功效。

最后，通过丰富的语料，让读者感受到书面语和口头语之间应有的区别，努力做到不以此代彼，即能用简单的口语表达的，不必复杂化；此举既可以使人更亲切自然地表达自己的想法，同时还能迅速拉近与交谈者的距离；此外，口语还可以为学习者提供一个深入了解英语国家文化特殊视野的有效途径。学生若能通过边学边说明白这一点，对提高英语学习的积极性定能产生良好的效果。

本书能为广大英语学习者提供些许有益的帮助，至少可带给大家开口说英语的启发、乐趣和信心，我们同时也相信，只要通过不懈的努力，学习者定会学有所获，最终达到自己认准的目标。必须承认的是，编者均非母语人士，故水平有限，顾此失彼之处在所难免，敬请读者大家“看看再说”。

编　者

2014.2.16 于山城重庆

CONTENTS

Chapter 1 Cultural Similarities
文化相通

一、思路讲解

要想迅速而准确地获得口语表达思路,不妨从英汉文化相通的角度“入口”。

根据《现代汉语词典》[8],广义上的文化指的是:“人类在社会历史发展过程中所创造的物质财富和精神财富的总和,特别指精神财富,如文学、艺术、教育、科学等。”而狭义文化则指的是:“运用文字的能力及一般知识。”

语言是文化的载体,语言蕴含着文化的沉淀。要想成为英语口语高手,不应该只停留在语言层面上的学习,还应该更多地了解西方文化传统和习俗,努力挖掘暗藏在语言背后的文化背景,只有对英语的文化底蕴有着深厚的认识或者了解,才有望更好地理解语言,进而使用语言。这一思路让我们明白在语言学习过程中不应忽略对文化趋势的了解,口语的提高应该首先存储文化背景知识,再巩固知识结构并提高能力去应用知识,在学习英语的过程中,研究文化内涵能为语言的学习提供实际指导,做到忠于原民族语言的独特风韵,使交流与沟通更加自然、顺畅。

在了解英语文化背景的过程中,我们不难发现英汉表达的文化内涵存在着诸多巧合。英汉两个民族在历史发展过程中通过劳动创造了物质财富和精神财富,形成了自己的文化。两个民族在生产实践中掌握了许多对自然界认识的共同知识,积累了许多共同经验,因此反映在语言表达上往往有许多惊人的共同之处,这便是语言中的文化共性。王治奎教授[5]曾指出:“人类具有通性,各种文化有相似或共同之处。这些相似性或共同性在语言中必然会有所体现。”而这种共同性和相似性为大家学习语言,且为理解语言和掌握语言提供了捷径,也为较快组织英语口语表达语料提供思路。我们不妨看看如下一些表达:

far and near 远近
ups and downs 沉浮,盛衰,高低
to burn one's boat 破釜沉舟
to be on thin ice 如履薄冰
to pour oil on the fire 火上加油
to strike while the iron is hot 趁热打铁
to lose/to save one's face 丢/保面子
Walls have ears. 隔墙有耳。
Look before you leap. 三思而后行。
It's never too old to learn. 活到老,学到老。
An eye for an eye, a tooth for a tooth. 以眼还眼,以牙还牙。

以上例证便是英汉语言中的一些内涵意义“庶几近之”的典型例子，了解和掌握这些表达，往往可以让我们口语交流显得生动、有趣、轻松不少。当然，如果能对此类表达背后的典故略知一二，不仅可以更加透彻地理解表达，更能丰富学生的文化知识。例如，“to burn one's boat（破釜沉舟）”，源于公元前49年，恺撒大帝率军渡过卢比根河时，下令焚船，表示不获胜宁愿死的决心。当年项羽渡河攻打秦军时，让部下破釜沉舟，烧庐舍，持三日之粮，也是志在必胜。英汉两个习语都用来表达同一含义，即下定决心，不顾一切代价，争取胜利。“Walls have ears.（隔墙有耳。）”，凯瑟琳女皇曾经在罗浮宫的房间墙内安置了一种特殊材料，偷听到很多机密的情报；古人言：“墙有耳，伏寇在侧。”英汉两种语言都用“墙长了耳朵”这个比喻形容秘密商量的事情被人偷听去了。“to catch sb. red-handed/当场捉住”，原意指凶手杀伤人后手中还有血迹，就被人逮住了。这句习语最早出现在19世纪初英国爵士级著名小说家斯科特（Sir Walter Scott）的作品。古时由于缺乏科学查案技术，判案免不了来自严刑逼供，或靠当场抓住，这点中外皆是。当年最常见的重罪之一，是偷宰别人的牲畜。家里有新鲜肉，并不能构成偷宰的证明，除非在偷宰的时候，被逮了个正着。此时，偷宰者的手，仍然沾满血迹，所以称为“be caught red-handed”。听说过“pipe dream”吗？知不知道“烟斗”怎么说？很简单，仅用一个“pipe”就可形容这种“一头带有小吹嘴的管状抽烟用具”。当然，谈起“pipe/烟斗”，免不了会想到19世纪提着烟袋吸食鸦片的烟鬼们。短语“pipe dream/白日梦”还真得从烟鬼们腾云驾雾的“感觉”谈起。在18、19世纪的英国，上流社会吸食鸦片并不罕见。据说，英国湖畔诗人Samuel Taylor Coleridge（塞缪尔·柯勒律治）就是在鸦片的作用下，创作出了流传后世的诗作*Kubla Kahn*（《忽必烈汗》），只可惜诗中的元大都与实际都城相差十万八千里远。在当时，“pipe/烟斗”常被引申为“鸦片”，如短语“on the pipe ”就很形象地再现了以“鸦片”为生的瘾君子形象，而“pipe dream”则用来比喻鸦片上瘾者陷入幻觉时的状态。大约1895年前后，“pipe dream”正式进入英语词汇，不过在书面语中，“pipe dream”不再与鸦片有任何瓜葛，而是用来形容“白日梦，幻想，空想”。“Ivory Tower/象牙塔”，根据圣经《旧约·雅歌》（*The Old Testament*，*Song of Songs*）第7章第4节，睿智富有的以色列王所罗门（Solomon）曾作诗歌1005首，其中《雅歌》全是爱情之歌。在第五首歌中，新郎是这样赞美新娘的：“… Your neck is like an ivory tower. Your eyes are pools in Heshbon, by the gate of Bath-rabbim….”（……你的颈项如象牙塔；你的眼目像希实本·巴特拉并门旁的水池……）。很显然，此处的“象牙塔”只是用来描述新娘那美丽的颈项。这个词后来被逐渐运用到社会生活的各方面，主要是指“与世隔绝的梦幻境地、逃避现实生活的世外桃源、隐居之地”。在汉语中，“象牙塔”原指忽视现实社会丑恶悲惨之生活，而自隐于其理想中美满之境地以从事创作的人，意为超脱现实社会，远离生活之外，躲进孤独舒适的个人小天地，凭主观幻想从事写作活动；“象牙塔”的外延含义主要是指“比喻脱离现实生活的文学家和艺术家的小天地”。再来说说“red tape”，是红色的带子吗？从字面意义看，“red tape”即“红色的带子”之意，但这有什么象征含义呢？原来以前的英国官方文件惯例上是用红色布带系成一扎一扎的，“red tape”的比喻由此而来。早在17世纪，“red tape”的本义“红色带子”就出现在英语中，但直到19世纪早期，这个说法才成为一个常见比喻，形容“官僚作风造成的延误”。在中国，官方文件或正式文件被称为“红头文件”，异曲同工之妙。在很多国家的官方机构里，都不同程度地存在着一些“形式主义”和“繁文缛节”，在英语中这个有趣的说法“red tape”，反映的就是这种复杂并浪费时间的“官僚作风”。我们再来了解一下“to beat around the bush”，意为“不直截了当地说；拐弯抹角；旁敲侧击”。这是一个与打猎有关的表达，以前猎人打草拨丛，寻觅猎物，中国不也有“打草惊蛇”的说法吗？通过旁敲侧击，来引出自己想知道的内容，也有不着正题，顾左右而言它之意。了解这些表达背后各自的典故既能增长背景知识，又能让记忆的过程变得有趣，更能达到地道和生动的交流效果。

常言道："实践出真知"，英汉两个民族有着悠久的历史和丰富的文化遗产，源于生活和劳动的丰富多彩的习语是文化遗产中重要的组成部分。习语是人民大众在劳动中创造出来的，它来自于普通百姓的生产活动和生活经历，与人和人生活的环境密切相关。大量比较发现，反映英汉文化各个方面的英汉习语有着许多惊人的相同处，归纳分析这些习语，可以帮助大家迅速熟悉以及系统掌握这些习语，为我们的表达提供思路和切入点，提高表达的效率。

1. 生活性

英汉文化重合现象在很大程度上表现在人类劳动经历的习语中。中国人和英国人在征服自然中，求生存的劳动生产和生活经历使得这两个民族产生一些相同的人生经验。它们均出自劳动人民之口，有着广泛的群众基础，具有长久和旺盛的生命力。例如：

Strike while the iron is hot. 趁热打铁。
A watched pot never boils. 心急水不开。
Still waters run deep. 静水流深。
As a man sows, so he shall reap. 种瓜得瓜，种豆得豆。
Such carpenters, such chips. 什么木匠出什么活。
Bad workmen often blame their tools. 人笨怪刀钝。
The best fish swim near the bottom. 好鱼潜水底。
A stitch in time saves nine. 一针及时省九针。
Wash your dirty linen at home. 家丑不可外扬。
A little pot is soon hot. 壶小热得快；量小易怒。
A bird in the hand is worth two in the bush. 双鸟在林，不如一鸟在手。
Fine feathers make fine birds. 人靠衣，鸟靠羽。
Like father, like son. 有其父必有其子。
Great minds think alike. 英雄所见略同。

以上习语分别出自铁匠、厨师、水手、农夫、匠人、渔夫、家庭主妇、猎人、亲人、勇士之口，是他们的切身体会和经验结晶。这些人生经验习语在英汉两个民族的民间广为流传，不仅形象生动，新颖别致，而且妙趣横生，给人启迪，而且多数可以直接套用表达。

英汉习语文化重合的生活性还反映在与人类自身相关的习语中。自然界中的人类，不论生活在哪个地区，不论属于哪个国家或民族，其生理结构、心理、情感、七情六欲都是相同的。"这种相同的生理学与心理学基础就使得人类各民族的认知结构有其共性，这就是乔姆斯基的'深层结构'(Deep Structure) 句法理论提出的生物学基础"[7]。"习语一般都运用恰当的比喻，并能引起联想"[4]。联想是全人类共有的天赋。人类本身以及赖以生存的一切外部条件都存在着种种共性，这种共性形成了人类对自身以及外部世界的种种共识。这种共识使得不同民族具备了"共有的非文化知识"，扎根于不同文化的习语便有了共性和重合，形成了"文化共核"(Cultural Common Core)的一部分[2]。《苏格兰谚语》一书的编者詹密斯 · 凯利曾经发现很多他认为纯属苏格兰的谚语却来自其他国家,并评论道:“全人类关于基本事物的见解何其相似”[7]。因为人类的认知过程正是从认识自身开始的。以“心/heart”为例足以说明这一点:

with a heavy heart 心情沉重
heart and soul 全心全意
heart to heart 心心相印
with misgivings in one's heart 心怀鬼胎
to have one's heart in the right place 富有同情心
to cry one's heart out 伤心欲绝
to allow the heart to rule the head 感情用事
to take sth. to heart 把某事放在心上
Our hearts burst into bloom. 我等心花怒放。

2. 思想性

具有深刻的思想性和教育意义是英汉习语的又一共性。它们不但在思想性方面存在共性,而且在所揭示事物本质方面有着惊人的一致性或相似性。习语的思想性是指习语丰富的文化内涵。如许多英汉习语都反映了“实践出真知”的唯物主义思想,都具有讴歌美德,鞭挞丑恶,激励上进等积极的教育作用。例如:

Life is a journey. 人生如旅程。
Practice makes perfect. 熟能生巧。
Life is not a bed of roses. 人生并不十全十美。
Adversity is a good schoolmaster. 逆境是良师。
Idleness is the mother of all evil. 懒惰是万恶之源。
An idle youth, a needy age. 少时懒散,老来寒酸。
Bread is the staff of life. 面包是生命的支柱;民以食为天。
Labor is often the father of pleasure. 劳动常常是快乐之父。
Many hands make light work. 人多好办事;众人拾柴火焰高。
A friend in need is a friend indeed. 患难中的朋友才是真朋友。

以上例证表明英汉习语的一个共性是喻事明理,它们具有深刻的思想性,是一部思想修养的教科书。它们不但语言生动,而且内容极其丰富,文化气息浓郁。这说明,虽然英汉两个民族生活的地理环境、社会背景、政治制度和宗教信仰各有不同,但他们在惩恶扬善的愿望上,在对真善美和假恶丑的判断标准上,有许多相同之处,这是英汉文化重合的另一方面[6]。

3. 简洁性

英汉习语除了广泛性和所蕴涵丰富的思想性之外,另一个显著的共性是简洁性。比较英汉习语的语言艺术特点,不难看出习语修辞巧妙、生动形象、语言精练、一针见血、节奏明快、韵律优美、和谐动听、顺耳入口、易识易记等特点,这又与口语表达所需言简意赅的特点不谋而合,更有助于口语学习者对语料的收集,以及流利的表达提供了便利。例如:

Money talks. 金钱万能。

No pains, no gains. 不劳无获。

Plenty is no plague. 多多益善。

Pain past is pleasure. 苦尽甘来。

Misery loves company. 同病相怜。

Cut the coat according to the cloth. 量体裁衣。

Bad news has wings/travels apace. 坏事传千里。

Beauty lies in the lover's eyes. 情人眼里出西施。

Constant dropping wears away the stone. 滴水穿石。

Opportunity knocks only once. 机不可失, 时不再来。

Penny wise, and (或 but) pound foolish. 贪小便宜吃大亏。/小处节约,大处浪费。/精明而不聪明。

语言是鲜活的,具有蓬勃的生命力,随着社会和时代的发展,语言的文化内涵和表现力得到了不断丰富。语言现象是人类对客观世界认识的反映。由于客观事物(包括人类自身及其赖以生存的外部环境甚至整个人类社会的文化背景)都存在着共同的联系, 人类的逻辑思维也有其同一性, 因此, 人们思维中的许多概念也有其同一性,也就是今天我们还能在英汉两种语言中找到语言表达的文化共通性的原因之一。如今,全球一体化使世界经济、科技、教育等交流联系更加紧密,文化交融更是得益于此。另外,我们也知道,英语之所以如此强大,其最重要的原因之一就在于其极具包容性,使我们找到了文化共鸣,有了更多的亲切感。这种文化亲和力是很多语言都较难复制的,也使其稳固的世界语言地位得到加强。受到这种语言背后的"似曾相识"的文化吸引,我们口语语料的收集变得轻松愉快,兴致盎然。再请看:

(1) be in the black 盈利

在财物报表中,亏损账目总是用红色墨水书写,盈利账目用黑色墨水书写,所以说一个公司 in the black ,则表示其运行状况良好,也即是"赢利"的意思。

例如: Having paid off all the debts, the company is now in the black. 还清所有的债务,公司目前运转良好。

(2) to give sb./sth. another chapter 翻开新篇章

英语中 chapter 有"章、回"的意思,也指"人生或历史上的重要时期"。

例如: Breaking the new world record gives him another chapter. 破世界纪录使他翻开了人生的新篇章。

(3) to leave sth. to chance 赌运气

to leave sth. to chance 的字面意思是"把……留给机会",这种消极的态度不就是在"赌运气"吗? 虽说"谋事在人,成事在天",但很多时候,凡事是要靠自己去争取,愿以下面这句话与大家共勉。

例如: Never leave anything to chance. 亲力亲为不赌运气。

(4) to strike a chord 引起共鸣,触动心弦

chord 弦，strike 敲击；拨动。to strike a spiritual chord with sb. 与某人精神上产生共鸣。

例如：Now you've struck a chord with me. 你这下说到我心里去了。

(5) a blessing in disguise 看似坏事的好事；塞翁失马；因祸得福。

从字面意思完全能理解词组的意思，英汉内涵的相通可见一斑。

例如：You never know, this might be a blessing in disguise. 塞翁失马焉知非福。

(6) to have both feet on the ground 脚踏实地；有理智

例如：Why are all your friends so dreamy? Can't you find a friend who has both feet on the ground? 你的朋友干嘛都这样充满幻想？你难道就找不到个脚踏实地的朋友？

(7) be black and blue 青一块紫一块；遍体鳞伤

例如：The shop-keeper was beaten black and blue. 店家被揍得青一块紫一块的。

(8) a blank look 发呆的样子；面无表情

blank"茫然的，无表情的"；look"面容"。

例如：I tried to explain, but he just gave me a blank look. 我想要解释，但他却对我面无表情。

(9) ants in one's pants 坐立不安

从字面意思讲，"裤子里有蚂蚁"，这能让人坐得住吗？汉语中有"热锅上的蚂蚁"等类似说法。

例如：The company financial report isn't due until next Friday. But the boss has ants in his pants and wants us to have it all ready for him on Tuesday morning. 公司的财政报告到周五才上交。但老板却坐立不安，要求周四早晨将一切弄好给他。

(10) to bite off more than one can chew 自不量力

bite off 是"咬下一口"，chew 是"咀嚼"，这个词组的意思是"吃得太多，不容易咀嚼"。中国人讲"贪多嚼不烂"。

例如：Listen son, you have a lot of responsibilities already. Are you sure you can manage football and your studies and your job? Be careful you don't bite off more than you can chew. 听着，儿子，你现在已承担很多责任。你能处理好足球、学习和工作的关系吗？小心"贪多嚼不烂"。

(11) be in the pink 身体好；气色不错

"红光满面"是形容一个人精神焕发，身体健康。

例如：All the family is in the pink. 全家身体安康。

(12) dog-eat-dog 无情的竞争

"狗咬狗"比喻坏人之间互相倾轧、争斗。dog-eat-dog 将这种惨烈描写得淋漓尽致。

例如：You have to be careful in this dog-eat-dog world. 在这个激励竞争的世界，你得处处小心。

(13) better half 贤内助

中国人将"爱人"称为"另一半"，传统的中国家庭提倡"男主外，女主内"，而且中国人相信"一个成功男人背后有一个贤内助。"没想到英国人也有如此看法。

例如：He attributed his success to his better half. 他把自己的胜利归功于他的妻子。

(14) a beginner's luck 初学者的运气

一般人认为初次接触的事物，尤其是初学者玩游戏的运气特别好。在重庆方言里头，有句话叫"黄棒手硬"，"黄棒"不是指黄色的木棒、铁棒。"黄棒"是指对某一专业一窍不通的门外汉,而当这个黄棒接触到某一专业时,“黄棒手硬”这一戏剧性的事情就会发生了。这个词还有一个“话粗理不粗”的说法,即“狗屎运”。

例如:His success is purely beginner's luck. 他的成功纯属新手的好运气。

值得提醒的是,我们今天的口语交流不要完全将过去和现在截然分开,习语的灵活使用会让我们的表达产生意想不到的效果。比如:

(1)我给你的是煮熟的鸭子。I'm offering you a bird in the hand.

a bird in the hand 已到手的东西;已成定局的事情;有把握的事物。不管是中文的“鸭子”还是英文中的“鸟”,意义均类似。“a bird in the hand”的反义词为“a bird in the bush”。

(2)可要趁热打铁。We mustn't let the iron grow cold.

比较:Strike while the iron is hot. 趁热打铁。

(3)一切都十分美好。Everything is rosy in the garden.

be rosy in the garden 非常好,称心如意

(4)不管做什么,请三思而行。No matter what you want to do, please look before you leap.

to look before you leap 三思而行

(5)你在家丑外扬。You're airing your dirty laundry to a journalist.

Wash your dirty linen at home. 家丑不可外扬。

(6)我愿亲手斩断。Fetch me the matches!

Fetch me the matches. 的前一句是 I'm sorry. But I've waited so long for those words. I can't believe I'm hearing them. You won't mind burning your bridges. 紧接的这句话字面意思为“给我火柴!”引申意思为“给我火柴,我亲自烧掉它”。to burn one's bridge 破釜沉舟

(7)她活泼好动,身体非常健康。She was lively and active and in the pink of condition.

be in the pink 身体好;气色不错

(8)她迈出了决定性的一步。She's crossed the Rubicon.

to burn one's boat 破釜沉舟。公元前 49 年,凯撒大帝率部渡过卢比根河(the Rubicon)时,下令焚舟。所以这里 cross the Rubicon 是“采取断然措施;迈出决定性的一步”的意思。

二、案例分析

下面是一些鲜活的典型案例,我们以此来说明英汉表达中的文化相似性,希望能有助于提高口语表达能力。

(1)恐怕我们也无能为力了。I'm afraid it's the end of our story too.

the end of a story “故事的结束”,引申为“就这样了,没办法改变了”。

(2)板着个脸 to keep a straight face

汉语中“拉长脸”就是这个意思。

(3)弥留之际 be on one's deathbed

deathbed 为“临死之人所卧的床”。

(4)筑起铜墙铁壁保护某人 to protect sb. with a ring of steel

a ring of steel 意为“一圈钢”。汉语中也用“铜墙铁壁”来形容严密的保护。

(5)我所有的钱 every penny I have

every penny 即“每个便士”,也就是“每分钱、每个子、每个铜板”。

(6)别灰心！Never say die.
“别说完蛋了/死定了”，就是“不要灰心”的意思。
(7)这一切来得太突然了。It all happened in a flash.
flash“闪电”，还有比“闪电”更快速、更突然的现象吗？
(8)笨驴 ass
ass = a foolish person = donkey，但这个单词常用以指小孩。
(9)我不想做没前途的工作。I don't want a dead-end job.
dead-end 即“死路，死胡同，尽头”，用这个词修饰 job，即为“没前途的工作”吗？
(10)想都别想/没门！Over my dead body！
与 no way 相比，虽然这个表达有些过激，但十分生动。
(11)落荒而逃 to run with the tail between the legs
“狗被打败后，夹着尾巴逃跑”的形象跃然纸上！
(12)居安思危 to prepare for war in time of peace
英语中的 war 成了汉语中的“危”，战争就是一种危难。
(13)金钱不能买尽一切。Money will not buy everything.
汉语“金钱不是万能的”。
(14)一分钱难倒英雄汉。A man without money is no man at all.
金钱不是万能的，但没有金钱是万万不能的。
(15)挥金如土 to throw money about like dirt/to spend money like water
花钱如流水。
(16)这个过程慢热。It's slow-burning.
这儿关键是对中文“热”的理解，“热”指过程，不是状态，所以用 burn 而不是 hot。
(17)向某人致敬；佩服某人 take off one's hat to sb.
这是英汉文化相通的经典案例——用脱帽来表示对别人的尊重、致敬。
(18)升官发财 climb the ladder
这里的 ladder 即指“社会地位的阶梯”。
(19)能工巧匠 a handy man
“能工巧匠”都是“手巧的人”。
(20)态度顽固 a pig-headed attitude
pig-headed 是“死脑筋，顽固不化”的意思。看来英汉文化中 pig 都难扮演好角色。
(21)某人天生具有的能力 sth. in sb.'s blood
在某人血液中的东西就是与生俱来的。
(22)就像过去一样。Just like the old days.
old days 即为“过去，昔日”。
(23)一段往事 a piece of history
“history”在此用作不可数名词。
(24)高手 a big dog
英国人对狗的喜爱可见一斑。
(25)你为什么瞪着我？Why are your eyes so white?
人生气就会怒目圆睁，眼白显得异常突出。第一个说这句话的人对生活的观察可谓细致入微，佩服佩服！

(26)脚踏两只船 two dates one day/have one foot in both camps/serve two masters/stand between two stairs

英汉两种文化对这个表达的内涵都有相似的延展。在英语中，“欺骗，爱情上对……不忠”还有一种表达，叫做 two-timing，“脚踏两只船的人”就是个 a two-timing jerk/two timer。

(27)木已成舟。The ship has already sailed.

“木已成舟”是比喻事情已成定局，不可挽回。而英国的海上贸易十分发达，船开出去了，订单还能改吗？

(28)英国佬 tea-drinker

地球人都知道，英国人爱喝下午茶，所以英国人有个别称 tea-drinker。中国人发现的茶叶，中国的茶叶品种繁多，品茶爱茶的人不在少数，可惜却没能获此“雅号”，不能不说是一种遗憾。

(29)熬夜；开夜车 to burn the midnight oil

字面意思“午夜仍点油灯照明，学习或工作”，即“开夜车，学习或工作到深夜”。

(30)自食其果 to eat one's bitter fruit

字面和内涵基本一致。

(31)被解雇 to get the bag

中文有“收拾包袱走人”的说法。

(32)像蜜蜂般忙碌 be as busy as a bee

看来在劳动实践中，英汉民族对蜜蜂的勤劳有着惊人的一致性。

(33)十之八九 nine out of ten

中英文数字完全重合。

(34)披着羊皮的狼 a wolf in sheep's clothing

对于披着伪善外衣的邪恶势力，英汉民族的认识是相同的。

(35)良药苦口。A good medicine tastes bitter.

这句英文谚语对应的中文谚语是“良药苦口利于病，忠言逆耳利于行”。

(36)一朝被蛇咬，十年怕井绳。Once bite, twice shy.

这是一句英文俗语，其对应的中文可谓“言到意到”。

(37)你吃错药了？Have you changed your pills?

在英国电视连续剧《唐顿庄园》第三季第七集里听到这句话时，我简直不敢相信自己的耳朵，英国人与中国人居然有这样惊人相似的表达。

(38)泪如泉涌 a stream of tears

stream“溪流”，此处形容“眼泪像小溪一样不断往外涌出”。

(39)我的话就是金科玉律。My word is law.

“金科玉律”比喻不能变更的信条。law 即“法律”，由立法机关制定，国家政权保证实施的行为准则。两者均突显权威性。

(40)天作之合 a (或 the) match made by heaven

“天作之合”就是老天爷配的姻缘，这个汉语词组与英文表达真是“无缝连接”，算不算一种“天作之合”呢？

(41)你是我的依靠。You are my rock.

rock 是“岩石”的意思,比喻十分坚固,在这里利用该单词的内涵来形容可以依靠的意思。中国人不是也讲“靠山”吗?

(42)我不是愤青。I' m not a cynical.

“愤青”特指一班对社会现状不满,而急于改变现实的青年。这个词最早出现在 20 世纪 70 年代的香港,而 cynical 是“愤世嫉俗的”。中文的“愤青”赋予 cynical 时代特征。

(43)让女孩子的心融化 to melt a girl' s heart

中文形容一个女人无情就用“铁石心肠”,怎么打动女人的心?“melt”就是用“热(情)熔化固体”,任你再硬的心,也给你融化了,“何意百炼钢,化为绕指柔。”中国人提问,英国人解答。

(44)通往地狱的路是由好心铺成的。The road to hell is paved with good intentions.

中国人不也说“好心办坏事。”

(45)长痛不如短痛。This is like pulling a tooth.

拔牙,痛苦万分,但“牙疼不是病,疼起来要人命”。如果给你两个选择“拔牙”还是“任其发展”,我看还是“长痛不如短痛”。汉语与英语的表达同样传神,更为难得的居然是“心往一处想”!

(46)吃老本 to eat through one' s savings

“老本”就是最初的本钱,savings 常用作复数,意思是“a fund of money put by as a reserve/收支的结余”,也就是“再投入的本钱”。

(47)名誉领导 a figurehead

figurehead 这个英语单词来自“船头雕饰”,引申为“有名无实的领导”。不知道该典故者似乎也可以这样理解,figure 有“象征,标志”的意思,所以就称为“名誉领导”。

(48)研究一下 to do homework

如今中国人出外旅游前都要“做功课”,意思是充分了解旅游过程和目的地的方方面面。可能大家不知道,其实 homework 这个词有“(会议、讨论等之前的)必要准备工作”的意思。简单的一个 homework 就把“研究”一词搞定,且十分生动。

(49)高枕无忧(即:不管事)的祖母 the hand-off grandma

重点掌握 hand-off,意思是“不干涉,不管”。中文中不是有“撒手不管”这一说法吗?

(50)一时失足 a temporary lapse

lapse 做名词是“失足、失误”的意思。temporary 是“暂时”的意思。“一失足成千古恨”如今有了新解,因为 To err is human. 就连 Homer sometimes nods. 谁还没个犯糊涂的时候?

(51)世事无常。Things change.

“世事无常”的中心思想就是世间的万物都是变化的,难以捉摸的,一成不变的事物是不存在的。中国学生使用得最好的英语单词就是 thing 了,对他们来讲,任何“事情”都可以用 thing 来一言概之,所以 Things change. 就不难理解了。

(52)不要迁怒于送信的人。Don' t shoot the messenger.

英文句子的字面意思是:“不要打死送信的人”,其实际意思则为:不要因为你不喜欢得到的信息而责备或者惩罚给你递送信息的人。明智的做法是把你的怒气针对那个给你发出信息的人。中国古代交战双方有约定俗成的规矩:“两军交战,不斩来使”。

(53)缘分 two in a million/a kind of luck

茫茫人海中的一种缘分,“众里寻他千百度”/God' s will / It is destined that…西方人理解

"缘分"为"上帝的旨意",中国人说这是一种"天意"或"命中注定"。karma 最后说说梵文音译的 karma。这是一个佛教名词,意译为"业",一种认为一个人的行为在道德上所产生的结果会影响其未来命运的学说。Karma 或 Karman 的字根是 Kar,是"去做"或"去行"的意思,所以业力之"业"原来是作业或行为的意思！但是今天佛教徒心目中的"业力",却代表一个极端复杂的多方面思想。在这多角的思想中,最根本的是说"业力者,即控制一切自然界和道德界现象之因果律也",其引申理解为"姻缘、轮回"。

三、实战演练

(1)饭量很小 to eat like a bird

小鸟能吃多少呢?

例如:为什么吃那么少呢? Why(do you)eat like a bird?

(2)有鉴赏能力 to have (got) an eye for sth.

中文里也讲"对……有独到眼光"!

例如:我恐怕看不懂这些设计。I am afraid I've not got an eye for designs.

(3)长相丑陋 to have a face that would stop a clock

"长得真有创意,活得真有勇气"。"长得很惊险"。注意使用的场合。再补充一句"只有内心不健康才叫丑。Ugly is something that goes up inside you."

例如:尽管长得不怎么样,但那位老人心地善良,深受人们的喜爱。Although he has a face that would stop a clock, this old man is so kind-hearted that everyone likes him so much.

(4)左耳朵进,右耳朵出。It goes in one ear and out the other.

跟中文如出一辙!

例如:我跟你说了多少次要按时上课。但我说的话总是一只耳朵进一只耳朵出。How many times have I told you to get to class on time! But my words just go in one ear and out the other.

(5)尚未确定。It's up in the air.

"be in the air"就是"在空中",即"未落实,未确定。"

例如:你知道开会的时间和地点吗? 还没决定呢。Do you know when and where the meeting starts? It's up in the air.

(6)对……了如指掌 to know sth. like the back of one's hand

容易理解,无须赘言。

例如:这条路我很熟悉。I knew the pathway like the back of my hand.

(7)大海捞针 to look for a needle in the haystack

中文说"大海捞针",英文是"a needle in the haystack":"在干草堆里",两者都不容易,这正是其近似或相通之处。

例如:在熙熙攘攘的购物中心找出朋友就像在大海捞针这么困难。It is nearly impossible to find a friend at a crowded shopping center. It's like looking for a needle in a haystack.

(8)抢风头,喧宾夺主 to steal the show

show 有"表演、炫耀"的意思,所以 to steal the show 有"抢风头、出尽风头"的意思。

例如:我可不愿抢了领导的风头。I wouldn't like to steal the show before these leading persons.

(9)浑水摸鱼,趁火打劫 to fish in troubled waters

此处的 fish 为动词,“打鱼、摸鱼”的意思,而 waters 则表示“(一片)水域”。

例如:他们想要做的就是挑拨离间、浑水摸鱼。All they wanted was to make bad blood between them and fish in troubled waters. 其中,“to make bad blood between…”是“在……之间挑拨离间”的意思。

(10)泼冷水 to throw cold water on sb./sth.

例如:办公室每个人都认为我的主意不错,可老板却对我泼冷水。Everybody else in the office thought my idea was great, but the boss threw cold water on it.

(11)希望好运 to keep one's fingers crossed

中国人祈祷的动作是双手合十,西方人是双手手指交叉,但心同此愿。

例如:我们的努力现在已无法改变现状,只有祈求好运了。Our effort can't change the situation now. So let's keep our fingers crossed.

(12)你知我知 between us/you and me

“between us /you and me”意为“你我之间的事”,也就是仅限“你我之间(的秘密)”。

例如:这是我们之间的秘密,我昨天考试作弊了。Just between you and me. I cheated on yesterday's exam.

(13)心眼好;心地善良 to have one's heart in the right place

中国人说一个人心眼不好就是“心术不正”,所以“心眼好”就是“to have one's heart in the right place”。

例如:他看上去凶巴巴的,但却心地善良。He looks very rough, but he has his heart in the right place.

(14)了解某人 to read sb. like a book

英文表达还有一说,即:“to read sb.'s mind”。

例如:你太了解我了。You read me like a book.

(15)求同存异 to agree to disagree

字面意思“同意存在不同意见”,“不再试图说服对方”或“尽管有不同意见,一方仍愿保留自己的不同意见,”其意接近中国的成语 “求同存异”。

例如:我有充分的理由跟他们保留不同的意见。I had every reason to agree to disagree with them.

(16)听命于某人 to eat out of sb.'s hands

中国人有句俗语“拿人家的手短,吃人家的嘴软”,与本习语有相同的含义。

例如:她很快就把全班管理得服服帖帖。She soon had the class eating out of her hands.

(17)打破僵局 to break the ice

字面意思“打破冰层”,比喻成“打破冷冰冰的场面而使气氛活跃起来”、“打破僵局”或“打破沉默”。

例如:为什么你不站出来打破僵局?Why didn't you stand up and break the ice?

(18)面面俱到 to cover all the bases

cover 是“覆盖”的意思,每个地方都“覆盖”到,就是每个地方都关注到的意思。所以“面面俱到,滴水不漏”。

例如:前两者适合于任何场合,无论是工作还是娱乐。The first two will cover all the bases whether at work or play.

(19)坚持某人的立场 to hold one's ground

ground 就是"场地"的意思,引申为"立场"。to hold one's ground 就是"坚守阵地不让步,不妥协;坚持自己的立场(或观点等);恪守自己的信念"。

例如:你知道什么时候该坚持,什么时候该妥协。You know when to hold your ground and when to compromise.

(20)老实人 direct people

"说话办事都非常直接的人"。说实话,第一次在电影里听到这个词,我吓一跳,"没有最巧合,只有更巧合。"

例如:澳大利亚人是说话办事都非常直接的人,他们通常都是想什么说什么。Australians are very direct people and usually mean what they say.

(21)耳边风 selectively deaf

字面意思为"选择性失聪的"。"耳边风"就是耳边吹过的风,比喻过耳即逝,不放在心上的话。两者都是指对不爱听的话选择不听,不上心的意思。

例如:医生都告诉我们抽烟对身体是有害的。可是,这种劝告对于有些人来说就像耳边风一样,毫无作用。The doctors tell us it's dangerous to smoke, but some people are selectively deaf to such good advice.

(22)很忙 to get enough on one's hands

中国人讲"手头上的事情太多了",就是对这个英文表达最好的诠释。

例如:他已经够忙的了。He's got enough on his hands.

(23)一开始就不顺利;起步便错 to get off on the wrong foot

get off 就是"起步,动身"的意思,从字面上不难理解英文词组的意义"开始就给人一个坏印象某人一开始就没给人一个好印象,或一开始由于某种行为而把事情弄糟了。"中文不也有"出师不利"这一说法吗?

例如:迈克和玛丽第一次约会时就出师不利,他打翻了一杯水。Mike got off the wrong foot on his first date with Mary when he knocked over a glass of water.

(24)脸皮要厚一点 to develop/grow a thick skin

"脸皮厚"在中文中既有褒义也有贬义,我们更愿意将其理解为"不要太敏感,不要太腼腆"。俗话说:"人要脸,树要皮",本来这是做人的美德,但不能过头;俗话还说:"没心没肺,活着不累"。大家生活在一个复杂的社会里,各种各样的人都有,做每一件事都能遇到麻烦或阻力,还有嫉妒者,甚至会被攻击谩骂,因此就要学着不太顾及脸面,脸皮要厚一点,不然就会心里不痛快,受压抑。面对这样一个相同的世界,英国人也有此做人的道理。

例如:作为一名经理,你必须学会不要太在乎人们的无礼,不要为此而影响到自己。As a manager, you have to learn to develop/grow a thick skin and not let people's insults affect you.

(25)目前最吸引人的问题、急待解决的问题 a burning question

汉语中有"燃眉之急"这一说法。

例如:校长是否受贿是时下学校最热门的话题。Whether the president has taken bribes or not is a burning question in the university.

(26)犹豫不决;拿不定主意 be of two minds

字面意思就是"三心二意"。

例如:我在犹豫到底穿什么礼服去参加晚会。I am in two minds about which dress to wear for the party.

四、巩固练习

1. 从文化相通的角度说说下面中文词组或句子的英语表达。

(1)很骄傲
(2)很忠诚
(3)纸老虎
(4)丢面子
(5)别兜圈子。
(6)开诚布公
(7)食多病多。
(8)人多心多。
(9)稳如磐石
(10)如坐针毡
(11)行将就木
(12)千钧一发
(13)轻如鸿毛
(14)火上浇油
(15)白纸黑字
(16)男情女愿
(17)资金紧张。
(18)以闪电般的速度
(19)给某人开绿灯
(20)去当绿林好汉
(21)披着羊皮的狼
(22)气得满脸通红
(23)人一有钱就变样。
(24)一阵雷鸣般的掌声
(25)就当成是积德吧。
(26)我对此充耳不闻。
(27)坏事传千里。
(28)把他的名字挂在嘴边
(29)救死扶伤
(30)有知情者
(31)女人的心海底针。(女人的心就像隐藏着秘密的深幽海洋。)

2. 从文化相通的角度说说下面英文词组或句子的中文表达。

(1)a red-letter day

(2) to burn the midnight oil to
(3) brawn and brain
(4) He's a snake.
(5) to propose a toast
(6) You are hard to read.
(7) Seeing is believing.
(8) to take the high road
(9) a position of power
(10) a moment of temporary insanity
(11) deep conversation
(12) No man is wise all the times.
(13) Poverty breeds strife.
(14) More haste, less speed.
(15) No cross, no crown.
(16) Easy come, easy go.
(17) Like father, like son.
(18) Old habits die hard.
(19) Beggars cannot be choosers.
(20) A rat crossing the street is chased by all.
(21) A rolling stone gathers no moss.
(22) Constant dropping wears the stone.
(23) The pen is mightier than the sword.
(24) People are people./To err is human.
(25) That's like the rich who say money doesn't matter.
(26) Your fault as a son is my failure as a father.
(27) An evil chance seldom comes alone.
(28) Penny and penny laid up will be many.
(29) Happiness consists in contentment.
(30) A fall into a pit, a gain in your wit.
(31) Barking dogs seldom bite.

3. 熟读并背诵下列句子。

(1) Art is long, life is short. 艺无止境，人生短暂。
(2) Man proposes, God disposes. 谋事在天，成事在人。
(3) Where there is a will, there is a way. 有志者事竟成。
(4) The spirit is willing, but the flesh is weak. 心有余而力不足。
(5) Be slow to promise and quick to perform. 不轻诺，诺必果。
(6) More haste, less speed. 欲速则不达。
(7) A high building, a low foundation. 树大根深。
(8) A heavy purse makes a light heart. 钱包重，心情轻松。

(9) Penny wise, pound foolish. 小事聪明，大事糊涂；因小失大。
(10) A little fire makes a great flame. 星星之火,可以燎原。
(11) Short pleasure, long lament. 欢乐一时，痛苦一世。
(12) A fat belly, a lean brain. 大腹便便，头脑空空。
(13) A bargain is a bargain. 契约终是契约;达成的契约不可妄毁。
(14) All covet, all lose. 贪多必失。
(15) Do well and have well. 善有善报。
(16) Enough is enough. 适可而止。
(17) Let bygones be bygones. 既往不咎。
(18) Merry meet, merry part. 好聚好散。
(19) Monkey see, monkey do. 近朱者赤，近墨者黑。
(20) Nothing venture, nothing gain. 不入虎穴，焉得虎子。
(21) Other countries, other manners. 国家不同，风俗各异。
(22) Time is money. 时间就是金钱；一寸光阴一寸金。
(23) Time flies. 光阴似箭，日月如梭。
(24) Time has wings. 光阴去如飞。
(25) Time is a file that wears and makes no noise. 光阴如锉,细磨无声。
(26) Money is the root of all evil. 金钱为万恶之源。
(27) Beauty fades like a flower. 红颜易逝。
(28) Easier said than done. 说着容易做着难。
(29) He who hesitates is lost. 当断不断,必受其患。
(30) Virtue never grows old. 美德永远不会老。
(31) A bosom friend afar brings a distant land near. 海内存知己,天涯若比邻。
(32) A near friend is better than a far-dwelling kinsman. 远亲不如近邻。
(33) A bad thing never dies. 遗臭万年。
(34) Harm set, harm get. 害人害己。
(35) A bad beginning makes a bad ending. 不善始者不善终。
(36) Those who live in glass houses should not throw stones. 己所不欲,勿施于人。

4. 用本单元所学的知识造句。

(1) 她计划进入影视圈只是痴心妄想。
(2) 我能洞察人的言行。
(3) 你真懂我。
(4) 还要我猜啊。
(5) 为了她他什么都肯干,他已经是对她百依百顺了。
(6) 他因从柜台抽屉偷钱而遭解雇。
(7) 我觉得这是他们一个非常糟糕的决定,而且他们最终将会自食其果。
(8) 不管什么事情,他总是犹豫不定。
(9) 要想成为一个有效的沟通者,你首先要学会如何打破僵局。
(10) 你不必赢得每个论点,求同存异。

(11) 百分之九十的被调查者说,他们喜欢新产品。
(12) 我们愿意像只打败的野狗一样,夹着尾巴逃离对这个令我们惭愧的问题吗?
(13) 在你开始详细的全方位的英语复习之前,先退下来想想什么才是你最需要学习的。
(14) 我们必须跳过所有的繁文缛节,以便迅速实现目标。
(15) 真是新手的好运气,我的一切进展顺利。
(16) 我们接受了太多的工作,应该寻求一些帮助。
(17) 我重新做人改头换面了。
(18) 告诉我真相,别拐弯抹角!
(19) 你错了,你不应该固执己见。
(20) 她把我对她的一再警告当作耳边风。
(21) 明天是我们与新客户的第一次会面,我们会努力不把事搞砸了。
(22) 一时失足不是死路一条。
(23) 想做一个好的推销员必须厚脸皮。
(24) 如何处理和利用城市再生资源已成为中国亟须解决的一个重要问题。
(25) 不要迁怒于送信者,应该找出肇事者。

5. 你能找到更多英汉文化相通的例证吗?请与大家共同分享本章的学习体会。

Chapter 2 Cultural Differences
文化差异

一、思路讲解

在学习这章之前，向大家推荐反映中西文化差异和冲突的《刮痧》、《喜福会》、《推手》、《喜宴》等经典影片，也请大家欣赏类似由著名导演 Spielberg. S 执导的奥斯卡入围影片 *War Horse* 等反映人类和动物之间情感的电影。

语言与文化相辅相成，文化包含语言并影响语言，一切的语言史都可以认为是文化的一部分。所以要想学好一种语言，不只是在学习过程中同语言本身打交道，还牵涉到文化背景知识的了解和掌握。现代人学英语的目的已转向沟通，在学习语言的基础上，了解所学语言国家的文化背景、风土人情，对于语言交流大有裨益。不同的文化会有不同的语言交际规则，文化相通是我们进行口语交流的捷径，但全面深入了解英汉文化差异可以让我们的口语交流更地道，少走弯路，少闹笑话。

1. 差异的根源

在地理环境、社会背景、历史渊源、民情风俗、思维方式、宗教信仰、民族心理以及道德标准等诸多方面，汉语与英语的发源存在着千差万别，这便是"文化差异"。这一差异不仅体现在语言本身的特点上，而且还反映在语言的使用上。文化差异在口语方面十分明显，口语中词汇变化快，语言风格多样，俗语的运用的渗透等，这给欲牢固掌握且运用自如的学习者增添了不小的难度。语言和文化是密不可分的。语言是文化的一部分，同时，语言又是文化的载体，古语云："知彼知己，百战不殆"，只有跳出语言背后的文化"陷阱"，才有望较为准确地掌握并运用它。如果不了解这些差异，我们的学习效果不仅会大打折扣，而且在交流中也会笑料百出，一头雾水。说英语就要了解英国人的文化，理解英汉差异，让表达更顺畅。通过对比分析，追本溯源，能够更好地理解和掌握英语语言的内在规律，有助于养成英语思维的习惯，减少汉语式英语的出现机率，从而习得更加地道的英语。对英语学习者来说，在母语和英语之间拥有良好的理解转换能力是口语交际能力的重要条件之一，了解东西方文化，准确地掌握和运用英语词汇，促进跨文化交流。

2. 差异的表现

1)制度政策

不同的国家有不同的社会制度和政府政策，比如中国的国家大政方针——"十二五规划"(the Twelfth Five-year Plan)、加拿大的"移民法"(Immigration Act)、美国的"人权法案"(Bills of Rights)、英国的"威斯敏斯特法案"(The Act of Westminster)。知道"grey area"这个英式英语表达吗？就是"灰区，次贫地区(指就业率较低，但还不够享受政府特别资助的地区)"，而"廉租房"(low-rent housing)是体现中国政府对低收入人群的人文关怀的例证。

对我们来讲，最熟悉的莫过于中西教育体制的差异。中国学生扎实的基本功，较强的阅读能力，出色的奥赛成绩等都是有目共睹的。“人生能有几回搏”的说教（preaching）铸造了不少高才生（top/top-notch student）。与其他英语国家相比较，我们的教育体制也有缺失。中国传统教育强调知识的传授，我们把它形象地比喻为“填鸭式”教育（duck-stuffing teaching），于是有了“死记硬背”（rote learning），有了铺天盖地的各式各样的考试，“考考考，教师的法宝；分分分，学生的命根”。美国教育强调学生能力的培养（ability cultivation），用各式各样的论文（paper）代替了考试，让学生充分展示自己的观点和看法。这种教育差异在“高考”这一词上得到体现：中国的“高考”英译为“College Entrance Examination/为了进大学的考试”。美国高考 SAT（Scholastic Assessment Test）用中文来讲就是“学术能力评估考试”。

学校教育（Schooling）有差异，家庭教育（Parenting）也有区别。在中国，孩子是“掌上明珠/the apple of one's eye”，父母对孩子的照顾无微不至，如帮助孩子洗衣服、整理卧室等。当然这有其个中原因：分数决定学生上的学校，所以在中国，为了取得较好的学业成绩，中小学生的课业负担重（heavy course burden），基本没有时间和精力关注书本知识学习之外的任何事情。在美国家庭中，父母教育子女健康成长而采用了包括归属法则、希望法则、力量法则等 12 条基本法则，（http://baby.sina.com.cn/edu/08/2310/0852123072.shtml），从中我们可以看到，美国人的家教几乎与读书、学习、成绩、升学无关，而是注重“做人/be an upright person/ to conduct oneself”，注重品德、修养的培育。这不由得让人想到中国的家庭教育，我们的家庭教育已成为学校教育的延续、延伸。家长几乎把全部心思、精力、甚至财力都用在了子女的学习辅导、成绩提高上，至于如何做一个诚实、勤劳的人（a person of honor/a person of diligence），如何做到生活自理、生活自立（self-starter/self-supporter），如何培养责任心（a sense of responsibility）和自制力（self-discipline）等内容，都“靠边站/be cast aside”。

在性教育（sex education）方面，由于受中国传统文化的影响，“性”在中国教育中似乎如同洪水猛兽（dirty things），无论家长还是老师都谈“性”色变（to hold an awkward attitude to sex），而对儿童则是尽可能“三缄其口”。近些年，性教育被提上教育历程，但是父母对子女以及学校对学生的性教育还是处于相对滞后状态，甚至有些家长用谎言来搪塞孩子们的好奇。西方国家则很早便开始对儿童进行正常的性教育（safe sex），让性不再成为禁区，而是一种自然的生活状态。在西方，性教育不是一次性的课程，而是从儿时一直到成年的一种不间断的教学，教师则由老师和家长共同承担。在西方父母的观念中，性是孩子不可避免将要知道的事情，与其让他们从同伴那里得到不正确甚至具有危害性的知识，还不如直接由学校和家庭来告诉他们，至少这样孩子可以得到准确的信息。知道 the birds and the bees 是什么意思吗？答案是“基本的性知识”。那知不知道为什么用 birds 和 bees 来表达这个意思呢？这里是以 bees（蜜蜂）采蜜用来隐喻男子射精；birds（鸟类）产卵用来隐喻女子排卵，用这两种动物来向孩子解释 sex，比较委婉，且易懂，容易让孩子理解和接受，“It's about time we told our daughter about the birds and the bees. /该是告诉我们女儿有关性知识的时候了。”再说一个例子：2013 年初，英国议会下院投票以压倒多数通过“同性恋婚姻合法化提案/ Marriage（Same Sex Couples）Bill”。很多英式英语爱好者都喜欢看《唐顿庄园》（*Downton Abbey*），里面的男主人公 Grantham 伯爵在第三季第八集淡定地说出了一句在该片历史背景（1910 年英王乔治五世在位时期）下让人瞠目结舌的话“If I shouted blue murder every time someone tried to kiss me at Eton, I'd have gone hoarse in a month. 如果在伊顿公学时每当有人要吻我，我都大声疾呼，不出一个月我就得哑了。”在这句话中，blue murder 意为“恐怖的喊声”，但这并不是“最恐怖”的，要知道“Eton 伊顿公学"是英国最知名的贵族男子学校。

2)宗教信仰

宗教——文化中不可或缺的成分,伴随着朝代的更迭,岁月的轮回,已经深入到西方人的骨髓与血液之中,渗入日常的行为、观念、精神和社会生活的各个方面,其影响力是毋庸置疑的。宗教带给我们的除了精神上的支持和生活中的信仰外,更带给我们一种自由、平等、仁爱、宽容的人生观和生活态度。我们以在欧洲美洲影响力最强的基督教为例,西方的近代文明和近代科学就是在基督教的神学背景和襁褓之中诞生的。除此之外,基督教更渗透到西方人生活的方方面面:《圣经》是最有影响力最为强大,世界排名第一的书籍,学校开设有圣经课,周末都去教堂,吃饭前划圣号念经,口头禅"God bless you!"几乎所有的重大节日都与宗教有关:圣诞节、复活节、圣灵降临节等。基督教带来人权思想,启蒙欧洲哲学,影响西方文学,开启欧洲教育,丰富西方音乐。

基督教只承认一个上帝,认为上帝是世间万事万物,包括人类的缔造者和主宰。人必须绝对服从上帝。上帝无所不知,无所不能。"Heaven is above all."(上帝高于一切。)/"God is where he was."(上帝无处不在。)/"Truth is the daughter of God."(真理是上帝的女儿。)而把上帝奉为至高无上的神的基督教却主张人平等。《新约·罗马书》说:"上帝使他们跟他有合宜的关系是基于他们信耶稣基督。上帝这样对待所有信基督的人,任何差别都没有:因为没一个人犯罪,亏欠了上帝的荣耀。"也就是说,除上帝外,人际关系是平等的。"Human blood is all of a color."(人类血的颜色都是一样的。)/"Every one is a master and servant."(每个人既是主人,又是仆人/凡人既主且仆。)/"Everyman should take his own."(每个人都应得到自己的一份。)/"Everyman is a king in his own home."(每个人都是家里的皇帝。)在《圣经》上记载着一个人所共知的故事,人类的始祖亚当和夏娃违背上帝的旨意,偷食禁果,犯了罪,这就是人类的原罪(sin)。"Our sins and our debts are often more than we think."(我们的罪和债常常比我们想象的多。)/"Sins are not known till they be acted."(罪未犯就不为人所知。)/"The sins of the fathers are visited upon the children."(父辈的罪孽,会殃及子孙。)这后一条谚语源自《旧约·出埃及记》,意思是说:人们有时由于父辈的罪孽而受到惩罚,后人要为前人的罪行承担责任。在西方,13这个数字被看作是不幸的象征,这来源于圣经中的一个故事。传说耶稣受害前和弟子们共进了一次晚餐,参加晚餐的第13个人是耶稣的弟子犹大,犹大为了30块银元,把耶稣出卖给犹太教当局,致使耶稣受尽折磨。参加最后晚餐的是13个人,晚餐的日期恰逢13日,"13"给耶稣带来苦难和不幸,因此,在西方国家13被认为是不吉利的数字。有很多楼层、门牌号都会直接跳过13,12之后直接是14,或用12A代替13表示。Judas(犹大),影射着"叛徒、奸细"的意思,而A Judas kiss, 则是"口蜜腹剑"之意。

3)历史典故

在英语语言中,许多典故都有其特定的历史背景和文学渊源,如源自于希腊罗马神话、历史事件、寓言故事等。它们语句短小精炼,寓意深刻明了,读起来耐人寻味,从各个不同的方面反映了该民族固有的文化特征和文化内涵,展示了英语语言民族文化的发展和演变,体现了不同民族的社会生活和价值观念,对英语语言文化产生了及其深刻的影响。如源自希腊罗马神话的Trojan Horse(特洛伊木马,比喻暗藏的敌人和危险)和I came, I saw, I conquer!(打败庞培时,恺撒说到"亲临、目睹、全胜!"充分表现了他当时胜利后喜悦,后来此语也成为语言精练的典范。)世界上最有影响力的寓言要数《伊索寓言》(*Aesop's Fables*)了,被誉为"西方寓言之父"。To mistake the shadow for substance是"以假乱真,捕风捉影"的意思,讲一条叼着一块肉从桥上走过，在桥下的河里看见自己的倒影，认为那也是一条狗，而且嘴里的肉比自己这块大两倍，于是张嘴冲下去，结果“竹篮打水一场空”，贪心一定会吃亏。Watergate 是美国首都华盛顿一座大厦的名字。1972 年 6 月 17 日，美国共和党为了争取尼克松连任总统，在竞选中派人潜入水门大厦民主党全国委员会办事处偷拍文件和安装窃听器，刺探民主党的竞选策略和活动情况，结果被警卫人员当场发现拘捕。案发后，尼克松被迫宣布辞职。在美国英语中，Watergate 常指“秘密的、非法的勾当”。自“水门事件”（Watergate Scandal）发生后，“门”（gate）一词也成了“丑闻”的后缀标志，如克林顿总统涉嫌与白宫女秘书有染被称为“拉链门”（Zippergate）等。我们再来看看文学中的典故，Catch-22 指“进退两难”。Joseph Heller 在 1996 年写了一部以战争为故事背景的小说 *Catch-22*（《第二十二条军规》），书中提到，在军中有一条规定，“一切精神失常的人员要停止飞行，必须由本人提出申请，而一个人在面临真正的迫在眉睫的危险时，对自身安全表示关注，就证明他不是疯子。”所以 Catch-22 就用来形容这种“任何自相矛盾、不合逻辑的规定或条件所造成的无法摆脱的困境、难以逾越的障碍”。

4）民情风俗

不同的国家和民族在漫长的历史进程中孕育出富有特色的地方文化，即便是同一个国家，不同地区的文化各有不同。“风俗是社会上长期形成的风尚、礼节、习惯等的总和”[8]。风俗是特定社会文化区域内历代人们共同遵守的行为模式或规范，风俗是社会道德与法律的基础和相辅部分。从古至今，民情风俗似一个极富魅力的百姓生活万花筒，从衣食住行到婚嫁丧葬，从农作田野到畜牧百工，从民间流传节日到百姓信仰崇拜，民俗风情丰富多彩、千变万化。正因如此，中英两国在民情风俗的差异体现在社会的方方面面，不胜枚举。

（1）亲属称呼中英不同

由于社会制度历史背景不同，中英两国人在亲属称呼表达上有差异。大家知道，中国历史上封建时期特别长，形成了浓厚的“家”的观念，因而亲属称呼较为繁复，分得较细致，有姨母、姑母、婶母、舅母；祖母、外相母；祖父、外祖父；伯父、叔父、姑父、姨父、舅父；哥哥、弟弟；姐姐、妹妹；表兄、表弟、表姐、表妹、堂兄、堂弟、堂姐、堂妹；侄子、外甥等。这些词都各有所指，用以称呼不同的人。在英国，金钱至上的观点使人们对“家”比较淡漠。在英语中，姨母、姑母、婶母、舅母都称为 aunt；伯父、叔父、舅父、姑父、姨父都称为 uncle；祖母和外祖母都是 grandmother；祖父和外祖父都是 grandfather；无论兄或弟都称为 brother；不管是姐姐还是妹妹都称为 sister；表兄弟、表姐妹、堂兄弟、堂姐妹都称为 cousin；外甥和侄儿都称 nephew，所以在英语交流中要知道这一文化现象，才不至于被这种关系搞晕脑袋。另外，英国更喜欢用“直呼其名”的方式来肯定个性的独立和拉近彼此之间的距离。英语称呼语比较简单，彼此熟悉的人之间直呼其名，正式场合用 Mr.，Miss，或 Ms. 等称呼，只有极少数职务、职称能用来称呼别人，如医生、博士、教授、总统等。在英语社会交往中，不论地位和职位高低，人们越来越愿意直呼其名——雇员、年轻人，乃至对上司、年长者以及子女对父母亲等都直接称呼他们的名字，这对讲究礼貌或礼仪的中国人来讲简直不可思议。

（2）见面打招呼中英不同

由于自然地理环境和经济生活水平不同，中英两国人在见面打招呼时的用语不同。英国是大西洋海岸的岛国，属海洋性气候，天气变化频繁无常，所以英国人对天气情况十分敏感，常常一见面就要谈论天气。因此“今天真是个好天儿啊！/It's nice, isn't it?”“今天真热呀！/It's hot!”“今天又是个雨天呀！/ Another rainy day today.”等，就成为见面打招呼的用语了。中国国土辽阔，属大陆气候，天气变化是十分明显，所以中国人对天气变化不像英国人那么敏感。但由于经济比较落后(underdeveloped),许多地区尚未解决温饱问题(problem of clothing and food),因此,人们一见面总习惯问一句"吃了没有?"以此作为打招呼的用语。但随着中国经济的腾飞,这种打招呼的倾向已逐渐改变。

(3)动物词汇内涵中英不同

分析英汉两种语言的文化内涵,可以清楚地发现动物词汇,不仅代表了动物的表象,也根深蒂固的烙印着历史文化与痕迹,表达着不同国家的语言特征,并反映了各自的文化风貌。因此应在跨文化交流中考虑两种语言中动物词汇各自的内涵,找到等价的表达词汇,而不要直接用目标语言的表面意义来理解。中英两国传统文化及人们对事物的理解和看法不同导致两种语言在动物习语表达上差异很大。英语形容人胆小的习语是"as timid as a hare/胆小如兔",汉语则说"胆小如鼠",因为鼠在汉民族文化里是胆小的象征,兔却是敏捷、迅速的象征。再如,汉语说"吹牛",英语说"to talk horse"。再比如说,汉语说"像热锅上的蚂蚁",英语说"like a cat on hot bricks/像热砖上的猫"。另外要注意以下情况:

①同一动物词汇在英语中是褒义,在汉语中却是贬义。狗(dog)在英语中是受欢迎的,但在中国,与狗相关的短语一般也都含有藐视之意:狐朋狗友、丧家犬、狗仗人势等等。"狗嘴里吐不出象牙"表示一个人不说好话;"狗急跳墙"是一个坏人陷入困境,试图做最后挣扎。在英国,人们称狗为人类最好的朋友,"You are a lucky dog./ 你是个幸运儿",狗是忠实、可靠和吃苦耐劳的象征。在英国文化中,猫头鹰(owl)象征着智慧(as wise as an owl)。然而,在中国有一种迷信,猫头鹰是一个不幸的鸟,象征灾难和死亡。中国俗语说,"猫头鹰进宅,好事不来"。在西方,蟋蟀(cricket)如莎士比亚在Henry IV中所写的那样,象征着幸福(as merry as a cricket)。但在中国,它经常会带给人们悲伤的感觉,它影射着贫穷的人。

②同一动物词汇在英语中是贬义,在汉语中却是褒义。中国人将"龙"(dragon)作为图腾信奉,有许多美好意义的关于龙的成语。"望子成龙"指父母希望孩子能有所成就。在古希腊神话中,龙是一种会喷出烟和烈火的怪物,它常被用来指"凶暴的人",英美人士受此影响,便认为龙是邪恶的,而"母夜叉"的英文表达就是dragon。由于受基督教文化的影响,dragon(龙)还含有"海怪或海魔"之意,如the Old Dragon就意为"魔王"。喜鹊(magpie)在中国是个受欢迎的鸟,它是好消息的使者,如"喜鹊闹梅"。西方人认为它代表着噪声,用来形容搬弄是非的人。

③英汉动物词汇中的民族文化差异。在中国,凤凰(phoenix)是太阳之灵,是一种神鸟,"百鸟朝凤","凤"是封建时代的皇后的特殊代号。在西方神话中,凤凰是神奇的鸟,传说它的寿命约有500年。死亡前,它会建一个巢唱哀歌,用火将自己烧尽,在灰烬中获得新生并不会再死去。因此,凤凰在西方代表重生或经济复苏。凤凰在英语也指代优秀的人。在中国,马(horse)有着悠久的历史,有关马的短语常被联想到战争,如"戎马生涯"、"金戈铁马"等。"厉兵秣马"是指准备战斗;"马到功成"意味着对成功的预祝。马也可以连接到做出贡献的人才,特别优秀的人被誉为"千里马"。在早期的英国,马是生产生活的主要交通工具,后来被用在赛马等娱乐活动,马代表勇气、大度、手段。如"A good horse should seldom spurred."(好马不用鞭。)/"A good horse can't be of a bad color."(好马无劣色。)等。

④英汉动物词汇的文化缺省。在北美,海狸被看成是勤劳的动物,具有独特的技术、能力、创造力,它的技巧和智慧为它赢得了"动物实干家"的美誉,这个动物也是"勤奋"的化身。"These young people beaver away at school."(这些年轻人很是用功)。然而,对大多数中国人来说,海狸只是一种动物,没有任何文化内涵。乌龟在中国人们的思想有两层含义,一个象征着

长寿；另一个意思是“愚蠢的人”。然而，“乌龟”在英国没有这种文化的内涵，它仅仅是一个缓慢而且没有吸引力的生物。蚕出生在中国，蚕丝制作出的真丝面料，深受世界各地人民的喜爱，著名的丝绸之路广为人知，蚕文化在中国源远流长。古诗有云：“春蚕到死丝方尽，蜡炬成灰泪始干”，这些内涵深刻影响中国人的思想。但“蚕”在大多数西方人的眼睛里只不过是蠕虫。

(4)颜色词汇内涵中英不同

由于人们生活在色彩绚丽的世界中，因此在人类语言里，也就存在着大量记录色彩的符号——颜色词。自古以来，色彩作为象征，代表一个民族、代表一定历史，代表特定的文化。从色彩的分类来看，汉语中的基本颜色词与英语基本对应。但由于英汉语言习惯不同，风俗各异，不仅表达色彩的方法和用词不尽相同，就是在同一领域对同一颜色的理解及象征意义也有差异。红色(red)：汉语中，“红色”象征着“吉祥如意、顺利成功、喜庆欢乐”。月老牵“红线”，“红娘”凑姻缘，结婚贴红双喜字，新娘子穿红嫁衣，以红头巾遮面，所以中国古代俗称婚嫁喜庆为“红事”。在说英语的国家，红色也有与幸福、吉祥、快乐等相关联，如“red-letter day”意为“纪念日，喜庆的日子”，“to roll out the red carpet for sb.”意为“隆重地欢迎某人”。但在说英语的国家中，人们对红色的喜爱远不如中国人，他们更多地把红色看着是残酷、狂热、灾祸、血腥等，如“red ruin”指火灾，“ a red battle”指血战。白色(white)：在中国，白色常使人产生卑贱、清贫的联想，白色还与死亡、丧事相联系，如“红白喜事”中的白指“丧事”(funeral)，表示哀悼。传统戏曲中白色脸谱(如三国的曹操和明代的严嵩)是奸诈阴险的象征。尽管白色在汉语里的联想，也有褒义的一面，特指“纯洁”、“清白”的意思，如汉语中的成语“清白如玉”、“洁白无瑕”，但中国人并不十分喜欢白色。而英语国家则不然，在西方文化里存在着“重白忌黑”的传统。在英美等西方国家，白色是“纯洁、素雅、光亮和坦率”的象征。白色为婚礼色，新娘在婚礼上要穿白色的婚纱以象征纯洁的爱情，因此，西方人的婚礼称为“white wedding”。此外，“a white lie”指善意的谎言，“white handed”指某人公正廉政，“white days”指吉日。由此可见，英语中的 white 这一色彩是很受英美人士欢迎的。绿色(green)：绿色无论在汉语还是英语国家，都是表示和平、满足、友善、希望和生机。绿色除了象征希望、自由和欢乐外，还象征着青春、信心和永恒，绿色为大自然的本色，体现朝气蓬勃、富有生命力。但在英语文化中，green 常用来表示“嫉妒”，如“green-eyed”(嫉妒的)和“green-eyed monster”(善妒之人)。蓝色(blue)：中国人喜欢“蓝色”这一天空和大海的自然色彩，把蓝色与美好的遐想、憧憬相联系，如“蓝色的梦想”，指美妙的梦想，渴望到达的境界，“青出于蓝而胜于蓝”更是一家喻户晓的汉语成语。英语中“blue”是个文化含义十分丰富的色彩语词。“blue”可用来表示社会地位高、有权势或出身于贵族或王族，如“blue blood”(贵族血统)。同时“blue” 还具有“下流，色情”的之义，如“blue jokes”指的是猥亵的笑话。在这一点上，与汉语中的“黄色”对应。紫色(purple)：关于紫色的喜好，中英文化是相近的。西方崇尚紫色。旧时西欧许多国家国王都穿“紫袍”。“紫色”象征显贵和尊严，象征王位、帝位，神权。因此在英语中，用“raised to the purple” 表示皇帝登上宝座，用“born in the purple”表示出生王室。在汉语里，“紫色”亦有“吉祥如意”、“大富大贵”的意思。有个成语叫“紫气东来”就是表示祥瑞之意[3]。

(5)中英无对应词的表达

由于文化内涵差异，英语和汉语中的部分词语在对方的语言中没有对应词。这些词语源于两种文化在社会、历史、自然、传说、宗教等诸方面的不同。例如：英语中的“garage sale”(车库销售)或者“yard sale”(庭院销售)，这两种销售方式在中国都不存在，它是一种典型的英美方式。夏秋季节天气晴朗时，许多人家打开车库大门和就在自家院子里，把自家不用的闲置物品标价摆出，供大家挑选购买。还有英语中的“cloud nine”（九号云彩），指愉快的心情、无比幸福的状态。在美国气象服务中，各种不同的云系都有各自的数字代号，而9号云系是一种叫作“积雨云”的特定代号。而“积雨云”的位置最高，因此，“cloud nine”就成了“处在世界顶峰”的形象代名词，用来形容一种情绪高涨的状态。再举一个例子，英语中有一个“a baker's dozen”（面包师的十二）。英国人是以面包为主食的，但那时有个别的面包师在制作面包时偷工减料，克扣分量，以这样的方法昧着良心赚顾客的黑心钱。后来，别的面包师也纷纷效仿。不法奸商的这种做法弄得民怨沸腾，最后官方不得不专门为面包师们制订了制作面包时投料的标准，凡达不到标准的就要受到处罚。这一措施果然奏效，面包的分量增加了。不过，在几百年前科学技术还不十分发达的情况下，手工投料制作面色很难做到个个合乎标准，而不符合官方标准的面包一经发现，面包师便会受到严厉的惩处。为了避免被罚，面包师们就在出售面包时每打多给一个，即十三个为一打。这样，也就逐渐形成了“a baker's dozen”这一短语。汉语中的一些词语在英语中也无契合词。比如“干部”经常被译为“cadre”，但是两者并不相同。事实上，“cadre”在英语中也不是一个常用词，许多英语国家的人都不知道这个词是什么意思。所以在翻译“干部”时，人们经常要找一些替代词如“official”、“functionary”和“administrator”等。但这些词也都不能准确地表达“干部”的含义。另外如秧歌、快板儿、文言文、粽子、麒麟、风水、观音、磕头、城管、知青、关系、房奴等，这些具有中国独特文化内涵的词汇，在英语中也很难找到对应的词汇，不过英语也很“大度”，将这些词语都收入进去了。

中英风情民俗的差异包罗万象，数不胜数：婚姻家庭、社交礼仪、饮食文化等，我们在后面的“案例分析”和“实战演练”中通过词组和句子做进一步生动讲解。

5）道德标准

中国与西方在文明的发展进程中都相当重视道德的作用，不断地有哲学家和思想家对道德原理和功效进行解释。但是中西方由于在文化特性和方法论上面有很大的不同，因此。在道德理解也有很大的不同。

（1）在歌颂勤俭，鼓励劳动，踏实工作方面，中英表现出的道德规范是一样的。“少壮不努力，老大徒伤悲”和英语中的“A lazy youth, a lousy age.”（少年懒惰，晚年糟糕/少时懒散，老来寒酸。）相对应。英语谚语中表示节俭的，有“Labor overcomes all things.”（勤劳压倒一切。）“Thrift is a philosopher's stone.”（节俭是点金石。）等。而在汉语中表示节俭的成语谚语就更多了，这里不一一举例。

（2）汉英对于表示谦虚，自知之明，诚实，名誉，知足等最基本道德品行方面的观点大多一致。例如，与“谦受益，满招损”对应的英文中有“Humility often gains more than pride.”。与“人贵自知之明”相对应的有“He is not wise that is not wise for himself.”（不自知者是不智的。）另外，汉语中有不少对妄想在行家门前班门弄斧的人加以讽刺的表达，如“孔子面前读经书”，“关公面前耍大刀”，英语中也有“Never offer to teach fish to swim.”以及“Don't teach your grandmother how to suck eggs”。

（3）在表述友谊、友情方面，东西方有较明显的差异。汉语中有这样的说法，“交一个朋友千难万易，得罪一个朋友三言两语”和英语中的“A friend is not so soon gotten as lost.”（交一个朋友没有失掉那么快）意思相同；“朋友易得，知己难求”就是“A faithful friend is hard to find.”最好的翻译。汉语中，“朋友”这个词本身就具有感情色彩（褒义），而在英语中似乎还有消极的意思和许多用来形容朋友的消极的谚语，“Love your friend, but look after yourself.”（爱朋友，但要照顾自己。）“Friends are thieves of time.”（朋友是时间的窃贼。）在西方的道德体系中，个人及自我永远是第一位的。西方友情观在拜金主义、功利主义的冲击下，友情是互惠互利的代名词，蒙着一层厚厚的功利注意色彩。“He that has a full purse never wants a friend.”（钱包丰厚的人从来不需要朋友。）“Hunger knows no friend.”（饥饿不识朋友），不仅如此，西方还讲究朋友落难时，千万不要伸出援手，以免殃及自身利益，如：“Never catch at a falling knife or a falling friend.”（千万不要接落下的刀或正在落难的朋友。）而中国文化传统中，特别是在儒家学说中，自身利益与国家、集体、家庭、朋友的利益比起来是小利益，这种文化氛围中，友情重于个人利益是公认的道德观。君子可以为朋友“两肋插刀”，可以“士为知己者死”。

（4）关于帮助和救济的看法，东西文化的根基决定必然存在截然不同的观点。中国的传统道德观念，讲究“礼、义、仁、至、信”。仁，就是要慈悲为怀，乐善好施；义，要仗义疏财，助人为乐。所以产生了“一人有难大家帮，一家有事百家忙”、“互帮互助，穷能变富”等无偿奉献的谚语。而在英文的谚语中却将这种朋友处于危难之中不愿相助的退缩心态描写得淋漓尽致。“He that has but one eye must be afraid to lose it.”（只有一只眼的人当然怕失去它。）意为“不借理所当然”。再看看这句，“Lend your horse for a long journey, you may have him returned with his skin.”（借马给人去远行，可能还你一张皮。）甚至钱还未借出，将可能产生的可怕后果都预料到了。“Lend your money, and lose your friend.”（借出你的钱，失去你的朋友。）还有些谚语直截了当劝人不要借钱和物给他人。“Lend and lose, so play fools.”（借出等于失去，所以装傻吧。）当然，英语谚语中也不乏鄙视借债者的说法，“He that borrows must pay with shame and loss.”（借债的人必然要用耻辱或是损失偿还。）

（5）中国人不愿在金钱问题的纠缠的另一个原因是怕扯皮，怕丢面子。一个有道德的人就会有好名声，通常也会有好面子，中国人讲的“面子”有受人尊重的意思。相关的谚语有褒有贬。“人怕不要脸，树怕剥掉皮”、“人不要脸，鬼都害怕”，还有“死要面子活受罪”，意为“打肿脸充胖子”。西方的传统道德观念认为，名誉很重要，人应该检点自己的行为，但只要自己不危害社会和他人，不违犯法律，他人如何评价自己并不十分重要，所以“面子”不“面子”的，都是“浮云”。“Sticks and stones may break my bones, but words will never hurt me.”（棍棒石头可能打断我的骨头，但话语决不会伤害我），其实说白了就是“难听的话不会伤筋动骨。”（Hard words break no bones.）相比之下，中国人要面子，而且很在乎周围人的评价，追其根源可能因为受“儒”而惊，人和环境社会是一体的，人只有在社会中得到的评估（好与坏）才是判断名誉面子的标准。同样，对于西方谚语中不在乎他人看法、社会评价的特点，不难看出个人主义、个人至上的影子。

6）思维模式

英汉民族地理环境不同，文化背景各异，形成了迥然不同的文化思维模式。思维支配语言，通过语言表达出来。在语言的传递过程中，其内容和形式都打上了思维的烙印。因此，某种语言所传递出来的信息容易被有同种文化思维模式的人群所理解，而有不同文化思维模式的人群对此信息有时很难理解，甚至产生误解。可见，思维方式对语言文字的影响不可忽视。

（1）整体（综合）思维和个体（分析）思维。

中国文化的思维模式根源于对自然界的朴素认识，按照自然界的本来面目把它当作一个整体来观察。这种整体思维也叫综合思维。而西方文化强调按照一定的程序进行思考，从已知推导未知，得出合乎逻辑的结论。这种在思维活动中把对象分为各个部分，逐一加以考察研究的方法正是分析思维的特点。中国人偏好综合,这导致了在思维上整体优先的特点。这种从整体到部分的思维方式,也反映在语言文字的表达上,如时间的表达方式和排列顺序是从大到小,由年到月,再到日、星期、时、分、秒;空间位置的叙述顺序也是由大到小,从国家到省、市、区、街道、门牌号;人物介绍时先说头衔,从大到小逐步列出其职务,最后再说名字。而英美人的表达方式则正相反。英语习惯从小单位到大单位,从小范围到大范围,从次要内容到主要内容的次序,这是西方人从局部到整体的思维方式在其语言中的体现。

(2)形象(具体)思维和抽象(逻辑)思维。

中国人习惯形象思维,在认识世界的过程中更加注重直观经验,以感觉、知觉、表象为依据,进行类比分析。这种思维借助于直觉体会,通过知觉从总体上模糊而直接地把握认识对象的内在本质和规律。西方人习惯抽象思维,在认识过程中借助于概念、判断、推理等思维形式反映客观现实,用科学的抽象概念、范畴揭示事物的本质。由于这一过程是按照逻辑规律进行的,所以也叫逻辑思维。西方人的抽象逻辑思维具有浓厚的实证、理性和思辨的色彩。英语民族善于抽象思维,体现在语言中还有一整套表达抽象思维的方式,如句中大量使用抽象名词,这些抽象名词含义概括,指称笼统,便于表达复杂的思想和微妙的情绪。这些名词大多是通过虚化手段,即加词缀,尤其是后缀等,从其他词类转化而来。如表性质、状态的后缀“-ness”、“-tion”、“-ity”、“-ence”、“-hood”等,如:absence, carelessness, youth, sensation, honesty, motherhood 等。此外,英语介词非常多,可表示虚泛的意义。汉族倾向于形象思维,汉语倾向于化抽象为具体,常常以实的形式来表达虚的概念,以具体的形象表达抽象的内容。因此在把英语理解为汉语时往往要把表达抽象概念的词义具体化和形象化,而把汉语说成英语时,则可以把具体的内容抽象化。如“lack of perseverance”译为“三天打鱼、两天晒网”,“perfect harmony”译为“水乳交融”,“As you sow, you will reap.”译为“种瓜得瓜, 种豆得豆”,无须绞尽脑汁地试图把“瓜”和“豆”这样具体的事物译成英语。

(3)主体思维和客体思维。

中国传统思维强调以人为本,把自身作为宇宙的中心,认为内心体验是一切认识的出发点。这种思维倾向侧重于向内探求,即认识自身、完善自身。但这种内倾性,并不突出独立的个体地位,相反,群体包摄个体,将自然包容于人心,以人为天,天人合一。通过主体与客体的融合去感受、领悟万物。这就形成了汉民族的主体性思维。由于主体性思维往往指向自身,寻求人与自然的和谐,在观察事物时以人为中心,在叙述事件或陈述观点时习惯从自我出发来叙述客观事物,倾向于描述人及其行为或状态,因此在汉语中常用人称,即以表示人或生物的词作主语,这也导致了汉语中主动语态使用得较多。与中国的主体意识不同,西方传统思维以自然为认知对象,认为只有认识自然,才能把握自然,只有探索自然,才能征服自然,因而主客二分,天人对立,划分内心世界与外部自然界,区分自我意识与认识对象。因此,西方人重视自然客体,强调客体的存在,思维的目标往往指向外界。在这种意识影响下,形成了客体性思维,把客观世界作为观察、分析和研究的对象。反映在语言上,英语常以非生物或抽象概念等非人称为主语,注重事物对人的作用和影响,使事物以客观的口气呈现出来。以下面的英语句子为例,以黑体标出的主语都是物称而非人称,汉语理解时必须改成人称主语才符合汉民族的表达习惯:

Not a **sound** reached his ear. 他没听到任何声音。

Something inside us seemed to stop momentarily. 我们顿时呆住了。

The sight of the old picture reminds us of our childhood. 看到那张老照片,我们想起了自己的童年。

二、案例分析

下面我们用更多的例子来帮助大家理解英汉表达中的文化差异，为提高口语表达能力提供大量的鲜活的典型案例。

1. 猫

在英国，“猫”用来指代一个人，有着不同的文化内涵及色彩。它象征着狡猾，代表低等动物，有贬义，如：copycat（模仿者），old cat（坏脾气的老太婆），cat's paw（受骗的人）。

（1）a fat cat 暴发户，有钱有势的人

字面意思：肥猫。

（2）When the cat's away, the mice will play. 山中无老虎猴子称大王。

字面意思：当猫不在时，老鼠就猖狂。

（3）to throw one's cat at everybody 招蜂引蝶

字面意思：拿自己的猫砸每个人。

（4）peephole 猫眼

“猫眼”是“门镜”的俗称。为什么要叫“猫眼”呢？因为光线通过它折射后在远处看它闪光的样子很类似波斯猫眼睛晚上发出的光线。中国人观察到它的外观，英国人注重它的功能——“窥视孔”，由此不难看出英国人很现实。

（5）There's more than one way to skin a cat. 条条大路通罗马。

比喻“采用许多不同的方法办事，都可以收到同样的效果”。“条条大路通长安”，“条条大路通北京”都同理，但这句英文句子却让“猫”遭了厄运。

（6）to put the cat among the pigeons 制造混乱；自找麻烦

不难想象把猫放进鸽子群的后果。

（7）cat out of the bag 泄露秘密

与 let 连用，意思是“让猫从袋子里跑出来”，通常喻指说走了嘴而泄露秘密。

（8）pussycat 温和的人

pussy 是 cat 的昵称，可译为“小猫咪；喵喵”。pussycat 一般是指“女孩子似的女人”，或指某人的“女朋友”。但中国人却用小鸟来形容这类人“小鸟依人”。也可形容像猫一样“胆小、温柔、屈服的男人”。

2. 马

（1）to change horses 中途换人

用这种方法思考可能有助记忆，古时候，人骑马打仗，人马一体，换马就是换人。

（2）to hold one's horses 不要急

这个词组来源于赛马比赛，发令枪响之前，所有的马在起跑线上，骑手要想尽办法勒住马缰，不让马冲出去。

（3）from the horse's mouth 由权威人士口中说出；来自可靠的消息来源

直译为“从马嘴里得到消息”，引申意就是“直接从原始来源处获取的消息，即指劝告、情报等来自直接参与者的，从可靠的人那里获得的消息”。马和消息可靠又有什么关系呢？要

知道，远在人们还没有使用汽车的年代，人们是依靠马作为他们主要的交通工具，认为马是十分可靠的。现在，汽车已经早就代替了马，但是这个俗语仍然被广为使用。

3. 猪

(1) Pigs can fly. 太阳打西边出来了。

“猪”能飞？这真是太阳打西边出来了。

(2) to live high on the hog 生活舒适

hog 是指“猪”，猪一般除了吃就是睡，生活舒适，所以用它比喻舒适的生活非常形象而贴切。与中文的“像猪一样”还是有区别，汉语的意思是说“很懒”，而不是像“猪一样舒适。”

(3) road hog 妨碍他人超车的驾驶员

hog 指的是“猪”的意思，road hog 在口语中比喻那些阻挠他人超越自己的蛮横驾驶员。hog 做动词是指占用某个地方。如：“hog to road / 占路中”，即紧挨着路中线驾驶使其他车辆无法超越；“hog the bathroom / 占用浴室”，使别人无法使用。

4. 狗

(1) She'd have found some other bone for us to fight over. 她也会另外找别的事跟我吵架。

这是与“狗”相关表达的延伸。狗与狗的战斗经常源自于对食物和异性的争夺，“bone”就是争夺对象，延伸为“争斗的导火索”。

(2) Keep your nose out of it! 别多管闲事！

能想象这样一副画面吗？一只狗用鼻子四处嗅，寻找食物或猎物。“把你的鼻子拿开！”就是不要“多管闲事！”把说话对象当狗看了，在英国还算客气，在中国，那就真不客气了。

(3) Throw me a bone! 别卖关子！

有人喜欢用骨头逗狗玩，这里的 me 用自己代替“狗”的位置，看见狗在西方国家真讨人喜欢。

(4) Let a sleeping dog lie. 别惹麻烦！

这已是一个耳熟能详的表达，无需多做解释。

(5) I know I'm a dog's body. 我知道我是被呼来唤去的命。

尽管英国人对狗十分友好，但它始终是动物，因为牵绳的始终是人。

(6) to bark up the wrong tree 攻击错了目标，错怪人，精力用在不该用的地方，一厢情愿

bark 是指“狗叫”，英文的意思是狗找错了目标对象，一阵狂吠。

(7) be out of the dog house 不再受冷遇，又受重用的

不管狗在英国有多么得宠，人住狗窝始终是对人的侮辱，所以“赶出狗窝”就是“不再受冷遇”的意思。

5. 鸟

(1) sb's cuckoo craze 某人又疯又傻

英国人认为“cuckoo/布谷鸟”十分愚笨。有部经典美国电影“*One Flew over the Cuckoo's Nest*”即《飞越疯人院》，该片名里就有 cuckoo 这个单词。

(2) to eat crow 被迫收回自己说的话

crow 是指乌鸦。吃乌鸦吗？乌鸦是人们都讨厌的鸟，它的肉也老得没法吃，因此要一个

人吃乌鸦是非常难受的。to eat crow 是指一个人犯了一个很难堪的错，而又不得不承认。可译为“食言，因犯错而丢脸”。

(3) like water off a duck's back 毫无作用；满不在乎；耳边风

鸭子有“出水而不带走一滴水”的好本事。鸭子身上的毛就像雨衣一样，水在上面待不住，一下全滑掉了。因此，water off a duck's back 即指“毫无作用；满不在乎”之意。

(4) to bury one's head in the sand 逃避现实

“将头埋在沙土里”。据说鸵鸟碰到危险时，就会把头扎进沙窝里，认为这样进犯的敌人就不会发现或伤害它。其实，鸵鸟庞大的身躯仍露在沙外，而只是将头埋起来起不到任何保护作用，所以把这条习语比喻成“闭眼不看眼前的现实”或“不敢正视现实”。鸵鸟在中国是后来引进的，汉语类似的表达也跟动物有关“缩头乌龟”。

(5) for the birds 无价值的；愚蠢的

出处不从考。但可以这样理解帮助记忆：为鸟儿准备的东西当然是数量上少，质量上要求不高。

(6) cocksure 过于自信；必定的，自以为是的

公鸡趾高气扬的神态帮助我们理解这个单词。

(7) He canceled on me/stood me up. 他放了我的鸽子。

“放某人的鸽子”在汉语中是“爽约”的意思，关于它的出处说法很多，不必深究。stand sb. up 译为“让某人空等一场”。英语中的“放鸽子”大概是奥运会开幕式放鸽子庆祝的意思。

(8) to talk turkey 直率地说或谈正经事

这里有这么一个有趣的故事：一个白人和一个印第安人约定去打一天猎，然后平分猎物。分猎物时，其他的猎物的分配都没有什么困难，直到最后，还剩下最后两只：一只乌鸦/crow 和一只火鸡/turkey。白人显得很公正地说道：“你可以拿乌鸦，那吗我就要火鸡；要么我要火鸡，你可以拿乌鸦。”印第安人说：“干嘛不对我直说你要火鸡呢？” to talk turkey 也可以说成 to say turkey，其意不变。

(9) to walk turkey 船在航行中前后左右地颠簸

在记忆这个词组的时候，不妨脑子里想象一下火鸡、公鸡等走路的样子：左右摇晃，一颠一颠的。

(10) to strut/swell like a turkey-cock 火鸡一样高傲，昂首阔步的人

火鸡虽然走路摇晃，但头始终高昂着。

(11) turkey-cock 雄火鸡

当某人因为生气而面红耳赤时，不妨以“He is as red as a turkey-cock.”来打比喻。

6. 牛

(1) A bull of Bashan woke the sleeping child with his noise. 一个大嗓门的人把那个酣睡的孩子吵醒了。

Bashan 约旦河以东的地区，因其广阔富饶的牧场而出名。中国说声音大有一个很形象的词语，叫“河东狮吼”，不过意义有别。

(2) a bull in a china shop 粗心大意者；粗人

本指一只在陶瓷店里的牛，如果稍不留意，店里所有的精细摆设都会被莽撞的牛弄坏，并由此引申出人和人之间不融洽、不协调的感觉，或形容某人粗枝大叶，笨手笨脚。

7. 羊

(1) an old goat 老古板

goat 一般指的是"山羊",而在俚语中则表示"令人讨厌的老头"。可能与山羊的脾性有关。中文中无此表达,类似表达有"老古董、犟得跟头牛似的"。

(2) a stone-cold fox 冰山美人

老外应该不知道"狐狸精"吧,但这个单词的汉语表达给人以大跌眼镜之感。

(3) He did the lion's share of the work. 他做了大部分工作。

"狮子"是森林之王,所以它占的份额是最大的。

8. 鱼

I'm not fishing with no bait! 我不是空手套白狼。

"空手套白狼"中的"空手"应该是指没有使用任何先进的武器,"套"表明了用了绳子这种最便宜和最原始的武器或工具,而且也表明用了计谋和智慧。"白狼"当然是不多见的狼了,稀少也就珍贵,表明"收获"很大。当然这么大的"收获"或"利益",风险也是不小的,毕竟是在没有武器的情况下抓到了一只大白狼,一定是艺高人胆大。意为:一个人以很小的付出或是暗指没有付出而取得了很大的回报。英文却讲的是"不用诱饵钓鱼的事"。一个说"鱼",一个讲"狼",内涵差不多。

9. 颜色

(1) out ofthe blue 突然

(2) to sing the blues 诉苦,哭穷;抱怨

(3) blue in the face 气急败坏;筋疲力尽;面红耳赤

(4) to tick sb. pink 逗某人笑

(5) Do you see any green in my eye? 你以为我那么好骗吗?

green 是"缺乏经验的"的意思。

(6) I can't even talk about it to everyone, except you, because anybody else would think I was yellow. 除你之外,这种事不能对别人说,因为他们会觉得我是个胆小鬼。

turn yellow 变得胆怯起来。

(7) greycation 同堂假期;和祖父母一起度假来分担费用的家庭假期

grey 代表"上年纪的人","-cation"为"vacation"的一部分,共同构成这个意思,有点"其乐融融"之感吧。

10. 苹果

(1) a bad apple 坏蛋;害群之马

不晓得与白雪公主吃下的毒苹果是否有关? 中国人说"坏蛋/bad egg"。但你知不知道,英国人说"好人"却可以用 good egg。

(2) Big Apple 纽约市

关于纽约市为什么要叫"大苹果",出处有三,读者不妨自己去搜搜看。记住"Meet you at Big Apple."是"纽约见!"的意思。

11. 国家民族

英国是个老牌的资本主义国家,曾号称“日不落帝国”! 英语中很多词汇来自于英民族对全球各国各民族的认识,有些很有趣,但也没少带损人的个人色彩。

(1)Greek gift 害人的礼物

(2)Pardon/Excuse my French. 原谅我说话粗鲁。

(3)an Indian giver 送东西给人后又讨回的人

(4)Spanish castle 空中楼阁,不切实际

(5)Spanish athlete 爱吹牛的人

(6)Italian hand 幕后操作,暗中干预

(7)Irish bull 自相矛盾,荒唐可笑的说法

(8)the luck of the Irish 非常幸运

(9)Dutch courage 酒后之勇

(10)to go Dutch 各人付各人的账

(11)Dutch uncle 严厉的批评者

(12)French window 落地窗

(13)to take a French leave 不告而别

(14)be ret/French Hat 贝雷帽

(15)Greek calends 永远不

calends 是罗马日历的第一天,希腊人不用罗马日历,所以“永远不”会有这一天。

(16)be Greek to sb. (某人)一点也不懂;一窍不通

此处的 Greek 指的是“希腊语”。对一个罗马人来说,希腊文是个陌生的语言,自然而然这句话就表示“完全不了解”的意思。

12. 上帝(神)

(1)God is always watching. 苍天有眼。

中国人说“人在做,天在看”。与这句英语句子的意思一样。但人家的宗教信仰决定了是“上帝/God” 在看。

(2)Those whom God wishes to destroy, he first makes mad. 上帝欲毁之,必先使其疯狂。

这句话出自古希腊历史学家 Herodotus 口中,其原本的见解是:上帝要使一个人遭难,总是让他忘乎所以。古希腊的悲剧家们纷纷受到其影响,对此言做了充足的演绎。较为出名的是古希腊悲剧作家欧底庇德斯的重复见解“Those whom God wishes to destroy, he first makes mad.”

(3)a man of clay 凡人;凡夫俗子

clay 在这儿是指“上帝造人的泥土;人的躯体, 肉体”。据传,第一个人就是用泥土造出来的。

13. 典故

(1)It was the last straw. 我真受不了了。

这句话大约起源于阿拉伯世界,完整的说法为 The last straw that breaks the camel back. 意

思是“压垮骆驼背的最后一根稻草”。要知道骆驼是沙漠世界中最有用的运输工具,背上的东西已经达到极限,这时候再放上去一根稻草,都可能把骆驼背压断。比喻在临界点附近的一个具有决定意义的小事件。

(2)The pot calls the kettle black. 五十步笑百步。

“五十步笑百步”比喻某些人嘲笑他人的不足和缺点却未意识到自己也有这样的不足和过失。英文的字面意思是“锅笑壶黑”。在烧柴火的日子里,有什么炊具不黑的吗?

(3)One land without two queens. 一山不容二虎。

这句话收集于热门电视剧《绯闻女孩》*Gossip Girl*。电视剧里的这句话可能来自于 Two Queens in One Isle 的说法,大不列颠岛上英格兰伊丽莎白一世和苏格兰玛丽女王的不和谐关系。

(4)There must be a story. 一定有名堂。

这里有个中国典故。“明堂”通“名堂”,与汉武帝和武则天修建“明堂”有关,说来话长,大家可以自己去查查这个典故。后来就将“稀奇古怪、别出心裁的东西”均称为“名堂”,看来带有 story 这个词的英文句子“It's a long story.”说的就是他、她,还有它。

(5)I just had to rip the band-aid off. 我必须快刀斩乱麻。

“快刀斩乱麻”是一个中国成语,北朝人高欢任东魏丞相时,他想测试几个儿子的智力,给每个儿子发上一堆乱麻,让他们尽快理清,大儿子一根根慢慢抽,越抽越乱,小儿子将乱麻分成两半然后再分开。只有高洋拿出快刀,几刀砍下去再理出一缕缕短麻来受到高欢的夸奖。比喻做事果断,能采取坚决有效的措施,很快解决复杂的问题。这句话的英文表达在生动形象方面不输于中文表达。band-aid 是“创可贴”的意思。你切乱麻,我撕创可贴。

(6)Small steps, we'll get there. 不积跬步无以至千里。

《大戴礼记·劝学》:“是故不积跬步,无以至千里;不积小流,无以成江海。”跬步:半步,一迈脚。

(7)Put this murderer behind bars. 将凶手绳之以法。

“绳之以法”出自《后汉书·冯衍传》:“以文帝之明,而魏尚之忠,绳之以法则为罪,施之以德则为功。”“绳”即准绳,引申为标准、法则,又引申为按一定的标准去衡量。英语表达很实在,该词的意思就是“把人抓起来关进监狱”,当然是依法进行。

(8)The fat's in the fire now. 生米已煮成熟饭了。

“生米已煮成熟饭了”这个成语出自明·沈受先《三元记·遣妾》:“小姐,如今生米做成熟饭了,又何必如此推阻。”表示“事情已无法挽回了”。英语“The fat's in the fire now.”用生动形象的方式表示“事情已无法挽回了”,脂肪或肥肉放进火里的后果,大家可以想象。

(9)There's my little worrywart. 你杞人忧天了。

“杞人忧天”出自《列子·天瑞》:“杞国有人,忧天地崩坠,身亡所寄,废寝食者。”后用以比喻不必要的忧虑。英语中 worrywart 是指“自寻烦恼的人;杞人忧天者”。

(10)to have a little walk on the wild side 红杏出墙

“红杏出墙”出自宋·叶绍翁《游小园不值》:“春色满园关不住,一枝红杏出墙来。”由于是红色的杏花穿出墙外,后常形容妻子有外遇。英文意思为“郊外散步”,这不是幌子、借口又是啥呢。

(11)They have a great deal to talk about each other when drinking with friends. 酒逢知己千杯少。

这句中文成语出自清·吴璿《飞龙全传》第三回:“二人也把别后之事,谈了一番。三人举杯大悦。正是:酒逢知己千杯少,话不投机半句多。”意为“酒桌上遇到知己,喝一千杯酒都还嫌少。形容性情相投的人聚在一起总不厌倦。”

(12)to usurp one's authority 越俎代庖

出处《庄子·逍遥游》:“庖人虽不治庖,尸祝不越俎而代之矣。”比喻超出自己职务范围去处理别人所管的事。usurp 意为“篡夺、夺取、侵占”,to usurp one's authority 意为“侵占别人的权力”。

(13)Sometimes we must endure a little pain in order to achieve satisfaction. 不如虎穴焉得虎子。

出自《后汉书·班超传》:“超曰:‘不入虎穴,不得虎子。’”不进入老虎洞,怎么能捉住小老虎。原指不亲历危险的境地,就不能获得成功。现也比喻不进行认真实践就不能得到真知。“入虎穴”就是 endure a little pain,“得虎子”就是 to achieve satisfaction。再介绍一句,“舍不得孩子套不住狼/ You've gotta speculate to accumulate.”英语句子的意思是“要投机才会有资本积累”。

(14)There are plenty more fish in the sea than ever came out of it. 天涯何处无芳草。

这是苏东坡所做《蝶恋花》一词的名句。有两个含义,第一是指大千世界机会很多,不要过分注重于某一件事儿而不知变通;第二是指男女之间没有必要死守一方,可以爱的人或值得爱的人很多,平时更常用的意思即此意。而英语里是拿“鱼”来说事,海里的鱼比跃出水面的鱼要多。虽然意思差不多,但感觉少了点意境。“天涯何处无芳草,何必单恋一枝花。”

(15)He looked like a rabbit in front of a snake. 他就像是惊弓之鸟一样。

出自《战国策·楚策四》、《晋书·王鉴传》:“黩武之众易动,惊弓之鸟难安。”意思为“被弓箭吓怕了的鸟不容易安定”,比喻经过惊吓的人碰到一点动静就非常害怕。英文将“他像是在蛇面前的兔子”。虽然中英文并不完全匹配,但内涵比较接近。

(16)to throw good money after bad 赔了夫人又折兵

东汉末年孙权想取回荆州,周瑜献计“假招亲扣人质”。诸葛亮识破,安排赵云陪伴前往,先拜会周瑜的岳父乔玄,乔玄说动吴国太在甘露寺见面,吴国太真的将孙尚香嫁给刘备。孙权与周瑜被人嘲笑“周郎妙计安天下,赔了夫人又折兵”。英语表达中 bad 后省略了 money,字面意思是“浪费钱之后浪费更多的钱。”

(17)The man who can smile and smile and be villain. 这人口蜜腹剑,笑里藏刀。

这是出自英国电视连续剧《唐顿庄园》的一个句子。“口蜜腹剑”出自宋朝司马光《资治通鉴·唐玄宗天宝元年》:“尤忌文学之士,或阳与之善,啖以甘言而阴陷之。世谓李林甫‘口有蜜,腹有剑’”。意思为“嘴上甜,心里狠”。形容两面派的狡猾阴险,多指蛇蝎心肠的人。对此的英语表达只能通过了解内涵的方式进行,“那个笑得很灿烂的人是个坏人。”意是出来了,但文化内涵丢失了很多,这就是文化差异最大的体现。

14. 缺省

(1)Not shed a tear until one sees the coffin. 不见棺材不落泪。

英语中没有这种说法,只能通过内涵的理解进行表达:To refuse to be convinced until one is faced with grim reality.

(2)Things have to come out somewhere. 纸包不住火。

“纸包不住火”比喻事实掩盖不了的。英语中,也常用这个表达:Truth will come to light sooner or later.

(3)social worker 社工

“社会工作者”是指从事社会工作“social work”的人,他们从事的是慈善工作“charitable work”。社会工作是非盈利的“non-profit”,旨在帮助他人和解决社会问题。而社会工作者是一种职业“profession”,需要专业技术“technical expertise”、职业道德“professional ethics”和奉献精神“devotion”。与社工相对的是义工“volunteer”,义工的工作是无偿的“voluntary”。目前在中国真正意义上的“社工”还很少,几乎没有。

(4)spring breaker 放春假的人

所谓的“春假”,其实是在复活节前一周放的假,所以每年都不一定,每个学校放假的时间长度都是统一的,一般放 8 天左右。中国没有这一假日。

(5)to melt away 化为乌有

“乌”通“无”,“乌有”就是“虚幻,不存在”。英语表达才有 melt away 十分形象,这个词指“雪的融化”,“形状”都没有了,“不存在”了。

(6)I' m Switzerland. 我保持中立。

这是一句非常生动的口语表达。“瑞士”是世界著名的中立国,历史上一直保持政治与军事上的中立,但瑞士同时也参与国际事务,许多国际性组织的总部都设在瑞士。

(7)a breadwinner 养家糊口的人

面包是英国人的主食,所以家里的主要劳动力就是“挣面包的人”。

(8)Trash doesn' t change. 狗改不了吃屎。

trash 在美式英语中有“流氓、无赖”的意思。“狗”在汉语中更多带有贬义,这句话的中文理解就不费劲了。

(9)Money talks. 金钱最重要。

资本主义的拜金意识跃然纸上。

(10)Chinese Feng Shui Kick 中国风水学

英语之所以成为全球 No.1 的“流行语”,其“兼收并蓄”特征无疑是最重要的原因之一。汉语最新流行语“房奴”、“知青”、“关系”、“城管”等都成了英语的“客人”!

(11)English occupied France 英属法国领地

英国有个别称“日不落帝国”,表明其在最强盛时期到处是殖民地。

(12)baby annoyer 狼外婆

annoyer 是指“招人讨厌的事或人”。“狼外婆”是中国孩子在小时候都听过的故事,英语只能意译。

(13)golden goose 摇钱树

源自西方民间传说,有只神鹅,每天都会下金蛋。虽然没有神鹅,但我们有摇钱树。

(14)My castle my rules. 我的地盘我做主。

地盘的边界在哪儿? 实在不好划分,还是城堡来得实在,是自己的。

(15)He is like a heat-seeking missile every time he sees you. 他每次见到你都像跟屁虫一样。

heat-seeking missile 意思为“热跟踪导弹”,可以对设定目标实行追踪和打击。“跟屁虫”指一天到晚围着某人转。这样一中一西的表达虽然载体不同,但内涵相似。

(16) south paw 左撇子

中国人把习惯用左手的人成为"左撇子",英语中可以用 left-handed 来表示,还有个说法叫 south paw,也是"左撇子"的意思。这个说法从 19 世纪晚期芝加哥的棒球运动中来。当时,棒球青年队的本垒板(棒球场一角上的一垒,由一块坚硬的橡胶板构成,投手击球时站在此处,跑垒员最后必须触到此垒,才能得分)方向朝东,也就是说,投手如果是"左撇子",那么他投球的那只胳膊应该是向着南边 south,而 paw 可以指"手爪",和投手戴的手套的形状差不多。

(17) Where is my brain? 我脑子进水了。

"我脑子进水了"可能是源自于现代生活的各种电器如果进水就不能正常工作,"脑子进水"人也就不能正常工作了。类似的表达还有"脑子进地沟油了","脑子被门夹了"。英语干脆直接,连"脑袋都不知道到哪儿去了?"

(18) I guess it's true what they say: you live by the gun, you get gunshot wounds. 前人的话不无道理,"常在河边走哪有不湿脚。"

英文意思是"常常玩枪,就会被枪伤。"

(19) Small strokes fall great oaks. 水滴石穿。

对于这中英两句话,我只能说两个民族对生活都有细致的观察,不过观察对象一个是石头,一个是橡树。

(20) to keep your hair on 别发火,保持冷静

汉英在这个表达上持截然不同的态度,汉语"怒发冲冠",而英语却说"让头发立起来"是"建议他人要保持冷静,不要生气或是过激反应"的意思。

(21) The evidence spoke itself. (smoking gun) 铁证如山。

汉语倾向于"证据确凿,像山一样不可动摇",又是"铁"又是"山"的,表示真的"十拿九稳"。英语理解为"证据自己说话"。另外还有一个词 smoking gun 也是"铁证如山"的意思:刚枪杀了被害者,火药枪还在冒烟呢? 属于被逮个现行。

(22) You'll come through this with flying colors. 你肯定会轻松战胜病魔的。

flying colors 是指"彩旗飘飘;胜利"的意思。英语用更加生动的方式让别人树立起战胜疾病的信心。

(23) name-calling 破口大骂

绞尽脑汁想 name-calling 怎么会是"破口大骂"的意思? 但如果想要越过中英文化差异的鸿沟,可否这样记忆该词:平时大家关系好都不会叫对方的全名,如果叫你的全名,一定是十分生气的时候,生气就会骂人。

(24) progressive dinner 百家宴

这个"百家宴"是指吃完一道菜换一家再吃。

(25) I must be in bad shape. 我一定很虚。

"虚"是一个中医词汇,是指"正气不足,以正气虚损为矛盾主要方面的一种病理反映"。这样将这个词用英语来表达呢? 只好说"身体不好。"

(26) to pop the question 单刀直入(求婚)

英文的字面意思好像是"突然提问",对,男士向女士提出"人生最大、最严肃的问题"——"愿意嫁给我吗?",男士是精心准备的,女士面对这"突然的提问"一定是十分幸福吧。

(27) shopping savant 购物达人/personal shopper 购物顾问,顾客购物参谋

介绍两个西方购物商场的出现的词汇。savant 是专家的意思,他们对购物有敏锐的感觉

和上乘的品位,所以许多大型商场会聘他们为“购物参谋”。

(28)to throw in the towel 认输,放弃

这句话跟拳击比赛有关。拳击比赛时,在一旁的教练扔出白毛巾,就表示认输。可与 throw up the sponge 互换使用。

(29)My imagination's running riot. 丈二和尚摸不着头脑。

“丈二和尚”指寺庙中比较高大的诸天、罗汉等塑像。俗用“和尚”来称呼罗汉等,人们无法用手触摸到高大的塑像,因而用“丈二和尚摸不着头脑”比喻弄不明情况,搞不清底细。to run riot 意思是“失去控制”,全句意思为“我的想象力失去控制”。就是“想不到,摸不清楚状况”的意思。

(30)I shall have arms like Jack Johnson if I'm not careful. 我得留心,别让杰克·约翰逊的粗胳膊长在我身上。

这里涉及文化背景,句中的“杰克·约翰逊”是世界第一位重量级拳王。

(31)Everyone's falling like ninepins. 大家怎么接二连三地病倒啊。

ninepins 是“九柱球的木桩;九瓶制保龄球柱”。大家生病接二连三的倒下,就像倒下的保龄球柱,非常形象。

(32)to keep one's nose clean 明哲保身/远离是非

记忆窍门:用鼻子吸食毒品的人要想改邪归正,最好的做法就是不再吸食毒品。

(33)be at sixes and sevens 乱七八糟

最有说服力的一种是说 sixes and sevens 和中世纪一种叫作 hazard 的掷骰游戏有关。骰子上最大的数字是五和六,当时有一个法语短语 to set on cinque[法语,five] and sice[法语,six]”,意思是“押 5 点和 6 点”,这是要冒很大的风险的。到了乔叟生活的时代,five and six 被改成了 six and seven,当然了,短语的意义也就发生了变化,因为这个数字根本不可能被掷出来,所以它的意思变成了“不惜冒一切风险”。为了掷骰赌博而不惜一切代价,那么这个人一定处于不理智的状态。到了 16 世纪,six and seven 就有“混乱、没有头绪”的意思。在莎翁作品《理查二世》中,约克公爵说:But time will not permit: all is uneven,and everything is left at six and seven. 说到这个短语在今天被使用的情况,恐怕给人印象最深的莫过于歌曲 *Don't Cry for Me, Argentina* 中的歌词:You won't believe me/All you will see is a girl you once knew/Although she's dressed up to the nines/At sixes and sevens with you.“尽管锦衣玉食,但生活却混乱不堪。”

(34)be wet behind the ears 乳臭未干的毛孩

英国人认为由于刚生下来的婴儿的耳朵里侧是湿的,就产生了这种说法。而中国人却认为是“还在吃奶的孩子,乳臭未干”。

(35)couch potato 懒人

在美国,很多人下班之后,如果没有所谓的“社交活动”,大多只能在家里当 couch potato,像马铃薯一样,一动不动地看着电视,吃着零食,直到睡着为止。

(36)to have sth. on the ball 有干某事的能耐

棒球,橄榄球,篮球是美国的三大球类运动 have sth. on the ball 是一条美语口语习语,意思是“有些能耐”。此语从棒球运动的术语中引申而来。当然,“没有能耐”就可以用 have nothing on the ball 来表示,而“很有能耐”则可用 have much on the ball 的短语来表示。汉语中类似的说法是“对……有一手”。

(37)My mama told me the only thing worth stealing is a kiss from a sleeping child. 我妈妈告

诉我唯一值得偷的东西就是偷吻一个熟睡的孩子。

中国人说/想过偷菜、偷税、偷笑、偷师等,还没有想过偷孩子的吻的。

(38) You two now speaking Chinese? 你们在说我听不懂的话。

这是两个老外的对话中的句子。类似于中国人说的"你在说爪哇语吗?","你在说什么鸟语?"再举个两美国人的对话的例子,A 听不懂 B 拐弯抹角的话,就冲他大吼一句 In English! 意思是"说听得懂的话! /说人话!"

(39) highway robbery 敲竹杠;勒索

字面上来解释就指"在高速公路上的抢劫案"。通常是用来抱怨商店索取的价钱太高,简直就像高速公路上的抢劫一样。上了高速路不管价格高低只有交钱往前开,中国人还没有高速路之前,称此行为"敲竹杠"。清末,沿海一带贩卖烟土成风。有个狡猾的云南客商,在毛竹刚生长时,就偷偷剖开嫩竹,藏进烟土,等毛竹长大后,便将毛竹做成竹杠、船篙。因此,竹杠外面,天衣无缝,一点不露痕迹。有一次,一个在关卡办事的绍兴师爷吸着长管旱烟,朝搁在船舱里的竹杠"笃、笃、笃"地敲了几下,准备把烟灰磕掉。谁知这"笃、笃、笃"一敲非同小可,吓得云南客商忙从船舱里钻了出来,以为绍兴师爷看出了秘密,敲敲竹杠,给他暗号。"敲竹杠"一词就产生了。

(40) He can pass out cigars later. 他有时间庆祝。

西方曾有习俗,婴儿诞生的时候父亲为了庆祝会分发雪茄。所以 pass out cigars 成了"庆祝新生儿"的意思,不过后来也用来泛指"庆祝"。

15. 其他

(1) to have a frog in the throat 嗓子哑了

在口语中"frog"就有表示"声音嘶哑"的意思。

(2) loan shark 高利贷者

英语中"shark"有贪得无厌,骗子的意思。

三、实战演练

(1) 你认为你能接他的班。You thought you could fill his shoes.

to fill one's shoes = to take one's place 很好地顶替;令人满意地替代。中国人说"接班"或"子承父业",但"穿旧鞋"表示接替却是英国人的说法。

例如: No one can fill his shoes, but we can all work to follow in his footsteps. 没有人能替代他的位置,我们能做的只有紧跟他的脚步。

(2) 玩真的了。The gloves are off.

西方人的决斗从一方抛出手套开始,丢手套表示开始决斗了,这引申为"开始毫不留情,真刀真枪干"、"强硬起来"了。

例如: The Chinese should take off the gloves and deal with Japanese economic aggression. 中国应该采取行动,以应对日本的经济侵略。

(3) 冷漠的人;沉默寡言的人;不友好的人 cold fish

每次看到这个词,脑海里就会浮现鱼缸里游来游去的金鱼,静静地在水里摆动鱼鳍,尽管主人给他好吃好住,但并不与主人交流,这是理解此表达的方法,仅是个人理解。汉语中对

“鱼”无此认识。

例如: Let’s not invite Joe to the party. He is such a cold fish. He’ll spoil it for everybody else. 我们不要邀请乔参加晚会,他沉默寡言,会扫大家的兴的。

(4)一模一样 two peas in one pod

即“一个豆荚里的两颗豌豆”,形容长得很像。

例如: Tom and Mike are like two peas in one pod. 汤姆和迈克长得一模一样。

(5)我们是一根绳上的蚂蚱。Sink or swim together.

“一条绳上的两只蚂蚱”, 比喻处在一个境地,意为谁也跑不掉、要死一起死要活一起活。

例如:I have a feeling we will sink or swim together. 我们已是一根绳上的俩蚂蚱。

(6)你在开我玩笑吗? Are you pulling my leg?

to pull one’s leg 乍一看,以为是“拖某人的腿”,而实际意思是“逗别人,开别人玩笑”的意思。据说,以前的贼通常是两人合伙抢劫的。一个用手杖或竹杖把人绊跌,另一个就趁机扑过去把皮夹子或者财物抢走。

例如: Don’t pull your teacher’s leg. 不要跟老师开玩笑。

(7)欠了一屁股的债 a long list of possession charges

这是一个古老的民间故事:后面还有一句:一屁股二肋行。传说某人欠债太多,不敢回家过年。年三十晚躲进庙中,藏在菩萨背后,自己也不知差多少债,无事时就将所欠债务,一条条写列在菩萨背后,因菩萨是泥塑的,非常高大,共写满了菩萨整个屁股带二肋。比喻欠债太多。英语的意思是“长长的财产债务清单”。

例如: Don’t lend him money any more. He has a long list of possession charges now. 别再借钱给他了,他已欠了一屁股债。

(8)与某人有过节 to have beef with sb.

beef 一直在英语中是褒义词,“牛肉”,健康食品,力量的源泉,beefy 是“强壮的”。但你知不知道,beef 在美式英语中有“抱怨,发牢骚,争吵,抱怨”的意思。

例如:I’m having a beef with my boss. 我和老板有点不愉快。

(9)把……掩盖起来 to sweep sth. under the carpet

“把……扫到地毯下”表示“把……东西掩藏起来”引申为“回避困难”,非常生动,容易理解。

例如: We'll be better off if we don’t sweep our problems under the carpet. 如果不回避困难,我们会过得好一些。

(10)你迫不及待了? Aren’t you jumping the gun?

“枪未响先偷跑”。在运动比赛中常用鸣枪作为“开始起跑”的信号,所以 to jump the gun 这个词组指的是“在正式鸣枪之前就先偷跑,操之过急”。在日常生活当中老美常用 to jump the gun 来指“太早行动”,也就是 to start too early 的意思。

例如: Don’t jump the gun before you really know what’s going on. 在你真正知道发生什么事之前别太早生气。

(11)那都是陈年往事了。That’s water under the bridge.

water under the bridge 就是“桥下的水、逝水、覆水”。

例如: Don’t worry about that mistake, it’s water under the bridge. 别担心这个错误,它已经无关紧要了。

(12)他绝不会袖手旁观。He's got broad shoulders.

broad shoulders 是"宽阔的肩膀"的意思,"宽阔的肩膀"就是"身体好,能担负重任"的意思,用于表示"能承担责任,决不旁观"。

例如: You can rely on him because he has got broad shoulders. 你可以依靠他,他绝不会袖手旁观。

(13)这山望着那山高。The grass is always greener on the other hill.

中国人比的是"山高",英国人比的是山上的"草"看谁更绿,虽然比的对象不同,但同样都表达了"不知足"的心态。

例如: Almost all people see that the grass is always greener on the other hill. They never feel satisfied with what they've already got. 所有人几乎都这山望着那山高,永远不会满足自己已得到的。

(14)不能跟某人比 can't hold a candle to someone

"连替某人举蜡烛为其照明的资格都没有",即"与某人相差悬殊"或"不能与某人相提并论",与汉语口语中的"连给某人提鞋的资格都没有"与"比不上某人"近似。电器发明之前,英国人和中国人一样只能靠蜡烛来照明。工匠在晚上做工时,会叫学徒给他拿着蜡烛;有钱人晚上从酒馆、戏院回家时,也有仆人拿着火把引路。仆人和主人的身份本来就很悬殊了,如果连做人家的仆人、给人家拿蜡烛都不配的话,那么双方在地位、能力等方面一定相差很远。

例如: No one can hold a candle to him when it comes to playing the guitar. 说到弹吉他,谁也比不上他。

(15)付出过高的代价 to cost an arm and a leg

"一条腿和一只胳膊的代价"不是"过高"的代价而是"惨烈"的代价,这个表达太震撼了。用 arm 来指"代价"的习语还有 to give one's right arm, 其意思是"付出极大的代价"。比如:He'd give his right arm to go abroad.

例如: Nowadays the apartment in the center of the city costs an arm and a leg. 现今位于市中心的公寓房可谓天价。

(16)平安无事。/一切安全。The coast is clear.

表示没有被发现或被捉住的危险。coast 是"海岸"的意思;clear 在这里是"没有任何障碍和危险"的意思。原句最早为海盗和走私犯的用语,意思要确保海岸上没有执法人员才能开始行动。

例如: Even though my parents grounded me, I have to see my girlfriend tonight. My plan is to sneak out of the house when mom and dad go next door to play cards. I'm not sure when the coast will be clear, but they should be leaving soon. 虽然父母罚我不许出门,但是今天晚上我一定要去会女朋友。我打算等他们到隔壁去打牌的时候偷偷溜出去。我不知道他们到底什么时候走,但估计快了。

(17)对……冷淡 to give one the cold shoulder

表示故意用一种不友好的方式对待某人。这里的 shoulder 是指"牛羊等连前腿在内的肩肉",因此,所谓 cold shoulder 就是"凉了的前腿肉"的意思。古时候有这样的风俗习惯:在招待贵客时,飨以美味佳肴;对于行商和乞丐,则给"凉了的前腿肉"吃。这就是 to give someone the cold shoulder 具有"采取冷淡态度"意思的来源。还有种说法是当客人停留时间太久,让主人感到不愉快时,主人就会拿出"羊肩肉/cold shoulder of mutton"来请客人吃。这种肉生硬难吃,这样客人就会明白主人的意思,乖乖告辞了。从此 cold shoulder 就有了"慢待别人"的意思。在日常会话中,to give sb. the cold shoulder, 既可以指表示"冷淡的耸肩动作",也可以指"采取冷淡的态度"。

例如: She walked into the room wearing a big smile, but everyone gave her the cold shoulder. 她满脸笑容地走进房间,但每个人都对她冷淡。

(18)面对惩罚、面对现实 to face the music

"to face the music/面对音乐",似乎是一件很美妙的事情。如果你这么理解的话,就错了,在英语中 to face the music 和"享受音乐的那种美妙感觉"相差十万八千里,它表达的恰恰是和"享受音乐"相反的一种感觉"不得不接受惩罚、承担后果"。为什么用 to face the music 来表达这个意思呢? 这个短语最早可以追溯到 19 世纪中期。有一些词源学方面的权威认为,这个短语来源于剧场。去过大型剧场的朋友一定知道,在舞台前方往往有一个乐池,乐队就坐在乐池中为台上表演的演员们伴奏。演员们在舞台上表演时,就直接面对着乐池中的乐队,to face the music 可能就是由此而来的。在舞台上,演员经常会由于紧张或怯场而造成忘词等尴尬的局面,只要音乐一响,演员就没有任何选择的余地,只能去"to face the music/必须承受出现的局面"。所以对于演员来说,音乐响起时,只能"硬着头皮上"了,所以也就是"不得不承担、不得不面对"。

例如: Everybody has to face the music for what he has done. 我们应学会接受真实的生活。

(19)该休息的时间了。It's Miller time.

因为美国美乐啤酒的电视广告而流行的惯用语。

例如: Everything's taken care of. Ah, it's Miller time. 每件事都安排好了。啊,轻松的时间到了。

(20)近在眼前 right under nose

这个英语短语是指东西就好像是在鼻子底下那么近,但却忽略了。通常用来形容要寻找的东西,虽在极明显的地方,但却没注意到。但中国人说"远在天边,近在眼前"。

例如: My pen was right there under my nose the whole time. It was just sitting there on the desk where I left it. 我的钢笔一直就在我的眼皮底下,在我刚才坐的座位上。

(21)拒不认错,不服输 not say uncle

not say uncle 起源于孩子们的游戏。据说,孩子们打闹时,占上风的一方把另一方压在身子底下,让被压在下面的孩子管他叫 uncle。如果那个孩子不这样做,就会面临一顿臭打。如果管他叫 uncle,这样意味着那个孩子"认输"了。所以,not say uncle 常用来指"不认输"或"不服输"。

例如: Never say uncle no matter whatever you come across! 无论遇到什么,我都决不放弃!

(22)精明的;通晓万事的 to know a thing or two about

这个短语直译为"略知一二",但其真正的含义却不"只知一二",而是"通晓万事"。

例如: Mark is a very good player and he knows a thing or two about coaching too. 马克是位好演员,他还善于传授技艺。

(23)说曹操,曹操到。to speak of the devil

devil 指的是"魔鬼",speak of 指的是"谈及、谈到"。to speak of the devil 直译就是"说到魔鬼",引申意为"谈到谁,谁就到了"。

例如: Speak of the devil! We were just talking about you! How did you know that? 说曹操,曹操到! 咱们刚还说你呢! 你怎么知道的? 再介绍一个更精彩的表达:Talk of the angel and you hear its wings.

(24)费体力的工作 elbow grease

古时候,英国的工人们在给贵族家帮佣的时候,为了把窗子、家具和地板清扫干净并抛光打蜡,总是在手臂和肘部涂抹上油脂,以节省力气和加强效果。后来人们就把"elbow grease"比喻为体力劳动,艰苦的工作,苦差事。

例如: The pot is so dirty that no amount of elbow grease will get it clean. 这个锅那么脏,费再大的力气也洗不干净。

(25)钱不是从树上长出来的。Money doesn't grow on trees.

"钱不是从树上长出来的",要靠自己辛苦努力挣得。就像中国人说的"天上不会自己掉馅饼。"

例如: You'd better not spend so much so quickly. Money doesn't grow on trees, you know. 你最好别一下子就花这么多钱。你知道钱不是白白从天上掉下来。

(26)解渴 to wet one's whistle

这是过去口语中的一种说法,表示"喝饲料,尤指喝酒"。这个短语的来历至少可以追溯到1386年。尽管短语中有 whistle 这个单词,它却压根和口哨没有任何关系。whistle 经常被用作指代"嘴"或"喉咙"的幽默说法,这种用法已经有很长时间了,特别用于和说话、唱歌有关的场合。to wet your whistle 这个短语之所以能够一直沿用下来,可能有以下两个原因:一是因为这个短语压头韵,读起来朗朗上口,很容易被记住。另一个原因就是嘴唇潮湿的时候确实比较容易吹口哨。

例如: This weather is so hot! Let's go and get something to wet our whistles. 天气那么热!我们去找点东西来解渴吧!

(27)学着做;跟同 to follow suit

to follow suit 本来是玩纸牌的用语,意思是"打出同组牌"。suit 是指同一组的纸牌,follow 是"跟随,跟着打出同组牌",可引申为"照着做;跟进"。

例如: All of his friends have dropped out of school. He's going to follow suit. 他所有的朋友都已经辍学了。他也会照着做。

(28)我一定会实现你的愿望/你咋说,我咋做。Your wish is my command.

这句话原本是《天方夜谭》中神灯里的精灵所说的名句,因无论主人要求什么,他也会照着都会使它实现。用在一般生活中,是强调对对方的承诺,只要对方高兴,自己就会拼命照办。可译为"我一定会实现你的愿望"。

例如: Your wish is my command. It will be just as you asked. 我一定会实现你的愿望。就如同你所要求的一模一样。

(29)二分之一的可能,二分之一的机会,碰运气的事 toss-up

当无法做出决定时,人们习惯会以为掷硬币 toss(up) a coin 的方式来解决,这就是碰运气,真反面各有一次机会,可解释为"都有可能;都差不多;半斤八两"等。

例如: They agreed to decide the matter by tossing a coin. 他们同意掷硬币来决定此事。

(30)我可不想当电灯泡。I don't want to be the third wheel.

the third wheel 是指那些"碍手碍脚、不合时宜"的人,也就是我们汉语中的"电灯泡"。至于它的来源,是因为自行车通常只有两个轮子,若再加一个轮子,一定是多余的。所以,久而久之,人们就用 the third wheel 来形容那些"不受欢迎、多余的人"。

例如：What do you think of "the third wheel" in romance? 你咋看爱情中的"小三"？

(31)你不必小心翼翼的。You don't have to mind your P's and Q's.

你知道 to mind your P's and Q's 的来历吗？它的意思是 be careful, behave yourself,也就是"小心、谨慎"的意思。从 17 世纪晚期开始,to mind your P's and Q's 被广泛使用,关于它的故事有很多。其中一种说法和酒店有关。当时,在英国的一些酒吧里有两种盛酒器具:品脱和夸脱。品脱大,夸脱小;为了在客人们结账的时候不出差错,酒店侍者必须在酒店的小黑板上记下客人们用的到底是哪种容器,P 代表 pints,Q 代表 quarts。因此,酒店老板也不断地提醒他们:注意你们的品脱和夸脱。另一种说法从课堂上来,小学生在拼写 p 和 q 时总是容易将它们混淆。P 反着写就成了 q,而 q 反过来写又变成了 p。这两个字母不但顺序相邻,而且拼写相似,难怪老师要说 to mind your P's and Q's。再来听听下面这个故事。这种说法中 P 指的是 pea cloth,一种粗呢布料;Q 代表 queue,指的是"(朝臣或水手们的)辫子"。年轻的贵族们总被提醒不要将假发上的粉末弄到粗呢夹克上;另一种解释是:水手们刚上船时,有一个惯例,就是将他们的辫子放在焦油里蘸一蘸,不过要小心把油弄到粗呢夹克上。听完了这些故事,你也明白 mind your P's and Q's 的意思了吧？

例如:She told her son to mind his P's and Q's at the banquet。她让儿子在宴会上要注意自己的言行。

(32)如果你想在 24 小时内爬三座山,那你身体得特别好。If you want to climb three mountains in 24 hours, you have to be as fit as a fiddle.

fit 是"身体好"的意思,fiddle 是类似小提琴的乐器。要是一个人说他 as fit as a fiddle, 那就好比是一把琴的弦和音调都调得很好。

例如:I think my health is important, so I don't smoke or drink. I eat lots of vegetables and fruit, and I do exercises three times a week. These things help to keep me fit as a fiddle. 因为我的身体是很重要的。所以,我不抽烟,也不喝酒。我吃好多蔬菜和水果。每个星期,我锻炼三次。这些都使我能保持身体健康。

(33)抢别人的风头 to steal one's thunder

英国 17 世纪大戏剧家约翰·丹尼生首次在自己的剧本 Appius and Vinginia 中使用了雷声这种戏剧音响手段。遗憾的是,这个剧不受观众欢迎,丹尼生为此收回了这个剧本。然而事隔不久莎士比亚的戏剧 *Macbeth*(《麦克白》)演出时使用了雷声轰鸣这种音响形式,丹尼生听后呼喊道:"My God! The villains will play my thunder but not my plays. / 天啊,这些小人们不上演我的戏剧却演出了我的雷声。"但本人认为在此处的"thunder"理解为"灵光一闪;创造发明"更有利于记忆,"窃取别人想出来的东西"。

例如:I couldn't believe how he stole our thunder——he told a reporter about the new drug, so the papers gave him the credit but not all the people who actually did the work. 原来这个人抢先一步对记者宣告这种新药。这一来报刊就把功劳都归给他，却忽略了真正为此付出辛劳的人。

各个国家的文化背景、风俗习惯等对她本国的语言产生着巨大的影响,语言是一个国家,一个民族不断繁荣昌盛的标志和象征。英语作为一种世界最广为使用的语言,更有其丰富的内涵和深邃的精神。全面了解英美文化,有利于学习以一种全新的思维方法去看待事物,避免不必要的麻烦和误解。

四、巩固练习

1. 从文化差异的角度说说下面中文词组或句子的英语表达。

(1)陷入左右为难的困境
(2)他喜欢捉弄陌生人。
(3)义愤填膺
(4)我跟乔治没有过节。
(5)发怒、狂怒,嗜血(成性),残暴
(6)纸包不住火。
(7)对牛弹琴
(8)我建议她先去避避风头。
(9)化干戈为玉帛
(10)传统百家宴
(11)我字字是肺腑之言。
(12)以毒攻毒
(13)装逼先生
(14)把某人照顾得很周全
(15)船到桥头自然直。
(16)我有些云里雾里的。
(17)随便什么张三李四现在都在找工作。
(18)盲从
(19)海市蜃楼般的希望
(20)长谈;谈到筋疲力尽
(21)直白辛辣的问题
(22)我知道这些话你都听烦了。
(23)一干人等
(24)我今天有点郁闷。
(25)真正地摔得狗啃泥。
(26)心乱如麻
(27)叫阵
(28)蠢人,摇摆不定的人
(29)你居然有脸来。
(30)成人礼
(31)乳臭未干的小毛孩
(32)谢天谢地哈利路亚!
(33)讨点钱(乞丐)
(34)醒酒偏方
(35)令朋友之间隔阂加深

(36)(尤指小孩)在朋友家过夜的晚会
(37)你让这个名字听起来那么高不可攀。
(38)我们可谓旗鼓相当。
(39)幸运符
(40)赶鸭子上架
(41)我看上两处房产。
(42)为什么在乎别人的眼光?
(43)我会守口如瓶。
(44)你们被禁足两个月。
(45)别打草惊蛇!
(46)他们是阳春白雪,我们是下里巴人。
(47)他是一个电灯泡。

2. 从文化差异的角度说说下面英文词组或句子的中文表达。

(1) to cast pearls before swine
(2) In the land of the blind, the one-eyed man is king.
(3) to cry up wine and sell vinegar
(4) as timid as a rabbit
(5) at a stone's throw
(6) to fish in the air
(7) as stupid as a goose
(8) be dumb as an oyster
(9) a black sheep
(10) to stick one's toe back in
(11) They who live in glass houses should not throw stones.
(12) You can run but you can't hide.
(13) to watch one's tongue
(14) When a pig flies...
(15) Why do you need to label everything?
(16) The writing is on the wall.
(17) The only way to deal with the world is to fight fire with fire.
(18) the herd effect
(19) Sometimes, even to deny these things is only to throw paraffin onto the flames.
(20) That's like asking the fox to spare the chicken.
(21) You should stand well clear when you light the blue touch paper.
(22) to rob Peter to pay Paul
(23) I can't have you grey-faced and in perpetual mourning.
(24) It's Greek to me.
(25) What a marathon!
(26) Don't have too many irons in the fire.

(27) a guidance counselor

(28) Sometimes she sacrifices something she loves for the greater good.

(29) to put sb. in the corner

(30) the spelling bee

(31) If the cap fits, wear it.

(32) I am in a relationship.

(33) We'll fail before we launch.

(34) the lifeline

(35) a catcall

(36) be busy as a bee

(37) to get a bee in one's bonnet

3. 熟读并背诵下列句子。

(1) God helps who help themselves. 自助者神助之。

(2) Man proposes, God disposes. 谋事在人,成事在天。

(3) The Lord (上帝) tempers(缓和) the wind to the shorn lamb. (原意:上帝让风轻抚剪过毛的羊)天无绝人之路。

(4) Making a silk purse out of a sow's ear. (原意:猪耳朵做不出丝钱袋来)巧妇难为无米之炊。

(5) Where there's smoke there's fire. 无风不起浪。

(6) Elbow grease gives the best polish. 只要功夫深,铁杵磨成针。

(7) Truth hath a good face, but ill clothes. 真理面目善良;但衣衫褴褛。(忠言逆耳)

(8) A broken heart can be as painful as a broken limb. 心痛也是种切肤之痛。

(9) We must strive to be worthy of the task we've been set. 我们必须尽力不辱使命。

4. 用本单元所学的知识造句。

(1) 也许你应该告诉你儿子一些<u>性知识</u>。

(2) 让他干吧,他是一个<u>踏实肯干的人</u>。

(3) 他是真正的<u>贵族</u>。

(4) 当自己与别人发生矛盾时,我们是<u>不依不饶</u>呢,还是化干戈为玉帛呢?

(5) 作为一家四口人中唯一<u>养家糊口的人</u>,他不能长期无所事事。

(6) 我的邻居是一个<u>冷漠的人</u>。

(7) 过去三年大家对这个问题都非常敏感,所以各国政府现在才了解他们不能<u>忽视这个问题</u>。

(8) 把这个疯狂的罪犯<u>抓入监狱</u>时,我们就睡得更香了。

(9) 在调查结果出来之前不要就爆炸原因<u>过早表态</u>。

(10) 所有那些现在都是不可改变的<u>既成事实</u>。

(11) 就因为你被拒一次,不等于你就的从此<u>甩手不干</u>。

(12) 扮演剧中的主角,父亲和母亲的两位明星都相当称职,但是扮演儿子的这位青年却<u>抢尽风头</u>。

(13) 他是一个<u>败家子</u>。

(14) 作为学生,我认为没有必要一天到晚<u>抱怨</u>家庭作业。

(15)下课铃声响起,我们都急着想走,但老师却让我们不要着急,听他讲完。

(16)一个爱说大话的人终会自食其果。

(17)他没日没夜地工作,看起来很忙。

(18)如果你不懂得明哲保身,迟早会陷入麻烦之中。

(19)这个老富婆真的是在制造麻烦,把钱留给她的园丁而不是子女。

(20)请原谅我难听的声音,今天我嗓子哑了。

(21)她的房间总是乱七八糟,连个落脚的地方都没有。

(22)他们对时尚一无所知,只是盲从。

(23)他已经损失了六千万美元。如果你再投资,将会是"赔了夫人又折兵"。

(24)老板在会上批评他,但他一点没听进去。

(25)安真是个好人,要是她别那么容易发脾气就好了。

(26)我已经道歉到口水都说干了。

(27)他是犯了很多错误,但不要对他太苛刻,他还是个孩子。

(28)我们要勇敢面对现实,不要做缩头乌龟。

(29)北京的房价咬死你。(在北京买房代价很高。)

(30)这儿的奶酪不如法国的好。

(31)好吧,大家既然寒暄已毕,那就让咱们来认真坦率地讨论实际发生的事情吧 。

(32)皮特先生辞去主席的职位,我是从他本人那里得到的确切消息。

(33)等一切安全了我会去找你。

(34)汤姆因称呼校长为老古板而被停职。

(35)你必须看看她好的一面。她真的是个温柔的女孩。

(36)一万美金!这简直是敲竹杠!

(37)汤姆不得不为他鲁莽的行为而面对惩罚。

(38)我学中文已经很久以了,但我还是不太懂。

(39)你又赢了,你真幸运。

(40)他的生意情况不妙,因此他想过舒适生活的希望破灭了。

(41)那个霸占车道的人不肯将车开到路边让我过去。

(42)汤姆总是逗我们笑。

(43)说到曹操,曹操到!嗨,马克!我们刚才还在说你呢。

(44)她十分独立,常说婚姻没有价值。

(45)他确信她会先给他打电话。

(46)她总爱在上晚班回来的路上喝点酒。

(47)我说不上约翰这次能否竞选成功,肯定有机会。

(48)我觉得她就是个老好人。

(49)我们只是随便挑选了一些学生组成了校篮球队,我们赢球完全是靠运气。

(50)我的祖父看起来像一个六十多岁的人。可是实际上,他已经八十岁了。而且他还非常健康:他不用装假牙,看东西也不用眼镜,每天还走四英里路。

5. 你能找到更多英汉文化差异的例证吗?请与大家共同分享本章的学习体会。

Chapter 3 Idioms & Slangs

习语俗语

一、思路讲解

语言是文化的载体，习语又是语言的精华。“习语”一词的含义甚广，一般指那些常用在一起，具有特定形式的词组，其蕴含的意义往往不能从词组中单个词的意思推测而得。习语通常包括成语、俗语、格言、歇后语、谚语、俚语、行话等，音节优美，音律协调，含蓄幽默，严肃典雅，言简意赅，形象生动，妙趣横生，具有浓厚的民族色彩和丰富的文化内涵。(http://baike.so.com/doc/1168526.html)作者认为，英语的习语是一个非常宽广的范畴，是人类从劳动中创造出来并经过长时间使用而提炼的固定短语或短句，和民族的历史背景、经济生活、地理环境、风俗习惯、心理状态紧密相连，它能把丰富的思想内涵精辟地表达出来，意义深远、富有哲理、富于含蓄、意在言外。

英语习语一般具有三个明显的语义特征：语言整体性(single linguistic unit)、结构凝固性(structural institutionalization)和不可替代性(irreplaceability)。对于一些习惯用语，我们不能仅从字面上去理解，要了解其中的文化内涵，这样才不会产生尴尬。有些习惯用语意思明显，易于理解记忆；有些则含蓄深刻，趣味无穷。习语常被用在口语中，积累并掌握一些习语有益于口头交流，使语言丰富、交流更地道。

在这个单元里所收录的条目我们尽量做到鲜活生动，增加文化信息含量，提供思考余地，加深对习语的理解、认识和记忆，有益于学习者透过语言现象了解英语民族的文化传统和习俗。习语是通俗化的口语，它能够提高语言运用能力，熟练掌握习语，有利于提升语言学习者的口语水平，增进文化交流。英语语言的学习不是一朝一夕的事儿，需要大家在日常生活中留心观察，细心体会，一点一点地去积累，相信大家只要持之以恒，慢慢就会在与英语国家人士的日常交往中如鱼得水，克服日常交往的障碍。

二、故事会

1. an apple of discord 争斗之源；不和之因；祸根

an apple of discord 直译为“纠纷的苹果”，出自荷马史诗 Iliad 中的希腊神话故事。传说希腊阿耳戈(Argonaut)英雄珀琉斯(Peleus)和爱琴海海神涅柔斯(Nereu)的女儿西蒂斯(Thetis)在珀利翁山举行婚礼，大摆宴席。他们邀请了奥林匹斯上(Olympus)的诸神参加喜筵，不知是有意还是无心，唯独没有邀请掌管争执的女神厄里斯(Eris)。这位女神恼羞成怒，决定在这次喜筵上制造不和。于是，她不请自来，并悄悄在筵席上放了一个金苹果，上面镌刻着“属于最美者”几个字。天后赫拉(Hera)、智慧女神雅典娜(Athena)、爱与美之神阿芙罗狄蒂(Aphrodite)，都自以为最美，应得金苹果，获得“最美者”称号。她们争执不下，闹到众神之父宙斯

(Zeus)那里,但宙斯碍于难言之隐,不愿偏袒任何一方,就要她们去找特洛伊的王子帕里斯(Paris)评判。三位女神为了获得金苹果,都各自私许帕里斯以某种好处:赫拉许给他以广袤国土和掌握富饶财宝的权利,雅典娜许以文武全才和胜利的荣誉,阿芙罗狄蒂则许他成为世界上最美艳女子的丈夫。年青的帕里斯在富贵、荣誉和美女之间选择了后者,便把金苹果判给爱与美之神。为此,赫拉和雅典娜怀恨帕里斯,连带也憎恨整个特洛伊人。后来,阿芙罗狄蒂为了履行诺言,帮助帕里斯拐走了斯巴达国王墨涅俄斯的王后——绝世美女海伦(Helen),从而引起了历时10年的特洛伊战争。女神厄里斯丢下的那个苹果,不仅成了天上三位女神之间不和的根源,而且也成了人间两个民族之间战争的起因。因此,在英语中产生了 an apple of discord 这个成语,常用来比喻 any subject of disagreement and contention、the root of the trouble; dispute 等意义。这个成语最初为公元2世纪时的古罗马历史学家马克·朱里·尤斯丁(Marcus Juninus Justinus)所使用,后来广泛的流传到欧洲许多语言中去,成了一个国际性成语。

例如: He throwing us an apple of discord, and we soon quarreled again. 他挑起祸端,我们很快又吵了起来。

2. Greek gift(s) 阴谋害人的礼物;黄鼠狼拜年,不安好心

Greek gift(s)直译是"希腊人的礼物",出自荷马史诗《奥德赛》以及古罗马杰出诗人维吉尔(Publius Virgilius Maro)的史诗《伊尼特》(*Aeneis*)中关于特洛伊城陷落经过的叙述。据《奥德赛》第8卷记述:许多特洛伊人对如何处置希腊人留下的大木马展开了辩论,他们有三种主张:有的主张用无情的铜矛刺透中空的木马;有的主张把它扔到岩石上;有的主张把它留在那里作为京观(古代战争中,胜者为了炫耀武功,收集敌人尸首,封土而成的高冢),来取悦天神。结果是后一说占优势,把那匹木马拖进城里来,终于遭到了亡国之灾。维吉尔的史诗《伊尼特》,写的是特洛伊被希腊攻陷后,王子伊尼斯从混乱中携家属出走,经由西西里、迦太基到达意大利,在各地漂泊流亡的情况。史诗第2卷便是伊尼斯关于特洛伊城陷落经过的叙述,其中情节除了模拟荷马史诗的描述外,还做了更详细的补充。当特洛伊人要把大木马拖进城的时候,祭司拉奥孔(Laocoon)劝说不要接受希腊人留下的东西。他说:"我怕希腊人,即使他们来送礼"。这句话后来成了一句拉丁谚语:Timeo Danaos, et dona ferenteso.(原文的达奈人 Danaos,泛指希腊各部族人)译成英语就是:I fear the Greeks, even when bringing gifts. 后简化为 Greek Gifts。可惜特洛伊人不听拉奥孔的警告,把木马作为战利品拖进城里。木马里藏着希腊的精锐部队,给特洛伊人带来了屠杀和灭亡。由此,Greek gift(s) 成为一个成语,表示"a gift with some sinister purposes of the enemy; one given with intent to harm; a gift sent in order to murder sb."等意思,按其形象意义,这个成语相当于英语的俚谚:"When the fox preaches, take care of your geese."也与汉语"黄鼠狼给鸡拜年——不安好心"十分类似。

例如: He is always buying you expensive clothes. I'm afraid they are Greek gifts for you. 他总是买昂贵的衣服给你。我认为可能他对你没安好心。

3. to meet Waterloo 倒霉;受毁灭性打击;灭顶之灾

一代天骄拿破仑在1815年的滑铁卢战役中被英国著名将领威灵顿和普鲁士陆帅吕歇尔彻底打败,滑铁卢是拿破仑遭受惨败的地方。"遭遇滑铁卢",对一个人来说,后果不堪设想。据说第二次世界大战期间,在准备诺曼底反攻时,温斯顿·丘吉尔冒雨去某地开会,其随员因路滑而摔了一跤,脱口说一句"To meet Waterloo!"丘吉尔竟联想到拿破仑兵败滑铁卢的典故,

恼怒地斥责他:“胡说! 我要去凯旋门呢!”

例如:John fought instead of running, and the bully met his Waterloo. 约翰没有逃走,他奋起反抗,终于打败了那个恶棍。

4. to send one to Coventry 断绝关系;受人排挤

其来源有二:一种是17世纪上半叶,英王查理一世以及由封建贵族、国教上层教士、王公大臣等组成的“骑士党”,另一方为由资产阶级和贵族组成的“园颅党”,该党以国会为代表,得到了城市小资产阶级、平民和信仰新教的农民的支持。此间,考文垂市(Coventry)被国会用来监禁顽固不化的战俘,使之断绝与外界的一切来往。因而该成语便有了上述译法。另一种是Coventry市居民在历史上素有反对驻军该市的传统,他们十分反感当兵的。若见有姑娘与士兵交谈,就会有人对其嗤之以鼻,自然而然地陷入孤立。因而,当兵的人常把被派往Coventry视为走向孤立与烦恼。

例如:The other workmen have sent him to Coventry because he supported the boss's point of view. 他因为支持老板的观点而受到同事的排挤。

5. (the) real Simon Pure 真正的,并非假冒的

该成语(the) real Simon Pure直译为“真正的西蒙·普勒”,源自英国女剧作家苏珊娜·圣特利芙(1667?—1723)的喜剧《良缘难结》中的一个人物。西蒙·普勒是宾西法尼亚洲的教友派传教士,当时颇有声望。有位上校,名叫费思维尔,爱上一位素不相识的安娜·拉芙利小姐,自叹无缘相见。后来他便乔装打扮冒充西蒙·普勒,以便骗取安娜小姐监护人同意他同小姐会晤。正当他因刚刚征得监护人的同意而得意扬扬时,真的西蒙·普勒出现了。在费了很大一番周折后,西蒙·普勒戳穿了费思维尔的骗局,证明自己才是真正的西蒙·普勒(the real Simon Pure)。因此,该成语表示“真正的”、“并非假冒的”的意思。

例如:The simon-pure cause lay in the fact that he would have everything his own way. 事情背后的真正原因是他要求凡事按他的方式进行。

6. the night of the long knives 采取背信弃义的行动

该成语直译为“长刀之夜”,指“采取背信弃义的行动,进行血的清洗的时刻”。该词源自英国历史,公元472年撒克逊人入侵,首领亨吉斯特邀请当地布立吞人上层显要赴会,席间在每个布立吞人身边都安排一个身背长刀的撒克逊人同坐。在首领发出约定信号后,撒克逊人立即拔刀直刺布立吞人,被杀者多达460名。另一说法是,希特勒为强化法西斯独裁统治,于1934年6月29日晚对褐衫突击队进行了大清洗,把可与之抗衡的军界头目数目人一网打尽。因此,该成语表示“采取背信弃义的行动,进行血的清洗的时刻”。

例如:Germans today believe that the night of the long knives happened because of an imminent coup. 现在德国人都相信当时的背信弃义是因为迫在眉睫的政变。

7. to keep one's powder dry 做好战斗准备,以防万一

该成语to keep one's powder dry直译为“保持火药干燥”,源自17世纪中期,英王查理一世挑起两次内战。当时新兴资产阶级组织了一支战斗力强,素有“铁军”之称的军队,组织者是克伦威尔(1599—1658),这支来自耕农和城市平民为主体的志愿骑兵纪律严明,具有很强

的战斗力。有一次,克伦威尔率军过河作战,要求部队“要相信上帝,但必须保持火药干燥”(put your trust in God, but mind to keep your powder dry!)后来人们就用“to keep one's powder dry”表示“做好战斗准备,以防万一;枕戈待旦”的意思。

例如: Honey, let's keep all our damages estimates handy. I don't trust Brown, he may find some excuse not to pay. Then we'll have to sue him in court so let's keep our powder dry. 亲爱的,我们做好损失预估。我不相信布朗。他可能会找借口拒绝赔付,那我们就做好准备上法庭。

8. a mare's nest 无稽之谈,虚无缥缈

成语 a mare's nest 直译为“母马之巢”。英国古代撒克逊人认为,人们夜间做梦是因为一个叫作马拉的精灵在人们熟睡之后,悄悄溜进卧室压在沉睡者的胸上造成的。此时人们感到压抑,呼吸困难,于是就有了各种各样的可怕噩梦。据说这个马拉精灵就像母鸡孵蛋一样,总是趴在家藏的珍宝上,它趴过的地方叫“母马之巢”。而所谓的“珍宝”只不过是人们的想象,并非实指,梦中发现“母马之巢”,不过是场空欢喜而已。因此,a mare's nest 指“无稽之谈;虚无缥缈。”

例如: It proved that everything was a mare's nest. 事实证明这一切都是子虚乌有。

9. an apple polisher 拍马屁的人

该成语直译为“擦苹果的人”,用来形容那些“讨好求宠的人”、“马屁精”、“迎合上司的人”等。“擦苹果”之事犹如人类社会一样古老,但这个说法却产生于不久以前,大约只有50年的历史。它来自学校的教室,曾有很长一段时间,有的学生经常在老师的桌子上放一只鲜艳的苹果,他们把苹果擦得鲜艳,锃亮,显得更加美味可口。学生希望这个苹果能使老师对他的差劲作业睁一只眼,闭一只眼,打个好分数。擦苹果的人形形色色,不一而足,包括政客和身居高位的人,差不多人人皆是。伟大的英国领袖奥利弗·克伦威尔曾送去很多礼物,企图赢得乔治·福克斯和他领导的公谊会的支持,但未能成功。克伦威尔说:“我看到已经出现了一些我无法用礼品,荣誉,官职或者高位笼络的人,但对于所有其他的教派和人士这却行得通。”另外,与之相近的有 soft-soaping 或 buttering-up,均表示“送礼,讨好人;拍马屁”。

例如: Nobody likes him because he's an apple polisher. 没有人喜欢他这个溜须拍马的人。

10. to wear the willow 痛失心爱之人

该成语直译为“佩戴柳枝”,喻指“痛失心爱之人”、“痛悼,哀悼”之意(grieve for the loss or death of someone one has loved)。出自《圣经·旧约》之《诗篇》第137篇。这一篇是因为以色列人被逐而哀悼的歌,歌词哀婉悲凉。诗中唱道:“我们曾在巴比伦的河边坐下,一追想锡安就哭了。我们把琴挂在那里的柳枝上。因为在那里,掳掠我们的要我们唱歌,抢夺我们的要我们作乐,说,给我们唱一首锡安歌吧。我们怎能在外邦唱耶和华的歌呢?”歌中的锡安(Zion)是耶路撒冷的一座名山,山上建有皇宫庙宇,是犹太人政教、文化和生活中心,象征着天国。后来在许多名家的作品中,“柳枝”就常常用来因失去心爱之人,特别是恋人而感到悲伤。莎士比亚在他的著名悲剧《奥赛罗》中,在奥赛罗因为听信谗言,错杀爱妻苔丝德梦娜之前,苔丝德梦娜唱了一首悲凉的歌子,歌中就多次用“柳枝”和“青青的柳枝”编成的“翠环”来表达失去心爱之人的哀伤。

例如:Her boyfriend fell in love with another girl and made her wear the willow. 她的男朋友另结新欢让她的爱付之东流。

11. under the rose 秘密地

under the rose 就是“秘密地”意思,罗马神话中的小爱神丘比特(Cupid),在希腊神话中也称为厄洛斯(Eros),在文艺作品中以背上长着双翼的小男孩的形象出现,常携带弓箭在天空中遨游,谁中了他的金箭就会产生爱情。丘比特是战神玛斯(Mars)和爱与美之神维纳斯(Venus)所生的儿子。维纳斯,也就是希腊神话里的阿芙罗狄蒂(Aphrodite),传说她是从大海的泡沫里生出来的,以美丽著称,从宙斯到奥林匹帕斯的诸神都为其美貌姿容所倾倒。有关她的恋爱传说很多,欧洲很多文艺作品常用维纳斯做题材。小爱神丘比特为了维护其母的声誉,给沉默之神哈伯克拉底(Harpocrates)送了一束玫瑰花,请他守口如瓶不要把维纳斯的风流韵事传播出去,哈伯克拉底受了玫瑰花就缄默不语了,成为名副其实的“沉默之神”。

例如:She told him the whole truth under the rose. 她悄悄告诉了他所有的真相。

三、案例分析

下面我们用更多的例子来帮助大家理解记忆英语习语,为提高口语表达能力提供大量的鲜活的典型案例。

1. 一字(词)多用

(1) to screw up

screw 当名词用时的意思是“螺丝钉”,当动词用则是指“旋转螺丝”的动作。to screw up 有“振作起来”的意思,比如:to screw up one's courage to do sth.(鼓起勇气做某事)。to screw up 也有“把事情搞砸”的意思,类似 to mess up 的用法,比如:Don't screw up again. 但在“You treat me like a screw-up./你把我当作衰人。”中,screw-up 用作名词。

(2) shot

请看看以下的表达,就会知道 shot 有很多的用法:to give me your best shot[让我看看你(们)的真本事];to give this poor me a shot(再给我一次机会);a big shot(大人物);to call all the shots(发号施令、大权独揽)。

(3) to turn back on

to turn back on 有两个意思:“拒绝帮助、不理睬”和“背叛”。以两个句子为例:How can I turn back on it?(我怎能袖手旁观呢?);Don't turn back on us.(别背叛我们。)。顺便说一下,“袖手旁观”还可以表达为 to sit on one's hands.

(4) catch

在美式俚语中,catch 有“隐藏的难题;不利的条件”等意思,所以当某人提出一个太优越以至于让人难以置信的条件时,就可以这么说“What's the catch? / 有什么企图?(条件是什么?)”来表示我们的怀疑,询问对方在玩什么把戏。另外,nice catch 原意是“接得好”,引申为“好身手”。

(5) knock

第一种含义是 to knock sb. out,该词组原意为用拳击击倒对手获胜,还表示击昏或灌醉某人,第二种含义是使某人经受不了或极为震惊。从上述含义也可以引申为把人迷得发晕的漂亮女孩或英俊男生,所以 knock-out 可指帅哥美女。knock-out 还可作形容词用,例如“a knock-out idea/绝妙的主意”。再来说说 knock off: knock sb.'s socks off 意为“让某人大吃一惊”。另外,knock off 还有“降低价格”的意思:“knock off $300 /再便宜 $300”。

(6) push

惹某人发火 to push sb.'s buttons

得寸进尺、贪心 to push one's luck

(7) ball

差不多 be in the ballpark(棒球场,可活动的领域)

尽全力 to play ball

(8) feet

害怕、胆怯 cold feet(沮丧,临阵退缩 get cold feet)

不合作、故意拖拉 to drag one's feet

(9) clock

没什么问的了。Clock's ticking.

我在工作。I'm on the clock.

打卡上班 clock in

(10) fall

别上当! Don't fall for it!

吵架,争吵 falling-out

替某人顶罪 to take the fall for sb.

(11) play

使诈 to play dirty

欲擒故纵 to play hard-to-want (或 get)

捣鬼 to play games

(12) think

专心思考 to hear oneself think

边想边说出、自言自语 to think aloud

把……不放在心上 to think nothing of

(13) blue

突然地、意外地 out of the blue

千载难逢 once in a blue moon

(14) bend

委屈自己 to bend over backwards

灵活掌握规则;(根据实际情况)放宽规定;通融 bend the rules

改变某人愿望 to bend sb.'s will

(15) suck

糟透了;烂透了。如:Everything pretty much sucks. 一切都乱糟糟的。

巴结某人 to suck up to sb.(她在拍你的马屁! She's sucking up to you.)

(16) number

伤人感情;彻底失败;嘲笑 to do a number on

知道底细 to have sb. 's number

(17) hang

因……而精神不安;放不下某人/某事 to hang up on sb./sth.

找到窍门 to get the hang of sth.(开心点,慢慢就上手了。Cheer up! You'll get the hang of it.)

(18) call

九死一生 close call(我们没有撞上那辆车,但也够惊险的了。We didn't actually hit the other car, but it was a close call.)

事业 calling

(19) oneself

趾高气扬、得意忘形、兴高采烈 be above oneself(她今天为什么这么高兴?Why is she so above herself today?)

极度兴奋、神志失常、忘乎所以 be beside oneself(她得知丈夫获得头奖,高兴得忘乎所以。When she was told her husband had won the first prize, she was beside herself with joy.)

表现不佳 to give a bad/poor account of oneself

表现出色、大显身手 to give a good account of oneself

2. 一意多达

(1)无路可走、无能为力;处于危险之中

智穷力竭 the end of one's rope

无路可走 the end of the line

冒险;处于危险之中 to put sth. on the line

(2)忙碌

to have one's hands full

be in the middle of sth.

to keep sb. on his toes

(3)欺负某人、专门针对某人

有人欺负你了吗?Is someone picking on you?

有人杠上了你?Does someone choose you?

(4)疯了

你疯了吗?Are you nuts?

你发什么神经?(怎么啦?)What's come over you?

(5)关系、门路

她在索尼公司有门路。She's got tie in Sony.

你还得找找关系。You might have to pull a few stings.(你不妨走走后门。)

(6)欺骗,出卖,上当受骗

不要出卖你的朋友。Don't double-cross your friend.

我没骗你,哈里逊先生和他的女秘书真有恋情。I'm not putting you on. Mr. Harrison and his secretary are having an affair.

她觉得我们会轻易上当。She thinks we're a soft touch.

(7)拍马屁

拍马屁 brownnosing

拍……的马屁;奉承者,谄媚者 brownnose

拍马屁的人 apple polisher

(8)顽固的人

怪人;脾气坏的人;老顽固 old crank

倔家伙 hard boiled

(9)富有的,有钱的,发财了

生于富贵 be born loaded

他腰缠万贯。He's loaded.

你挣大钱了。You are flush.

兴旺发达;暴发 be in high cotton

(10)生气

(为小事)生气、发怒、怒气冲天 to get hot under the collar (真搞不懂你们为什么要大惊小怪 I don't know why you're getting so hot under the collar.)

惹恼、惹怒某人 to get in sb.'s hair

你把我惹毛了。You send me over the age.

我气死了。I'm pissed.

你要把我惹火了。You're starting to piss me off.

我拿话来激她(或痛骂)。I jump all over her.

(11)恋爱

你就是我要找的(恋)人。You're the home for me.

谁和谁是一对。X and Y are an item.

他死心塌地爱上了她。He falls head over heels in love with her.

(12)婚外情,外遇

有外遇 to have an affair

和某人有一腿 to have a fling with sb.

(13)甩了某人

甩了某人 to blow sb.

甲甩了乙。A has dumped B.

(14)……的人

受人喜欢的人(物)peach (干点好事。Be a peach.)

精明的人、生气勃勃的人 bright spark

未加工的钻石(可造之才,内秀外粗的人)a rough diamond

木头木脑的人 a feeble-idiot

专门破坏他人乐趣者;扫兴者 a spoilsport

自作主张的人、不受约束的人 a free-wheeler

大嘴巴 a nutcracker

(政府、警察、父母亲、老师等)有权有势的人 a big brother

游手好闲者;赖债不还的人;落魄者 a deadbeat

老相好(情人)an old flame
优秀的人 a lulu(她男朋友是个网球高手。Her boyfriend is a lulu at playing tennis.)
(15)洗手间
厕所 John(can)
(家里)洗手间 bathroom
(公共场合)洗手间 rest room(washroom)
男卫生间 men's room
女卫生间是 ladies' room

3.褒贬差异

(1)对女士的追求
(褒)爱上某人 to have a crush on sb.(我很喜欢你。I have an enormous crush on you.)
(贬)向某人展开追求(调情,挑逗) make a pass at sb.(女孩对试图挑逗她的男子怒目而视。The girl glared at the man who tried to make a pass at her.)
(2)对女性美丽的描述
(褒)十分引人注目的,非常漂亮的,异常惊人的 drop-dead(无敌性感的 drop-dead sexy)
(褒)十分引人注目的 catchy(这女孩真吸引人。The girl is catchy.)
(贬)小妞 chick(菲利克斯总是邀请一大群漂亮小妞参加他的舞会。Felix always invites lots of beautiful chicks to his parties.)

4.简洁易记的表达

(1)在任何情况下 thick and thin
是好是坏我都陪你走过来了。I have stood by you, through thick and thin.
(2)允许有小误差 give or take
通常大约 20 分钟,允许有 3 分钟的误差。Generally it is about 20 minutes, give or take 3 minutes.
(3)一半对一半 half and half
所以我得说双方都有错误,我认为损失应由双方承担,我们就对半负担吧。I must say the error was on both sides and I think the loss ought to be shared.
(4)事情的真相 what's what
请向吉姆打听,他知道事情的真相。Please ask Jim. He knows what's what.
(5)选这个还是选那个 choices, choices
choice 是"选择"的名词,重复两次是强调自己不知该选哪个才好。有时我们也会说 Decisions, decisions!,表示"不知怎么决定才好"。
(6)光明正大地,诚实地(愿赌服输)fine and square
(7)曲折 twists and turns
(8)忍无可忍。Enough is enough.
(9)明白了 asked and answered
(10)很难界定 yes and no
(11)又是这个又是那个;各种各样的东西 this and that

(12)没有前科 no priors

5.简洁生动的表达

(1)奶妈 wet-nurse(保姆 dry nurse)

(2)遭挤兑 be out of favor(得宠 be in favor)

(3)旁敲侧击或拐弯抹角地得知 fish

当 fish 做动词,后接 for,表示"间接探听;企图用不正当手段攫取;转弯抹角地引出"的意思。

(4)忍气吞声,低头认罪 to eat dirt

(5)打破常规,独具匠心,别出心裁 to think out of the box

(6)制造麻烦 to make the feather fly

(7)惹某人生气;把某人惹翻了 to get sb.'s back up

(8)连篇的谎话 line of lies

line 在俚语中可指"故事、说法"。

(9)爱吃甜食 to have a sweet tooth

(10)与男人有关的感情问题 man trouble

A: What's the matter, man trouble? B: How did you guess? 甲:怎么了? 关于男人的感情问题? 乙:你怎么猜到的?

6.习语理解帮手

(1)to play second fiddle 居次要位置,当配角

一个交响乐团,为了造成良好的音响效果,除了要有第一小提琴手外,还须要有第二小提琴手。否则,如果只有主角而无配角的话,整个演奏效果还是好不了。因此,play second fiddle 表示"当配角"。

(2)go-to guy 能人,热门红人,关键人物,最有可能得分的球员

go-to guy 就是"需要时靠得住的人",或者是"此人会以有效的行动来完成某件事"。"go-to guy"这个习惯用语原来是来自体育界,具体地说是来自职业篮球。比方说,在一场篮球比赛中,对方球队比你们的球队多了一分,而比赛还有十秒钟就要结束了。在这关键时刻,你就会想把球传给那个最可能投篮得分的球员。这个球员就是 go-to guy。我们就拿大名鼎鼎的篮球健将乔丹来举一个例子吧:"Michael Jordan is over 40 now, and that makes him older than anybody else on the team. But in the frantic last few seconds when his team is a point or two behind, put the ball in his hands - he's still the best go-to guy in the game! /乔丹现在已经四十出头了,他是那个球队里年纪最大的一个球员。可是,当他的球队落后一两分,比赛到了最后几秒钟的紧张关头,把球传到他手里就行了。他仍然是篮球界里最靠得上的球员。"

(3)to take no prisoners 态度强硬;毫不留情

prisoner 就是"在战争中抓获的敌兵"。to take no prisoners 这个说法是出自一个神秘的军官。他在战争中命令他手下的士兵杀死那些已经举手投降的敌军。所以,to take no prisoners 这个习惯用语就是指"对人强硬的人、很难对付的人"。"This new manager knows the business, I guess. But he's really tough on our staff - he takes no prisoners. You make one mistake and he'll fire you without giving you a chance to do better, and you'll be out looking for another job. /我猜想

这个新来的处长很懂行。但是他对雇员实在是很厉害;他毫不留情。你出一次错他马上就会解雇你,不给你任何改进的机会。这样你也就只好另找工作了。"

(4)the son of a gun 王八蛋(昵称:这小子)

大家还记得有一首由卡伦·卡朋特演唱的经典歌曲《什锦菜》(*Jambalaya*)吗?歌曲旋律动听,和声优美,《什锦菜》唱的是 Joe 和 Yvonne 结婚后将迁居密西西比河,过上幸福的生活。其中有一句歌词就是 *the son of a gun*,以示亲昵关系。

(5)dyed-in-the-wool 彻底的、道地的

这个词组最早出现于 16 世纪,dyed 来源于动词 dye(染色),最初,人们用 dyed in the wool 来形容"生染毛织品的一种方法",即 the process of dying sheep wool before it was woven into cloth(加工羊毛之前就把原毛染色)。据说,这种染色法在原毛制成其他毛织品后更不容易褪色。现代,人们更常用它的比喻意,既然毛色在毛织品出现之前就已成色且不容易脱褪,那形容某人"憎恶爱好它物的程度至深",完全可以用 dyed in the wool 来形容,其内涵和汉语中的"根深蒂固"很相像。

(6)to sell sb. down the river 出卖朋友

出卖朋友 to sell sb. down the river 这个说法得上溯到一百五十来年前美国实行黑奴制度的时代。不少人看过《汤姆叔的小屋》这部小说或者电影,了解当年美国黑奴的悲惨处境。当时一名黑奴的最大悲剧可能就是被转卖给密西西比河下游的另一个主人。因为那意味着妻离子散的命运和在棉花地里累断筋骨的操劳。当年很多黑奴就死于这种非人的待遇。所以 to sell sb. down the river 就是"出卖某人、令人陷入厄运"的意思。例如:"I might have been sorry to my friends, but I have never sold and will never sell them down the river./我也许做过对不起朋友的事,但是我从来没有也永远不会出卖他们。"

(7)the milk of human kindness 人类的善良天性

源于莎士比亚《麦克白》第一场第五幕"I fear thy nature; it is too full of the milk of human kindness./我为你的天性担忧,它充满了太多的人情乳臭"。the milk of human kindness 大概是"妇人之仁"的意思,是 Macbeth 所不喜欢的一种品性。不过随着时间发展,这个词逐渐被大家当褒义词使用,"人情味"、"恻隐之心"等。例如:"There's less and less the milk of human kindness these days./现在这个社会里人情味越来越淡了"。

7. 固定表达

(1)积习难返。Old habits die hard.

(2)日本谚语说:"冒头的钉子挨敲打。"Japanese saying "The nail that sticks out must be pounded down.

(3)自作自受。You reap what you sow.

(4)善有善报。One good turn deserves another.

8. 习语改写

(1)真是一刻不得闲啊。No rest for the wicked.

There is no rest for the wicked.

(2)(不幸或失望中的)一线希望;乌云周围的白光 silver lining

Every cloud has a silver lining.

(3)她丈夫经常外出就餐,与不三不四的人鬼混在一起。Her husband and often dined out and kept rather disreputable company.

keep rather disreputable company 是由习语“to keep company/结伴”扩充而来,表达了憎恨与厌恶之情。

(4)Don't be foolish enough to indulge in name-calling. 不要太傻,总是张口就骂人。

name-calling 源自于习语“to call sb. names/骂人”,在此句中作名词用。

(5)Where there is smoke, there is a meeting. 有烟必有会,无会不抽烟。

此句改自英语谚语:“Where there is a will, there is a way. /有志者,事竟成。”形象生动,收到了嘲讽的修辞效果。

(6)He intended to take an opportunity this afternoon of speaking to Irene. A word in time saves nine. 他打算今天下午找机会跟艾琳谈谈。一语及时省九语。

将原有习语“a stitch in time saves nine/ 一针及时省九针”中的名词 stitch 改成 word,比喻贴切,言简意赅。

(7)Of poetry I do not read much and when I do I choose the dead lion in the preference to the living dog. 对于诗,我读得不多,要读的时候,我宁可选择死狮,而不要活狗。

the dead lion 和 the living dog 源自英语习语:“A living dog is better than a dead lion. /下贱而活着比高贵而死的强。”

(8)One woman shopper said to another, “Mary, let's spend money like water——drip…drip…drip…”一位女顾客对另一位说:“玛丽,咱们花钱得像细水一样——滴…… 滴……滴……慢流。”

to spend money like water 原意是“花钱如水;大手大脚”,这儿对此谚语的使用却打破常规,一连加上三个 drip 予以引申,语义发生变化:不是大把花钱,而是锱铢必究,细水长流,收到出人意料的表达效果。

四、实战演练

1. be in a rut 墨守成规、一成不变

rut 本身指“车轮驶过留下的印痕”,引申指“从过去延续下来的老一套,老规矩”。be/stuck in a rut 指“处于墨守成规、一成不变、不思进取的一种状态”。

例如:I quit because I don't want to be stuck in a rut. 我不想陷入窠臼所以才辞职。

2. to turn the table 扭转局势

to turn the table on sb. 这个短语和“桌子”没什么关系,它的意思是“to suddenly take a position of strength or advantage that was formerly held by sb. else /反败为胜,转弱为强。”但也可以采用“形象记忆法”来理解这个习语:掀翻桌子就是推翻目前的状况,就是“扭转局势”。

例如: She played badly in the first set, but then she turned the tables on her opponent and won the match. 她开局不利,但后来扭转局势战胜对手赢得比赛。

3. be strong for 对……特别偏爱(或注重)

这个词组不管从内涵还是字面都不难理解。另外再介绍一个美式英语的表达"to go it strong on/坚决支持,热烈拥护"。

例如:I'm not very strong for this brand. 我对这个品牌没有特别的偏爱。

4. to look over one's shoulder 提心吊胆、小心提防

看到这个词组,脑子里是否有这样的画面:一个人因为害怕,头不停地往后转,留意背后动态。

例如:You should work freely and boldly, and think independently instead of always looking over your shoulder. 你们要放手大胆去做,要独立思考,不要畏首畏尾。

5. rain check 改期

rain check 是美国流行口语,典故出自露天举行的棒球比赛。棒球是最受美国人欢迎的运动之一。如果球赛进行时天公不作美,骤然倾盆大雨,不得不暂停,观众可领"雨票",或用原票存根作为"雨票",球赛改期举行时可凭之入场。

例如:I can't play tennis this afternoon but can I take a rain check? 我今天下午不能去打网球了,要么改天吧?

6. to make a meal of it 把事情做得过头

笔者有一位朋友,是个中国人,她信奉"要抓住男人的心,首先要抓住男人的胃",每天"四菜一汤"地张罗着。但她的澳大利亚老公却"不领情",抱怨说她在饮食上浪费了太多的时间和精力。由此可见,中西方都认为"做饭"是"大费周章"的事。

例如:Let's not make a meal of it. 咱适可而止吧。

7. crash 睡觉、住宿、过夜

在美国俚语中是指"在临时的床铺上睡觉,尤其在困极时"。是否可以这样记住这个词:crash 在计算机领域是指"死机",而且这个词有"发出猛烈声音倒下"的意思:一个人累极了,磕磕绊绊地找到床铺,一头倒下睡着了。

例如:Thanks a lot for letting me crash at your house last night. 谢谢你昨晚让我留宿你家。

8. by ear 不用乐谱(演奏);到时候再看着办;走着瞧

to play sth. by ear 口语中表示"凭记忆演奏乐曲(即不看乐谱)",也表示"事先无准备而根据情况采取行动;临时现做"。

例如:I have not decided what to say when he comes, I will play it by ear. 他来时我不知道要说什么,只有见机行事。

9. to fall asleep at the switch 玩忽职守

该习语来自源于铁路扳道执勤工人在上班是睡着了的行为,常用来比喻"玩忽职守"或"坐失良机"。

例如:His father often falls asleep at the switch. 他父亲总是坐失良机。

10. to hit the spot 满足要求

to hit the spot 本指“射击时正中红心”,也可以代换为 to hit the bull’s eye,在一般口语中则表示“完全正确”或“食物正合某人的胃口”。

例如:What you said just now really hit the spot. 你刚才所言极是。I’m hot and thirsty. A cool drink would just hit the bull’s eye. 我又热又渴,一杯冷饮正合我的胃口。

11. to give sb. a wide berth 回避,敬而远之

该习语源于航海用语,始见于19世纪。berth 系海上用语,常指船与灯塔或沙滩等之间留出的回旋“余地”或“安全距离”,在日常用语中比喻“和某人保持一定的距离”。

例如:Shall we give them a wide berth? 我们是否离他们远远的吗?

12. to hold the bag 背黑锅

to hold the bag 是一条脍炙人口的美语习语,意思是无可奈何地“背他人甩掉的包袱”或“独担本应与他人共担的责任”,即“背黑锅”。该词组在美语口语中还可指“一无所得”或“分得最差一份”。

例如:When the ball broke the window, the boys scattered and left George holding the bag. 球击碎玻璃窗后,孩子们一哄而散,让乔治一人背了黑锅。You still want to work for him this year? Don’t forget you just held the bag last year! 你今年还想给他干活?别忘了你去年在他那儿可一个子儿也没挣着呀!

13. be under the weather 身体不适的

weather 即天气, under 有“受……所影响、处于……状况之下”的意思,被天气影响而不舒服,固有 under the weather 一说,该习惯用语指“生病的”,当然也指一般不明原因的小病痛,类似形容词 sick 或 ill 的用法。

例如:I’m a little under the weather. 我身体有点不舒服。

14. to change one’s tune 改变某人的想法

tune 在这里可不是“音符”而是代表“想法”。to change one’s tune 按照字面意思来解释就是改换曲调,但其应用范围现在大大扩展。该词组最初出现在近四百年前的一首民谣里,咏唱侠盗罗宾汉劫富济贫的故事。另外再提提 to sing a different tune,按照字面意思是“唱不同的调子”, 它和 to change one’s tune 都可以用来表示“改变主意或者决定”,但是 to sing a different tune 作为习惯用语更为古老,来自14世纪的年代。to sing a different tune 往往还含有“某人的言行一反既往”的意思。那请你再猜猜 to dance to another tune 的意思?对,也是用来比喻“改变以往的作为和态度”。

例如:Now that he’s been elected governor, he certainly sings a different tune about big business. Now he refuses to tighten regulations on chemical wastes although he promised to during the campaign. 如今他已当选州长,对待大企业当然就改变了论调。虽然他在竞选时曾经答应要对大企业的化学废料处理严加规定,但是现在他却拒绝这样做。又如: Adams used to swear that they would never get married; but soon after meeting Bonnie he changed his tune and is now a happily married man. 亚当斯曾经发誓他绝不结婚的，但遇见邦尼之后不久，他改变了想法，现在可是位快乐的已婚男。

15. to put on an act 装腔作势

act 意是“戏剧的一幕”，或“较短的节目”，故其字面意为“上演一幕戏”，或“表演一个节目”。在中西方文化中，人们常用“演戏”来形容某人的装腔作势，所以本短语也即“装腔作势”、“炫耀自己”或“装模作样”之意。

例如：She smiled cheerfully, but I knew she was only putting on an act. 她笑得倒欢快，但我心里清楚，她只不过是在装模作样罢了。

16. to cramp one's style 因……而无法施展其才能

cramp 意思是“限制在狭小的范围内而阻碍或妨碍人的某人/某事的活动/发展”，style 则指“才能，风格”。

例如：He complained that bringing his wife to parties rather cramped his style. 他抱怨说，带太太参加舞会使他无法施展舞技。

17. to roll in the aisles 使某人捧腹大笑

roll 原指“转动”或“打滚”，在特定语言环境中还有“笑得无法抑制”之意；而 aisle 指“剧院、礼堂等处坐席间的纵直通道或走道”。to roll in the aisles 意思是“（使人）捧腹大笑或大笑不止”。

例如：He said something that rolled the other boys in the aisles. 他说了几句，逗得其他男孩捧腹大笑。

18. run-of-the-mill 一般的

mill 指的是“研磨机”，run-of-the-mill 表示“通过研磨机的转运而进行研磨”，引申为“平平常常的”，即研磨机转运是再自然、平常不过的了，一般常用作贬义。

例如：It's a run-of-the-mill detective story. 这只是一个平淡无奇的侦探故事。

19. A-1 第一流的、极好的

源自于船舶语言，根据英国《劳埃德船舶年鉴》，船体及设备均属第一等的标志符号为 A-1。

例如：The house is really A-1. 那间房子确实是一流的。

20. to mess around (with sth.) 玩弄某物；把玩某物

mess around 或 mess about 都可表示“玩一玩”，其后可接 with sth. 表示“玩一下某样东西”，也可接 with sb. 表示“与某人在一起鬼混或浪费某人的时间”。

例如：They were just messing around with the phone when it dropped and broke. 他们正玩那电话，结果它掉下来摔坏了。

五、巩固练习

1. 请翻译和理解以下谚语。

(1) Lookers-on see most of the game.
(2) Do not quarrel with your bread and butter.
(3) When one will not, two cannot quarrel.
(4) When wine sinks, words swim.
(5) Merry meet, merry part.
(6) Grasp all, lose all.
(7) Short pleasure, long lament.
(8) Least said, soonest mended.
(9) Fortune favors fools.
(10) Men make houses, women make homes.
(11) Let bygones be bygones.
(12) Hear all parties.
(13) Tall trees catch much wind.
(14) Experience must be bought.
(15) Lies have short legs.
(16) Soon learnt, soon forgotten.
(17) Even a worm will turn.
(18) Everybody's business is nobody's business.
(19) Great minds think alike.

2. 熟读并背诵下列俗语警句。

(1) What is done by night appears by day. 若要人不知,除非己莫为。
(2) All are not friends that speak us fair. 说我们好话的未必全是朋友。
(3) Accidents will happen in the best regulated families. 家规再严,事端难免。
(4) All shall be well, and Jack shall have Jill. 有情人终成眷属。
(5) No man is born wise or learned. 没有生而知之者。
(6) No man is content. 人心不足蛇吞象。
(7) Nothing is so necessary for travelers as languages. 外出旅行,语言最要紧。
(8) Nothing is to be got without pains but poverty. 世上唯有贫穷可以不劳而获。
(9) Not to advance is to go back. 不进则退。
(10) No way is impossible to courage. 勇者无惧。
(11) Observation is the best teacher. 观察是最好的老师。
(12) Old sin makes new shame. 一失足成千古恨。
(13) One false move may lose the game. 一着不慎,满盘皆输。
(14) One good turn deserves another. 行善积德/善有善报。

(15) Out of office, out of danger. 无官一身轻。(Out of debt, out of danger. 无债一身轻。)

(16) Promise is debt. 一诺千金。

(17) Reading enriches the mind. 开卷有益。

(18) Seek the truth from facts. 实事求是。

3. 请欣赏下列各句,并比较其译文之得失。

(1) One should love animals. They are so tasty.

每个人都应热爱动物,因为它们很好吃。

人人都应爱护动物。(它们)挺好吃的!

(2) Love the neighbor. But don't get caught.

要用心去爱你的邻居,不过不要让她的老公知道。

爱你的邻居吧! 可别让人逮着。

(3) Every man should marry. After all, happiness is not the only thing in life.

再快乐的单身汉迟早也会结婚,幸福不是永久的嘛。

男人都该结婚。幸福毕竟不是生活的全部。

(4) The wise never marry. And when they marry they become otherwise.

聪明人都是未婚的,结婚的人很难再聪明起来。

智者不婚,婚者不智/智者不婚,婚者昏也。

(5) Love is photogenic. It needs darkness to develop.

爱情就像照片,需要大量的暗房时间来培养。

爱情似照片,暗室出效果。

(6) "Your future depends on your dreams." So go to sleep.

"现在的梦想决定着你的未来,"所以还是再睡一会吧。

"梦想决定未来,"还是睡去吧。

(7) There should be a better way to start a day than waking up every morning.

应该有更好的方式开始新的一天,而不是千篇一律的在每个上午都醒来。

日始哪时不可以,何必清早醒来时!

(8) "Work fascinates me." "I can look at it for hours!"

"工作有意思耶!""尤其是看别人工作!"

"工作太吸引人啦!""我一看就是几小时!"

(9) When two's company, three's result.

两个人的状态是不稳定的,三个人才是!

两人成欢/"结伙",三人"成果"/"结果"!

(10) A dress is like a barbed fence. It protects the premises without restricting the view.

服饰就像铁丝网,它阻止你贸然行动,但却不妨碍你尽情观看。

连衣裙恰如刺篱笆,护着房屋,但不碍观瞻。

(11) The more you learn, the more you know; the more you know, the more you forget; the more you forget, the less you know. So why bother to learn.

学的越多,知道的越多;知道的越多;忘记的越多;忘记的越多;知道的越少,为什么学来着?

学多知多,知多忘多;忘多知少。何劳神学呢!

4. 请用本单元所学的知识造句。

(1)关于遗产的继承产生看分歧,最终导致了他们之间的争斗。
(2)他自动提议帮忙,可能有诈。
(3)利润对许多企业家的收益计划来讲并不是最重要的。
(4)我常常喜欢自言自语。
(5)他突然辞职,使人感到意外。
(6)这种机会真是千载难逢。
(7)在旅途中,吃饭方面很容易将就一下,结果顿顿都是快餐。
(8)难怪在比赛中惨败,他们已好几个月没训练了。
(9)别忘了打卡,否则领不到钱。
(10)简,别跟我捣鬼,我对你的诡计和手段一清二楚。
(11)他觉得走二十英里不算什么。
(12)别跟我说大话,我知道你的底细。
(13)一旦掌握诀窍,迈克发现用筷子吃东西很简单。
(14)我们无能为力。
(15)我只是猜你应该也很忙。
(16)我现在很忙,你能过会儿给我打电话吗?
(17)汤姆好像发达了,挣了很多钱。
(18)每次我想到这事,我就非常生气。
(19)乔被那家大公司开除因为他们认为他太自由散漫。
(20)选这个,选那个!有这么多的大学可以念,我选哪一所呢?
(21)我想他肯定是警察,他不断地转弯抹角地打听消息。
(22)我已听够了你的连篇谎话,让我清静一会儿。
(23)我绝不会出卖朋友。
(24)你可是大善人一个啊。
(25)俗话说"善有善报",我相信你有好报的。
(26)她有点小题大做了,这活居然花了她五个小时!
(27)咱们干吗不顺其自然呢?
(28)他怎么能坐失这次的良机?
(29)泰德没有去上学,因为他不舒服。
(30)我向你们保证我们会给你们送去的货物一定是一流的质量。

5. 借助词典理解下列习语并造句。

(1)be in full swing
(2)for my blood
(3)to serve sb. right
(4)to live sth. down
(5)in stitches

(6) to blow (sb./sth.) off

(7) to see eye to eye with sb

(8) be few and far between

(9) Don't give it another thought.

6. 请收集更多的中英文习语与大家分享。

Chapter 4 Reverse Thinking
逆向思考

一、思路讲解

“逆向思考”不是指单纯的意义上的反向思考，而是指换一种方式思考。“逆向思考”在本单元也可指“转向思考”或“多角度思考”。这种思考方式既可以是反义词的选择，也可以是通过内涵的理解，换一种表达方式或单词词组，还可以是句子结构方式的改写。总之，就是让大家进行多渠道多方位多层次多模式的思考，不因某个单词或表达形式不熟悉，而让口语交流而出现“断流”或“卡壳”现象，即不在一棵树上吊死。

在口语交流过程中，非英语母语国家的交流者受历史、文化、思维方式、语言的掌握程度、语言使用频繁程度、社会经验等因素的影响，会出现短暂的“失语”现象，不知该如何重启对话以及相应语言表达模式，陷于表达忧虑之中，这也是学生害怕口语交流的主要原因，使流畅或零障碍的交流变得似乎不可能。我们应该意识到非母语国家的说话者在交流中出现“卡带”的现象是不可避免的，妨碍英语口语交流的原因很多，比如受历史和文化影响较多的相应的俗语、俚语和谚语的表达；又比如美国的篮球文化和英国皇室文化；再比如思维方式：中国人的螺旋思维和西方人的直线思维等。再加上语言掌握的熟练程度和语言使用的频繁程度的影响，常常让我们的英语口语表达“捉襟见肘”。

随着国际交流的日趋频繁，英语作为全球最通用的工作语言让我们倍感“说好英语”的重要性，只有充分认识到汉英表达上的差异，并想尽办法搭建沟通桥梁才是建立良好交流的“王道”。实际上，大家要认识到口语最本质的特点就是“简单”。中国学生由于缺乏真实的英语交流的语境，受到书本英语影响较重，说出来的都是“书本气息”浓郁的“书卷味中国式英语口语”。要想改正这种英语表达的“非真实性”和“非生活化”的缺点，首先应充分利用真实的语言材料收集口语表达方式，比如 TED 公开课、哈佛公开课、网易公开课、探索频道、NBA 的现场转播等，让自己有更多的时间和机会浸润在真实的语料中；而这一章要谈到的“逆向思考”将是对大家帮助很大的口语习得方法：用不同的手段立即找到交流的思路，迅速回归表达，消除表达障碍，凸显幽默精神，体现语言表达的新颖性，避免了千篇一律的枯燥表达方式，实现表达的多样化，使交流者更好地融入跨文化交际之中。通过“逆向思考”，还可以帮助大家重拾信心，重建话题，消除“失语症”。怎样才能做到呢？看看下面的“案例分析”，你或许能得到启发。

二、案例分析

为帮助大家理解英汉表达中的文化相似性，从而提高口语表达能力我们将以下面提供的充足例子作为典型案例。

(1)我一直处处迁就你。I have been holding myself back.

"迁就别人"就是"克制自己",舍己为人!

(2)我经常加班。I have been working late, a lot.

"加"怎么讲?"班"怎么说?其实不用这么麻烦,"加班"就是 work late,而且句尾补充的 a lot 特别体现出口语交流的轻松随意的特点。

(3)我不怕投诉。I can handle complaint.

为什么"不怕投诉"?因为"我搞得定。/I can handle it."

(4)什么都豁出去了。You have nothing to lose.

未见 You have nothing to lose. 不知要翻译出"豁出去"得费多大周章,原来可如此轻松搞定。

(5)我有点不能专心。I have a little trouble concentrating.

这句话倾向于隐性否定的表达,就是不用常见的 not、no 这些否定词,用意义上表达否定的单词,比如这句话中的 trouble。

(6)我听不懂你说的。I can't follow what you say!

"听不懂"别人说些什么,自然就"I can't follow/跟不上" 说话人的思路,相信现在的你一定能"follow what I say"。

(7)我不是读书的材料。I'm just not the school type of person.

"读书"就是到学校学知识,"不是读书的材料"转向表达为 not the school type of person 非常生动。那举一反三,"不是做生意的料"和"不是搞体育的料",你一定知道怎样表达了。

(8)不是按照标准程序。It's not by the book.

"标准程序"应白纸黑字写在书上,供大家参考执行,所以这句话用简单的方式表达了这个意思。该结构有时候也用来表达贬义意义,说明人的人品低,有时候也用来调侃,比如说"某人很糟糕,没优点"。

(9)你是我见过的最烂的人。You are the most ridiculous man I ever met.

中文里的"烂人"是个贬义词,用来说明人品低,很糟糕,没优点,有时候也用来调侃。英语表达中的 ridiculous 在体现"烂人"的意思是指这个人的行为荒诞可笑,不按正常人的标准和道德规范行事。

(10)他对我甜言蜜语。He told me everything I want to hear.

什么是"甜言蜜语"?就是指说别人想听的话,顺耳的话,虽然有欺骗虚伪的成分在里面,但有时候这种话能融洽人与人之间的关系,其作用不容小觑。

(11)你应该忘掉这事。You should drop this thing.

邓丽君的歌里曾经有这样一个句子"把我俩的过去丢进河里,埋在土里",就是要忘记过去的意思。所以这里的"drop/丢"很好地表达了"忘记、忘掉"的意思。

(12)皆大欢喜。Everybody wins.

用两个字生动地表达了这个意思,不是"win-win/双赢"而是"大家、每个人"都赢,这难道不是"皆大欢喜"的事?

(13)我将倾囊相助(传授)。I teach everything I know.

"囊":口袋,引申为钱财力量。"相助":帮助。倾囊相助:倾尽自己的所有来帮助别人。理解了"倾囊相助"的本意,这个词的英语表达就有了很简单的思考思路。

(14)她看起来有点眼熟。There is something familiar about her.

这句话的句子结构是将整个思路反过来,起到了表达新颖性的目的。

(15)修心养性是极其重要的。The culture of the mind is vital.

"修心":使心灵纯洁;"养性":使本性不受损害。通过自我反省体察,使身心达到完美的境界。受文化影响,英文中无完全一致的表达,转向思维在这儿就尤显重要。虽然 the culture of the mind 不能全面深刻地反映这个词组,但基本意义还是涵盖了。

(16)此举不合礼仪。It is not considered couth.

couth 是"有教养的、温文尔雅的"的意思。中文词组形式用英文句子形式表达出来,而且中英文的句构形式也是相反。

(17)地球变暖真让人受不了。This global warming is killing me.

"受不了"用英文怎么表达? I can't stand sth.,还是 I can't take this anymore,亦或是 I can't bear sth.? 但句子里的 killing 就轻松地表达了相同的意思,这就是转向思考的好处。

(18)抽筋了。That's cramp.

"抽筋"在此句中应为动词,但在英语表达中单词做动词要考虑时态和语态,转向思考为名词 cramp 就会让表达轻松很多。考考你:如果抽筋现象得到缓解,"好了,不抽筋了"英文怎样表达? 对,就是 And release!

(19)城堡的每个角落 every inch of the castle

其实中文里的"角落"在这里的内涵有延伸,就是指的城堡里的每个地方,反向思考为"每一寸地方"。你不会认为汉语方言里的"犄角旮旯"、"旮旮角角"等只是指某个地方的角落吧?

(20)他们做到了。They got their wish.

"做到了"就是"得偿所愿"、"达到愿望"的意思,从这个角度理解,英文的 to get one's wish 就再自然不过了。

(21)你已长大成人。You are not a boy any more.

"长大成人"就是"不再是孩子了",反向思考让表达变得简单。对女孩子该怎么说呢? You are a girl any more.

(22)我不能说完全没有动心。I couldn't say I wasn't attempted.

说实在的,"动心"这个中文词的英文表达真还需要动动心思去考虑一下。转向思考一下:"动心"不就是想"跃跃欲试"吗?

(23)别费口舌! Save your speech!

中文中用"你省省吧!"来表达这个意思,到也应了 save 这个词。

(24)我们能做到。It can be done.

中文的主动语态用英文的被动语态表示出来,被动语态在此发挥了作用。

(25)不明白 to miss the point

point 就是"要点"的意思,to miss the point 就是"错过要点",要点都错过,当然就"不明白"了。

(26)管好嘴。Lips are sealed.

这又是一个从中文的主动语态转向到英文被动语态的例子。"管好嘴。"最好的办法就是"上封条/seal"呗。

(27)但愿比外卖好吃。I hope it beats takeout.

老实讲,这句话太生动了,一个"beat/战胜"将意境完全表达清楚了。

(28)你给我台阶下。You gave me an out.

"给台阶下"就是"给出路/out",这里的 out 从副词转成了名词。

(29)男人生病时很难伺候。Men make awful patients.

应该说谁生病都难伺候。但这句英语表达通过转向的方式,把意思言简意赅生动地表达出来,这种功力也只有母语国家的人才能做得到。

(30)还没完。It's a work in progress.

"还没完"表示"……正在进行之中",反向思考派上用场。

(31)拭目以待。Only time can tell.

"拭目以待"就是"擦亮眼睛等着瞧,形容很迫切。"从对这个词的理解来看,存在着一种被动无助的感觉,只有等的份。所以反向理解为 Only time can tell.

(32)不用送!I'll see myself off.

"不用送"不就是"自己送自己/ to see oneself off"吗?

(33)那跟我无关。It's news to me.

"无关"就是"没关系,不关心",那也就是当"新闻"看。

(34)我对此事暂不表态。I reserve judgment on this issue.

"不表态"就是不做评论,不给意见,英语转向理解为"reserve judgment/保留意见"。

(35)别忧心忡忡的。Let go of the stresses and strains.

"别忧心忡忡的"反向理解为"别拽着压力;让压力走开/let go off"。

(36)有人找你。You've got a visitor.

"有人找你"反向理解为"你有访者要见你"。

(37)你没有把握好机会。You've let this chance slip through your fingers.

"没有把握好"反向理解为"让……从手指间溜走"。

(38)她情绪不对。She was in strange mood.

"情绪不对"就是"情绪变得陌生、奇怪"。

(39)谢谢老妈。Thanks, Mom.

在此是讽刺对方干涉自己的行为,就像老妈一样。若欲直接表达拒绝对方干涉时,可说"None of your business./不干你的事"。或"Mind your own business./管好你自己的事"。

三、实战演练

(1)对……不反感 get the stomach for sth.

"不反感"就是有"胃口"的意思。

例如:其实我对英语不反感,但背单词实在让人头疼。Actually I get the stomach for English, but memorizing words is killing me.

(2)我不知道他被什么耽误了。I don't know what's keeping him?

"被……耽误了"就是"被……磕绊住了","被……留住了","keep"很好地解决了这个问题。

例如:他的出行计划被临时的任务给耽误了。The accidental assignment kept him from his trip.

(3)他的话萦绕在我脑子里。I couldn't get his words off my head.

中文中有"挥之不去"一说,表示某事或某人在脑子里"萦绕",用英文来讲就是不能

"get…off/从……下来"。

例如:对过去岁月的回忆常常萦绕在他的心头。Memories of the old days couldn't get off his head.

(4)他们让我感动。They strike me.

说到"感动",肯定大家不易想到 strike 这个词。你知道 strike 作为动词有这样的意思"给……印象,给……以深刻印象;引起……的感情或情绪等;感动,影响"。

例如:你对她印象如何? How does she strike you?

(5)我不介意。I'm OK with that.

"不介意"这个词大家都知道用 don't mind 或 don't care 来表达,但口语中有一更简单更形象的表达方法,即 OK with sth.

例如:实际上我不介意和其他人共事。I'm OK with other people working together actually.

(6)我很讨厌你这种表达方式。I'm a little bit of uncomfortable with the way you express yourself.

"讨厌某事"就是"对某事感到不舒服",comfortable 反义词 uncomfortable 就派上用场。

例如:我虽然讨厌他,但我不把他看作是敌人。Although I am uncomfortable with him, but I didn't treat him among my enemies.

(7)不出所料 right on schedule

schedule 是"时间表"的意思,right on schedule 就是"一切按照时间表的安排进行",也就是"不出所料"的意思。

例如:领班报告说工作如预期进行相当顺利。The foreman reported that the job was progressing right on schedule.

(8)沉默的反抗 silent treatment

这个词让笔者想起另一个词"冷暴力",顾名思义,指不通过殴打等行为暴力解决问题,而是表现为冷淡、轻视、放任、疏远和漠不关心,致使他人精神上和心理上受到侵犯和伤害。

例如:沉默的反抗无助于事情的解决。Silent treatment is not going to make the problem go away.

(9)美美地睡了一觉 full night sleep

依作者之见,"美美地睡一觉"就是指"睡到自然醒,一觉睡到大天亮"。这里的 full night 起修饰作用,应理解为"一整晚的"。

例如:因为感冒,他整整一宿无法入睡。Because of the cold, he couldn't have a full night sleep.

(10)我觉得女人们会相当吃这套。I see women really responding to that.

汉语口语中的"吃这套"就是"接受、有回应"的意思。

例如:我觉得睡前故事对孩子来讲相当管用。I think children will respond to sleeping story.

(11)我看人很准。I am a really good judge of character.

"看……很准"恐怕来自中国的八卦算命,be a good judge of sth. 意为"对什么做出正确的判断"。如果不转向思考,恐怕很难搭起沟通的桥梁。

例如:我认为他很会判断别人潜力的大小。I count him a good judge of potential.

(12)我目光太短浅了。I was thinking too small.

英语口语中 think too small 是"思想狭隘,目光短浅"的意思。从汉语的"目光短浅"转向到英语中的“思想狭隘”,如不了解这些知识,那就真的要埋怨自己“目光短浅,思想狭隘”了。

例如:说到这个话题,可能我们想得太狭隘了。Perhaps we tend to think too small when it comes to this issue.

(13)你一定有门路。You must know someone.

这句话的表达思路是:首先应知道什么是“门路”? 就是“途径,方法,窍门”。在特定的环境下,最好的办法就是有“人脉关系”。所以转向思考可让我们找到表达的捷径。

例如:他能在这么好的公司找到工作,他在公司一定有门路。He has got a position in such a decent company and he must know someone there.

(14)看起来眼熟。The face is so familiar.

中文是个省略句,省略了“某人”,但英语句子补上的是“某人的脸/the face”,从另一方向思考句子的表达。

例如:尽管这人看起来眼熟,但是我却叫不出他的名字。Although the face is so familiar, the name of the person is on the tip of my tongue.

(15)我向你保证。You have my word.

一说“保证”,恐怕大家会思考用 guarantee 或 pledge,或 ensure 或 assure 呢? 用动词还是名词呢? 词组搭配怎样? 其实转念一想,You have my word. 简洁明了。

例如:我向你保证,周末抽时间来陪你。You have my word, and I'll spend some time with you on the weekend.

(16)打气 to steel one's nerves

这里的 steel 是动词,“使坚强”、“打气”的另外一个思路不就是让人“精神坚强起来。”

例如:朋友的鼓励为处于低谷的我打气。The encouragement from my friends steeled my nerves when I was in trouble.

(17)做……于事无补。Doing sth. won't change anything.

“于事无补”就是“对事情毫无补益”的意思,转向思考就是“改变不了什么/ won't change anything”。

例如:有些人认为光埋头工作于事无补。Some people believe that working hard only won't change anything.

(18)怎样忘掉过去? How to turn the page?

现在有一流行词“翻篇儿”,不正是“忘掉过去”的意思吗?

例如:忘掉过去就是新的一天。Turning the page is another new day.

(19)一言难尽。Don't make me started.

“一言难尽”就是“一两句话说不清”,心里不舒服,不想说。反向理解就是“别让我说这件事。”

例如:一言难尽。我不想说这破事。Don't make me started! I don't want to talk about the failure.

(20)作为老人你肯定不常出门。You're old and pretty much house bound.

housebound 就是“被束缚在房子里”,意为“足不出户”的意思。

例如:他就喜欢待在家里,打电子游戏成了他唯一的爱好。He is a housebound boy and playing computer games is the only hobby for him.

(21)我不想无礼。The last thing I would wish to be is rude.

"The last thing I would wish to be …"是对"不想"的转向思考,英语的这个表达也带有极大的强调作用。

例如:我最不想做的事就是伤你的心。The last thing I wanted to do was to break your heart.

四、巩固练习

1. 从逆向思考的角度说说下面词组的英语表达。

(1)文化不发达的社会
(2)搬家
(3)不愿透露
(4)大麻烦
(5)咒语
(6)别管闲事
(7)捣乱
(8)中场休息
(9)摒除杂念
(10)老老实实
(11)伤人的词
(12)捕捉些灵感
(13)敞开心扉
(14)遵命
(15)宣传造势
(16)体面的工作
(17)客满
(18)天生一对
(19)意外之喜
(20)没有放下架子
(21)钱的正面
(22)养老院
(23)可折叠式后座
(24)情侣帽
(25)别为难人家
(26)早点休息
(27)小心措辞
(28)不要走开

2. 从逆向思考的角度说说下面句子的英语表达。

(1)这孩子真不给面子。
(2)这是不许碰的。

(3)我知道如何克服。
(4)她是一个文化修养很高的女子。
(5)我接受你的条件。
(6)这是天生的。
(7)我没空。
(8)他们看上去没意见。
(9)我真实绝望透了。
(10)我看算了。
(11)我和他没有过节。
(12)倾心于某人。
(13)你肯定错过了。
(14)我会指点你。
(15)屋里所有的人都哭得稀里哗啦。
(16)他们加密了。
(17)那段婚姻早就千疮百孔了。
(18)你在开玩笑。
(19)她现在处于千钧一发的境地。
(20)我不插手。
(21)你胡说八道。
(22)还有件事。
(23)别动某物。
(24)别管闲事!
(25)别再说什么。
(26)别反悔!
(27)别往心里去。
(28)别扯远了。
(29)别费口舌。
(30)别自取其辱!
(31)你看起来干劲十足。
(32)我还没有打听多少。
(33)硬撑着,硬挺着。
(34)我就不拐弯抹角了。
(35)如果我是你,就不掺和进来。
(36)他不是未成年人。
(37)没有挑明。
(38)没什么能帮我。
(39)我无能为力。
(40)它无聊极了。
(41)说得好!

3. 用本单元所学的知识造句。

(1)问题是她的哥哥对猫很反感,所以她不敢在家里养猫。
(2)不是每个小孩都是弹钢琴的料,别逼她。
(3)避免事故发生的最好办法就是按章操作。
(4)天啊! 我找遍房间所有的角落也未发现钥匙。
(5)他准是被拥挤的交通给耽误了。
(6)美妙的音乐还在我脑海里萦绕。
(7)他见义勇为事迹让她很感动。
(8)但是我倒是不介意吃盒饭。
(9)我讨厌大冷天的这么早起床。
(10)我讨厌遭受无言的冷遇。
(11)保证每晚睡眠充足。
(12)他是一个有眼光的艺术评论家。
(13)我向你保证按时来上课。
(14)她看起来很伤心。让我为她打打气。
(15)哭有什么用,好好准备下一次考试吧。
(16)在逆境中要学会如何忘掉过去迎接新生活。
(17)真是一言难尽,恐怕我不能告诉你。
(18)老年人应多出去参加社交活动,不要老待在家里。
(19)实际上,去购物是我最不想做的事了。

4. 请体会学习下面的句子,进一步了解逆向表达法的精妙之处。

(1)他需要有人跟他说说。He needs someone to fill in the blank.
(2)这让我很矛盾。I am feeling kind of caught in the middle of all that right now.
(3)我会让他尝到苦头的。I am not gonna let him get away with this.
(4)我今天还不够倒霉吗? As if my day could get any worse?
(5)欢迎自由提问。We're open for the questions. (open 是"公开的,开放的,自由参与的"的意思。)
(6)你怎么一点都不顾虑他们,不顾虑我们? How could you have such little regard for them, for us?
(7)所以你省省力气吧,别跟我争了。/行行好,别在这事上较真了? So do yourself a favor and don't try to fight this.
(8)我们曾经有佣人,现在我们就是佣人。We used to have help. Now we're the help.
(9)我想让她慢慢接受。I want her ease into this.
(10)你还耿耿于怀,是吗? You're not gonna let that go, are you?
(11)她不喜欢黑色。Black is not her color.
(12)我受之有愧。I've done nothing to deserve.
(13)你现在有你的生活。You moved on with your life.
(14)我让你丢脸了。I am sorry that I embarrassed you.

(15)也不是那么糟糕。It's not a total zero, all right?

(16)我从没往心上去过。I never gave it a second thought.

(17)算了吧！Let's face it!

(18)她没有前途。She is going nowhere.

(19)闻起来很细腻。It has an exquisite nose.

(20)我们不想说这些。We want to keep this story to ourselves.

(21)她就是忙碌命。She needs to be needed.

(22)没得商量。The matter is closed.

(23)你会认为我太不矜持了。You'll think me rather forward.

(24)我们还是打开天窗说亮话吧。I will not be coy and pretend I do not understand your meaning.（coy 扭捏、腼腆）

(25)我说了不讨论此事。I have asked for silence.

(26)我们回不到从前了。Things have changed between us.

(27)我可一直注意防晒。I always keep out of the sun.

(28)肯定是无心的误会。It was an honest mistake.

(29)我会叫他们不要多嘴。I'll try to keep them quiet.

(30)别到处现眼了，抓紧干活儿吧。Keep your histrionics to yourself and hurry up about it.（histrionics 装腔作势的态度和举止）

5. 通过观看英文电影、电视、讲座等，收集一些"逆向思考"的表达，并与同学分享。

Chapter 5 Connotative Understanding

内涵相助

一、思路讲解

"内涵"是一种抽象的感觉，是某个人对一个人或某件事的一种认知感觉。(http://baike.so.com/doc/3087203.html)有道字典对英文 connotations(内涵)的解释是：The connotations of a particular word or name are the ideas or qualities which it makes you think of. 与前一章"逆向思考"的利用反向或多向思维模式诠释相同意义不同，本章的"内涵相助"是指英汉之间通过内涵而不是字面意思理解表达出相同意义，是同向思维模式的近义表达方式。

通过观察和梳理，笔者发现口语交流中利用"内涵相助"的方法很多，主要有以下几种手段：

(1)因中英历史、地理、气候、制度等因素造成的文化差异和缺失，需要"吃透"内涵，找到合适的同义表达。比如"扶不起的阿斗"(disappointing child)；"我愿毛遂自荐。"(I would like to nominate myself.)；"我们倒也可以将计就计。"(This could work to our advantage.)

(2)某个词和词组有多个意义，通过语境帮助，筛选出合适的意义，"内涵相助"使表达更精准。比如这句话"作为一个有经验的管理者，在处理这个问题上我会更灵活。"中的"我会更灵活"是指"身手敏捷"吗？当然不是，这儿是指"灵活掌握原则"的意思，(I'll be more flexible.)。再看看这句"在强大社会压力下，总统决定辞职。"，你的选择是"under tremendous public press"还是"under tremendous social press"呢？

(3)通过内涵的理解，把汉语中语意复杂的单词换成简单的恰到好处的英文表达，而且"简洁"也符合口语特点："好吃街的东西可真多，有牡蛎，各种小吃，美味的手抓食物……"这里的"手抓食物"可能会让大家犯糊涂，"手抓"怎样表达呢？finger food 准确且简洁地表达这个内涵。"夜宵"也可准确且简洁地表达为 midnight snack。再说说"维持一个长久幸福的婚姻"(keep long-lasting happy marriage)。再试一下这句话："我不想连任。"(I'm not intended to run for the second term.)

(4)通过内涵理解，将禁忌的单词替换掉："他仍旧想念已故的妻子。"(He still misses his late wife.)在这里 late 替换了 dead。"你可能因为年事已高忘了我是谁了。"(You may not remember because of your advanced age.)用 advanced age 替换了 be old。

(5)通过对内涵的理解，用更形象的表达来替换意义相同的原词："我忘了时间。"(I lost all track of time.)；"很快忘记我"(to get over me fast)。

(6)通过内涵理解，解决专业术语的表达难题："恋父情结"(daddy issues)；"他很自闭"。(He is closed-off.)。

二、案例分析

下面我们用鲜活的案例帮助大家进一步了解“内涵相助”的思路。

(1)我尽职了。I am committed. 我不中用了。I' m out of commission.

这两个汉语句子的英文表达都涉及一个同根单词 commit,这个单词做动词有“使……承担义务”的意思,be out of commission 根据同根动词的意义理解为“不能使用的,退役的”。

(2)事情进展太快了。The thing is moving a little fast. 你是不是在跟某人耍手段? Are you making some kind of move against sb.? 大家伙,动作快一点。Come on, guys, we' ve gotta get a move on. 招牌动作 signature move 。

这里的四个例子都是利用 move 一词多义,分别匹配内涵相应的汉语表达:第一句:动词“移动,改变位置”。第二句:名词“步骤;措施”。第三句:名词“移动,行动”。

(3)你在执行任务。You are on the case.

be on the case 是“着手做”的意思。

(4)请把酒杯斟满酒。Please charge your glasses.

charge 有 fill or load to capacity 的意思,此处的“斟”就利用了这个意义。

(5)把这段感情带到下一步。Take this relationship to the next level.

说到“感情”的英文表达,很多人恐怕还得想一想,到底是用 feeling 还是 love 好呢? 请看看 relationship 的解释:A relationship is a close friendship between two people, especially one involving romantic or sexual feelings. 这个词尤指爱情或性的关系。

(6)他们是绝佳的一对。They are a golden couple.

我们先来看看 golden 在此句中的意义:If you describe something as golden, you mean it is wonderful because it is likely to be successful and rewarding, or because it is the best of its kind. 意思是“黄金般的,绝佳的”,其实笔者认为“黄金般的”都没有完全准确地表达出此处 golden 内涵。那现在你知不知道“生活中的黄金搭档”用英文怎么表达呢?

(7)他背叛了你。He cheated on you. 你认为你能骗我。You think you can screw with me. 不要欺骗你的朋友。Don' t double-cross your friend. 他因诈骗与欺诈被监禁了两年。He was jailed for two years for fraud and deception.

怎一个“骗”字了得? 一个中文的“骗”字英语中有这些表达应对,但请注意词性,前三个为动词,最后一个为名词。

(8)你在吵什么? What are you fussing about?

这里的“吵”不是“吵架”的意思,更倾向于是“因大惊小怪而发出的吵闹声”。

(9)宅男 homeboy;杂役 busboy;报童 paperboy

在这三个“boy”中,homeboy 除了“宅男”的意思外,还有“喜欢在家消遣的男人;家庭第一主义的男人”的意思;busboy 是指“在餐馆里打杂的小工”,比较一下,footman 是指“在宫殿里或有钱人家的仆人”。

(10)我可以和你谈一下吗? Can I talk to you personally?

作者认为这里的 personally 有“画龙点睛”的作用,是对中文这句话内涵透彻理解的绝佳例子。

(11)你站在那儿对我评头论足。You just stand there judging me.

"对某人评头论足"的英文表达是 to judge sb. 。那再试试这句话怎么说"别因为那个看扁人。/I hope you don't judge me for that."

(12)我可以走了吗？Am I released now?

宣布下课的时候，教师经常说 You are dismissed. 或者 You are released. 还记得吗？如果记得，说明你是个好学生，而且也知道这句话的英语表达，真是 win-win 双赢。

(13)破借口 a fake excuse

"破借口"就是"漏洞百出的借口"，也就是"不成立的借口，假借口"。fake 就是"假的，伪造的"。

(14)这歌很上口。This song is catching. 有什么企图？What's the catch? 名言、流行口号：a catchphrase

通过这三个例子，我们可看到 catch 的用法：第一句中的 catching 是"具有感染力"的意思。第二句中的 catch 是"a drawback or difficulty that is not readily evident/隐藏的困难或缺点"。第三个是"引人注目的，吸引人的词组/句子"的意思。

(15)我不想参与。I do not want to get involved.

"参与"的英文表达大家学过不少，如 join，take part in，participate in 等，其实这儿使用的 be involved 对内涵理解得更透彻，不想参与的事自然不是好事，不是好事用"卷入"不是更体现出要表达的意义。

(16)我是乐队的主要成员。I'm sort of an integral part of a musical number.

这里的 integral 把"必不可少"的内涵凸显出来了，因为该词意为"必需的，作为整体存在的 /existing as an essential constituent or characteristic"。

(17)这个政策很严格。The policy is very tough. 我最近过得不怎么样。I had tough days recently. 我比想象中的要坚强。I'm tougher than I look.

能记住一个单词的多个意义当然是最好的，但记忆的方法不要死记硬背，而是"多用"，作者认为"使用"是记忆单词最好的办法。

(18)胜算不大。The odds aren't good. /The odds are against us. 我和他有几面之缘。I used to see him at the odd thing.

the odds 是"可能性，机会"的意思，而 at odd times/hours/moments 是"偶尔；在闲暇的时候；用零碎的时间"的意思，现在口语中也用 at the odd thing 表示这个意思。所以提醒一下大家，一定不要只记单词本身的意义，在交流的语境中你会发现另一片新天地。

(19)那是什么表情？What's that face?

大家可能没有注意到 face 有"the feelings expressed on a person's face /表情"的意思，当你了解了这个意思，这个简单的 face 就会在口语交流中发挥它神奇的力，比如"摆着一张苦瓜/臭脸"怎么说？对，to wear a sour face。再引申一个，"败兴而归"怎么讲？to return with a sour face

(20)他是一个乖乖男。He did everything by the book.

做什么是都按照书上写的做，不是"乖乖男"是什么？那"乖乖女"呢？知道你会表达了！但我们换一个说法 regular girl，这个词的内涵意思是"做什么是都按部就班"。我们看到"乖乖男"的表达用了 book 这个单词，那考考大家以下词组怎么表达？"通讯录/contact book"，"记事本/an appointment notebook"。再给你说一个很有意思的表达，你知道"招惹某人"怎么说吗？"be in sb.'s bad books/进入某人的黑名单"。看看这个例子："就因为个金表，我可不愿招惹她。/I wouldn't be in her bad books for a gold watch."

(21)一切都还顺利吗？Is everything under control？

control是一个值得大家注意的单词，这个单词掌握好了，会让我们的表达收到惊喜。比如"我自有分寸。/I got everything under control."；"某人的地盘/sb.'s control"；"最出格的事/ the most out-of-control thing"；"控制狂/control freak"；"质量监督/quality control"。对最后两个词组多说两句："控制狂"应该是种病态，用这个表达替换了专业术语，这是我们前面讲过的"内涵相助"的方法之一。"质量监督"的"监督 — 监视、督促"总是让我们有很多负面的联想，谁愿意被人看着，管着，个人理解，用control语气就要缓和很多，效果一样好。

(22)成熟的办法 grown-up approach

第一次听到这个词组，为其对"内涵相助"手段的"成熟"应用拍案叫绝。说到"成熟"，再看看下面两个表达："他们都长大了。/They're so grown up."；"长大成人/to reach one's maturity"。

(23)我累惨了。I am exhausted.

"惨"该怎么理解？看看exhaust的理解："If something **exhausts** you, it makes you so tired, either physically or mentally, that you have no energy left. / 使精疲力竭"。

(24)你在下战书吗？Is that a challenge？

中文里的"战书"指的是"敌对一方向另一方提出交战的文书"。challenge意为"If you **challenge** someone, you invite them to fight or compete with you in some way./向……发出挑战"。"战书"还可以说成written challenge to war，不过这个句子的表达简洁生动，不需要用write这个动词来使整个句子的表达变复杂。

(25)我对他太严格了。I was too hard on him.

hard是英语中的活跃词汇，掌握起来难度不大，但需要用更多的语料帮助大家拓展对这个词的认识。"我也不会让你为难的。/I don't want to make it harder for you."；"你能否不让事情复杂化？/Can you please not make it any harder?"

(26)咒语解除了。The curse lifted.

恐怕大家没想到"解除"用lift轻松搞定。作者这样理解lift的用法：凡是不好的事情都会像障碍物一样堵在那儿，解决的办法就是"拿开，挪开，提走……"。对lift的"官方"解释是："If people in authority **lift** a law or rule that prevents people from doing something, they end it. /解除（法令等）"。比如"解除关税/to lift tariff"。

(27)我找了你一整夜。I've been reaching you all night.

也许有人会说"这句话这么简单，分分钟搞定。"但作者想说的是reach一词在此处的精妙使用。同样的"找"，为什么不用find，look for，discover呢？因为reach还含有"联系上"的意思，不一定是出去到处找。再说说"他很难找到。/He is hard to keep track of."这里的"找"用了keep track of，表明了这人行踪不定。"内涵相助"可让我们的表达更生动准确。

(28)爱心包裹 care package

说到"爱"，大家都知道love，那"爱心"该怎么说呢？care做名词有"关爱"的意思，了解内涵，问题迎刃而解。扩展几个词组："临终关怀/hospice care"、"无微不至的关爱/constant care"、"贴心的朋友/caring friend"、"爱抚/caress"。

(29)你太讨厌了。You are sick.

"讨人厌"就是"让人恶心"的意思，sick因此派上用场。"有点恶心/a burst of sickness"。

(30)一个好机会 a big break

大家可能不太清楚,break 有“时来运转”的意思:A **break** is a lucky opportunity that someone gets to achieve something.

(31)同性恋 queer

社会的多元化发展使“同性恋”不再是个隐秘词汇,很多人都知道“男同性恋”是“gay /玻璃、飘飘”,“女同性恋”是“lesbian /蕾丝、拉拉”,那 queer 又是什么意思呢? 我们请“内涵帮助”:queer 本义是“奇怪的”,做形容词,“怪人”,做名词,这里用 queer 就是对男同性恋的贬称,即 an offensive term for an openly homosexual man。

(32)爱上一个不该爱的人 to love a wrong person

怎样表达“不该爱的人”,如果用定语从句的方式,就把句子弄复杂了,“内涵相助”派上用场:“不该爱的人”就是“所托非人”,如果说“如意郎君”是 Mr. Right,那“不该爱的人”就是 Mr. Wrong。

(33)听到你的消息 to hear a word from you

可能大家忽视了 word 有表示“消息”的意思,如果此处表达为 news,就显得不够地道了。

(34)麻烦不断的小青年 a mess-up kid

说说 mess,其作动词有“把事情弄糟;制造脏乱;玩弄”,同义名词也很好理解的意思。“搅乱某人的思维/ mess with one's head ”,“情感上一片混/emotional mess”。说到“恶作剧,混乱”,这里延展一个单词“shenanigan /恶作剧;诡计”,例如:“如果他们胆敢胡闹…… /If they pull any shenanigans...”。

(35)吸引人的条件 a solid offer

这里的 solid 是“实实在在的,不是‘水’的”的意思。我们试试用 solid 来完成下面的表达:“稳定的婚姻/ solid marriage”,“足够的证据 /solid alibi”。说到“吸引人的,诱人的”,最常见的表达该是 tempting 一词,如 “tempting offer/诱人提议”,“The good news is that prices are still temptingly low. /好消息是价格仍然低得诱人。”那请大家再想想,不使用 tempting,这句话怎么说?“我已经出了很高的价格。/I make a very generous offer. ”。那“丰厚的工资”呢?“generous salary”。最后说说 offering,“休战礼物/ a peace offering”。

(36)工作动员会 career intervention

这里的 intervention 是“干预,介入,调停”的意思,职场上的 career intervention 类似于现在学校里的“心理干预”,大家要知道 intervention 是一个积极词汇,是希望别人的介入和干预的意思,不要把它和“interference/干涉”混淆起来。说个段子让你记住这两个词的区别:金正恩希望中国对朝鲜事务进行 intervention,不希望美国对朝鲜事务进行 interference。再跟你说个“动员会,鼓劲会”的说法,即 pep talk。请看例子:“身残志坚之类的理智谈话/ handicapped pep talk”。

(37)这是我的办法。This is my shot.

从内涵的角度来看 shot 用得比 way 好,因为 shot 有“尝试”的意思。再看 shot 的另一个用法:“你对我的鼓励真是一针兴奋剂。/Your encouraging words were a real shot to me.”

(38)你这是拖我后腿。You're trying to sabotage this.

如果你犯疑怎么表达“拖后腿”,老外更是一头雾水:人还分前腿和后腿? 那“拖后腿”是什么意思? 只有理解好内涵,才能说好这个句子。sabotage 就是“妨害;对……采取破坏行动”的意思,与“拖后腿——比喻牵制、阻挠别人或事物使不得前进”相对应。所以请大家记住:学好母语才能更好地掌握英语。

(39)对某人很凶 be harsh on sb.

harsh 就是"unkind or cruel or uncivil /残酷的,苛刻的,严厉的"的意思。"苛刻的条件/harsh terms"。比如"harsh words /刺耳的话语"。

(40)独处 alone time

类似的表达有 to leave sb. alone,也可以换一个表达"让我们清静清静。/Leave us in peace"。

(41)消除痛苦 to ease the pain

在这儿能不能用 get rid of 来代替 ease 呢?"If something unpleasant eases or if you ease it, it is reduced in degree, speed, or intensity. /减轻;减缓",所以从内涵上讲,这两个词还是有区别的:to get rid of 是完完全全去掉,而 to ease 是缓解,减轻的意思。"减轻罪恶感/to ease guilty","舒缓放手时的疼痛/ to ease the pain of letting go"。

(42)看来有人是飞上枝头当凤凰了。The sad caterpillar has turned into an extravagant butterfly.

在汉语中有个时髦的词,叫"凤凰男",你知道这是什么意思吗?"凤凰男是指家境贫困的农村男孩通过自身努力和他人帮助,进入大城市并获得成功"。我们可以通过内涵理解用 ugly duckling 或 phoenix man 来表达这个词组。但个人感觉还是不够贴切,显得有点别扭,直到眼前这句话的出现,"The sad caterpillar has turned into an extravagant butterfly. /忧伤的毛毛虫终于蜕变为高贵的蝴蝶"。

三、实战演练

(1)她还是很灰心丧气。She's still pretty down in the dumps.

"down in the dumps/ 伤心,忧郁",dump 当动词讲时,有"抛弃某人"的意思,所以一个人如果被人甩了,当然心情不好了。那表示"心情不好,沮丧"还有哪些说法?"他有点不高兴。/He seems a little down. ";"我今天心情(有点)低落。/I feel low today. ";"我心情很低落。/I am so down. "

例如:简丢了工作后,很伤心。After Jane lost her job, she was down in the dumps.

(2)动起来! Let's boogie!

boogie 原意是"跳摇滚舞;跳迪斯科;情不自禁地,尤其跟着摇滚乐或迪斯科乐跳起舞来;跳霹雳舞"。引申为"着手工作,认真开始工作"。

例如:该着手工作了。Time to boogie.

(3)我担心她认出我。I'm afraid she spots me.

"认出"某人,是用 identify 还是 recognize? 可能根据书本所学,你还会想到 single out,能否有更简单一点的单词选择,对,就是 spot!

例如:高个子在人群中是很容易认出的。A tall man is easy to spot in the crowd.

(4)我深表遗憾。I have many regrets.

这里的"深"是"十分,特别"的意思。而英文表达这儿利用了 regret 的名词复数形式,将中英文的内涵有机结合在一起。

例如: We have many regrets tonight because we didn't expect to lose the game like that.

(5)我为这个国家卖命。I dedicate my life to this country.

这句话透着一股浓浓的抱怨味道,“卖命”就是指“为某人、某集团所利用或为生活所逼而拼命干活”有时也泛指“下最大力气干工作”。dedicate 有“把时间、精力等用于”的意思,如果这个单词能用于传递正能量,那不是更好。

例如:他把毕生精力用于保护我们的自然资源。She dedicated her life to natural resources.

(6)瞧不起人 to think less of sb.

轻视一个人最冷酷的做法莫过于忽视他、冷落他、眼里没有他、心里不想他。

例如:对什么都不在乎是不对的 。It is wrong to think less of everything.

(7)袒护某人 to cover sb.

cover 作名词就是“盖子,封面”,作动词“掩盖,掩护”,所以 cover sb. 就是“袒护某人”的意思。李××之母护子心切,尽管社会诟病很多,虽然其做法不可取,但作为母亲,也值得理解和同情。

例如:别替他说话。Don't cover him.

(8)花哨的东西 something fancy

fancy 是一个活跃词汇,意义和词性较多,这里先说它的两个意思。fancy 作形容词,有“花哨的,装饰性的”的意思。“高档餐厅/ fancy restaurant”,因为“ If you describe something as fancy, you mean that it is very expensive or of very high quality, and you often dislike it because of this./ 阔气的,高档的”。

例如: My parents sent me to a fancy private school. 我父母把我送到了一所高档的私立学校。

(9)真相 lowdown

“真相”在口语中有一个表达是 lowdown,“ If someone gives you the lowdown on a person or thing, they tell you all the important information about them. /实情、内幕”。延展一个与 low 有关的单词,即“节水马桶/ low-flow toilet”。

例如:我可不想告诉你真相。I'm not about to tell you the lowdown.

(10)合理的价格 a decent price

大家经常用 decent 表示“体面的”意思,这里的 decent 是通过内涵理解,表示为“公道的”的意思。怎么说“像样的饭菜”? 就是“a decent meal”!

例如:在那儿你不用花太多的钱就可美餐一顿。You can get quite a decent meal there without spending too much.

(11)优秀品质 wonderful attributes

很少有学生能用 attribute 一词来表达“品质”之意,因为同学们在书本上更多地是了解这个词作动词的用法。那么 attribute 作名词到底是什么意思呢? “An attribute is a quality or feature that someone or something has. / 特性”。

例如: Politeness is an attribute of a gentleman. 彬彬有礼是绅士的本色。

(12)我要好好求老板给他两个星期的假。I need to sweet-talk our boss into giving him two weeks off.

sweet-talk 这个词字面和内涵十分匹配,“好好求”无非就是“说点甜言蜜语”,不过要提醒大家,这个词略带贬义。

例如:别给我灌迷汤了,我不会再给你钱的。Don't sweet-talk me into it. I won't give you money anymore.

(13)我们都有过去。We all have baggage.

"谁没有过去呢?"但这儿的"过去"该怎样理解呢? 从内涵来讲 baggage 用得很不错,因为它是指"感情或思想上的包袱"。再请大家说说这个词组"过去不堪回首的经历/past negative experience"。

例如:好消息让他解除了思想包袱。The good news took the baggage off .

(14)我可没觉得惊喜,我有些措手不及。I wasn't surprised. I was blindsided.

blindside 作动词,指"攻其不备/surprise sb. in a negative way"。

例如:我连挨两记闷棍。Twice I've been blindsided.

(15)即使这个情况比她们预料的糟乱得多。Even the mess is much bigger than they bargained for.

bargain 对大家来讲并不陌生,但 bargain for 或 bargain on 却很少使用,"If you have not **bargained** for or bargained on something that happens, you did not expect it to happen and so feel surprised or worried by it. /预料"。

例如:这项政策的影响出乎政府的预料。The effects of this policy were more than the government had bargained for.

(16)她的健康状况急转直下。Her health takes a turn for the worse.

"急转直下"的"转"采用"turn"是字面和内涵的完美结合,想想"急转弯"怎么说? sharp turn。再说说"事情会有转机的。/Something will turn up.","越来越坏/go from bad to worse"等。

例如:我们但愿有所改善,然而事情却每况愈下。We were hoping for an improvement but things had gone from bad to worse.

(17)她是家人。She's blood.

这是在口语中才能听到的表达。"血浓于水"说的就是有血缘关系的亲人比什么都重要。我们再学一个词组"be in one's blood/ 对某人很重要;天生就有的,骨子里存在的",这个习语表示某种东西对某人来讲很重要或因遗传影响具有某种禀性或特征。

例如: He spends money like water. It's in his blood and can't be changed. 他挥金如土,这是天性没法改变。

(18)这件事不容我们置喙。It's not for us to have an opinion.

"置喙"中的"喙"是指"鸟嘴"的意思,"不容置喙"就是"不容插嘴,不需要发表意见"的意思。了解中文内涵之后,你就会觉得英文的理解十分到位。再记一个表达"别胡说八道。/Don't give me the bull."

例如:人人似乎都想对此事品头论足一番。Everyone seems to have an opinion on this issue.

(19)当一切都进行得很顺利时,不要总想惹是生非。Don't always try to start something when everything is running smoothly.

"惹是生非"就是挑起事端的意思,所以 to start something 非常到位的理解。其实同义词的表达还有:"你最好还是走吧,别自找麻烦! /Don't ask for trouble. You'd better run away."

例如:老板似乎在生气。现在找他谈话是自讨苦吃。The boss seems to be annoyed. To talk to him now is to ask for trouble.

(20)没有附加条件 no strings attached

"no strings attached = without strings",这算是固定词组表达方式。"high-strung /极度紧

张的”,strung 是 string 的过去分词。string 的意思是“用线、绳等悬挂;系住某物”,high 在此是形容线或绳已拉得非常紧,比喻极度紧张。

例如:这位上了年纪的女演员非常紧张,而且傲慢专横。The aging actress was very high-strung and overbearing.

(21)侥幸猜中 lucky guess

这个词中英文字面和内涵匹配,理解起来不难。“lucky guess”还可以理解为“蒙对”。

例如:他并非真知道答案——那不过是个侥幸的猜测。He didn't really know the answer——it was just a lucky guess.

(22)to have something cooking 有计划

cook 原意是指“烹调;做饭”,而在口语中 cooking 是指“在筹划中(经过策划而)发生”。

例如:你今年圣诞假期有什么计划? Do you have anything special cooking for Christmas vacation this year?

四、巩固练习

1. 利用“内涵相助”的方法说说下面中文词组的英语表达。

(1)警方征用

(2)午餐高峰

(3)给予回报

(4)平凡百姓

(5)日常的活

(6)胡思乱想

(7)重要的会议

(8)案底

(9)逃课

(10)国宴

(11)大卖家

(12)耍手段

(13)艳舞

(14)更有点人性

(15)配不上他

(16)情侣衫

(17)情书

(18)被取消掉

(19)一次性相机

(20)处于劣势

(21)赞赏的眼光

(22)竞争的第一要诀

(23)滞纳金

(24)押金
(25)全额退款
(26)十分光彩照人
(27)正规程序
(28)明确的答复
(29)理想的工作
(30)艰难的过渡期
(31)真人秀
(32)抨击某人
(33)老夫老妻
(34)又一次失望
(35)亲密关系的开始
(36)突然有一天
(37)心灵伴侣(心灵相通的人)
(38)相当英俊
(39)白马王子
(40)很耗脑力的
(41)赶走某人
(42)别耍滑头
(43)尖锐问题
(44)搞定这事
(45)时机的敏感性
(46)说清楚点
(47)大开眼界
(48)没有意识到
(49)这工作的诀窍
(50)富含深意的歌曲
(51)做一个大胆的猜测
(52)擅长说话的人
(53)一杯又一杯
(54)固执的儿子

2.利用"内涵相助"的方法说说下面中文句子的英语表达。

(1)有得有失。
(2)这太难了。
(3)很丢人!
(4)她很忙。
(5)他是我的偶像。
(6)你在出价吗?
(7)我被开除了。

(8)他受不了这个。
(9)放回原处。
(10)我不喜欢这个。
(11)我染了发。
(12)事已至此。
(13)遵守自己的感觉(跟着心走)。
(14)你差点就被停课。
(15)我四海为家。
(16)我不能丢下朋友。
(17)我头痛欲裂。
(18)都是您胡思乱想。
(19)你脑子进水了?
(20)她真粘人。
(21)我知道规矩。
(22)她的个头和我差不多。
(23)我们应该大胆迈进一步。
(24)你认为是一夕成功?
(25)他是学校最受欢迎的男生。
(26)你已无路可逃。
(27)今天是什么好日子?
(28)用得着这么丢人现眼吗?

3. 熟读并背诵下列句子,进一步体会“内涵相助”的使用方法。

(1)让我把话说完。Let me get through it.
(2)他能呼风唤雨。He is manipulative.
(3)我受到好评。I was well reviewed.
(4)我可不帮你们把风。I'm just not standing guard.
(5)你要我违背本性。You ask me to be someone I am not.
(6)这是个善变的世界。This is a slippery world. (slippery 不稳定的)
(7)她的忍耐达到极限。She was pushed to her breaking point.
(8)我是指要包罗万象。All I mean is it needs to be inclusive.
(9)你在我门前鬼鬼祟祟地干什么? What are you doing lurking outside my door?
(10)我不想再打扰你。I don't want to take up any more of your time.
(11)我承诺我将既往不咎。I promise I can make everything go back to the way it was.
(12)一旦背叛我,我将会变成冷血的人。Once you betray me, I'll become an ice woman.
(13)你能给你那老公做点思想工作吗? Can you talk some sense into your husband?
(14)很少有男人能从一而终。Constancy is rarely found in men.
(15)做好事的不一定都是“雷锋”。Good deeds aren't always done for the purest reasons.
(16)我们先探探口风,再寻找蛛丝马迹。We'll ask indirect questions and scan for clues.
(17)桑普森是个厉害角色。Sampson is a very sharp player.

(18)别拿我当挡箭牌。Don't use me as an excuse.

(19)就算我要遭殃,也得拉他垫背。If I go down, I'll take him with me.

(20)你用不了多久就能做出一番红火的生意。You should have a roaring trade in minutes.

(21)A. 你甚至都没听到我的委屈。B. 你有什么委屈? A. You don't even listen to my side of it. B. What's your side of it?

(22)原来你这么懂得随机应变。I didn't know that your loyalty was contingent on the circumstances. (contingent adj. 因情况而异的)

4. 用本单元所学的知识造句。

(1)这里有几条在我感觉有点儿不开心时曾帮助过我的建议。

(2)这个曲子我喜欢!咱们跳一段吧。

(3)你有多少遗憾? 多少次你希望自己拥有足够的勇气去做某事?

(4)这名法官毕生致力于反腐败斗争。

(5)如果我不参加你的婚礼,你不会对我有看法吧?

(6)她为何要包庇那个试图要杀死她的人呢?

(7)哈里带我到一家高档餐厅庆祝我们的结婚纪念日。

(8)只是要告诉我真相,你就没事。

(9)再三考虑之后,觉得他值得好好吃一顿。

(10)回到学校学习这个主意是诱人的,为什么不这样做呢?

(11)"喜新厌旧"是人类的一种正常的特性。

(12)我要跟我妈灌些迷汤,说服她给我一部新车。

(13)我们思想上的包袱太多了。

(14)他抱怨该决定让他感到意外。

(15)别指望会有立竿见影的疗效。

(16)克服困难寻找幸福是人类的天性。

(17)我们都在报纸上提出了自己对道德教育的看法。

(18)你最好保持沉默,否则你会自找麻烦。

(19)他最近有点神经质,因为他工作压力一直很大。

(20)那个计划已经筹划了一个星期了。

5. 你能找到更多在口语交流中"内涵相助"的例证吗? 请与大家共同分享本章的学习体会。

Chapter 6　Gelivable Affixes (Roots)

词根/词缀给力

一、思路讲解

英语学习的最大“拦路虎”之一是生词,扫清拦路虎就等于扩大词汇量。口语交流中出现的“失语”或“词不达意”或多或少都跟词汇量不足有关。不过,我们发现扩展词汇量有捷径可走,那就是“一个中心(词根),两个基本点(前缀和后缀)”。英语词汇中由词根,前缀,后缀结合在一起的词很多,占有相当大的比重。英语词缀是掌握记忆词汇的一个重要环节,牢记词根可以起到举一反三的效果。

词根是英语语素,它是指不能再分的最小单位,能代表一个完整的意思并独立存在,称为“root”。词缀是指加在词根之前或之后的一个最小语素,它也有一定意义,但是不能独立存在,必须依附于词根。词缀是放在单词前后以构成新词的附属成分,可分为前缀和后缀,一般前缀改变词义,后缀改变词性。(http://wenda. so. com/q/1363601938068520)《牛津简明英语词典》对“词缀”是这样下定义的:“放在词根(Root)、词干(Stem)或单词(Word)的前部(指Prefix)、后部(指Suffix)或中间(指Infix),用来修饰其意义的添加成分。”[1]。

在口语交流的过程中,利用词根词缀不仅能让词汇量得到提高,也能使表达更加简洁,英汉转换的思维更加流畅,不需要转弯抹角地考虑时态、语态以及句型结构等。说到利用词根词缀扩大词汇量,不知大家是否注意到,最近很多中国词就是利用这个方法进入英语中的,比如“taikonaut”(特指中国宇航员),“taiko”源自中文的“太空”,后缀“-naut”指“驾驶员、操作员”。按国际惯例,拥有载人技术的国家都能享受一个专有名词,外媒在报道“神六”时创造了“taikonaut”。再比如说2010年,中式英语“ungelivable/不给力”风靡网络,似乎标志着一个从“中国人背英语单词”到“中国人造英语单词”的跨越性时代拉开帷幕,《纽约时报》称此事“非常酷”。比如将“Chinese/中国人”与“consumer/顾客”合成的单词“Chinsumer”,意指出国旅游时挥金如土的“中国购物狂”。“antizen”译为“蚁族”,是把“ant/蚂蚁”,加上“-izen”作为后缀,用来形容80后大学生低收入聚集的群体。反映中国电影人雄心壮志的“中国坞/Chinawood”以及喻指中国提供动力发动全世界经济的“领头龙/Leading Dragon”。

本章中所提到的词缀不仅是传统意义上的词缀,是指广义上的词缀,比如“well-”,“-bound”以及临时拆词的“-mance”等也算是词缀。另外,也希望大家明白,尽管利用词根词缀扩展生词有别于传统意义的生词记忆——方便、简单、快捷,但“天下没有白吃的午餐”,相应的词缀和词根记忆还是要下工夫,而且难点在于容易混淆词缀的用法:否定词缀该用“im-”还是“un-”呢?后缀表形容词是用“-ible”还是“-able”呢?这些都是应该下“死”工夫的地方,不能偷懒。建议大家利用“多用”的方式记忆单词,学过的见过的生词通过课堂、英语角、英语活动、考试等途径展示出来;有时候也可采用自言自语的方式,随时随地把生词进行复习;还可以利用电影的字幕,采用关闭声音,自己看字幕先说一次,再打开声音进行对照等方式。

二、案例分析

下面我们用更多鲜活的案例来帮助大家深入理解和实践英汉表达中的"词缀词根给力"这一方法。

(1)他对你不高兴。He is displeased with you.

be displeased with sb. 记忆窍门:词缀里的 d 和原词里的 p 字形颠倒:d-p,颠倒所以不高兴。

(2)他不能挑三拣四的。He can't be a chooser.

从中文的"挑三拣四的"形容词转化为 chooser,名词。choose + (e)r,表示"挑三拣四的人,挑剔的人"。再看看这句话"他学得很快。/He's a fast-learner."这个例子呢?"一年级学生/ first-grader"。

(3)我们相互间疏远了。We are untouched with each other.

"保持关系,保持联系"英文表达是 keep in touch with,利用 touch 这个词根加上否定前缀 un-和表示形容词的后缀-ed 完成了表达。记忆窍门:"u"很像缺了一截的圆环,就可以理解为断开了联系。

(4)山峦起伏的 hilly

这个单词是典型的名词后跟-y 或-ly 构成形容词的构词方法,既然说到"山峦起伏的",那我们以描述"山城"重庆的自然风光来复习此构词法:"多雾的/ foggy","多河流的/ streamy","多云的/cloudy","多雨的,潮湿的/ drippy","麻辣的/spicy","好吃/tasty/yummy"……

(5)真的是隐形的吗? Is it really invisible?

"隐形"就是"看不见", visible 可看见的 + 否定前缀 in-。记忆窍门:"隐"音通 in-,就记住了这个词的否定前缀。

(6)我喜欢资源回收。I'm a recyclist.

recycle 是"重新利用,再用"的意思,后缀-ist 表示"……的人"。记忆窍门:表示人,后缀是加-er 还是-or 抑或是-ist? 一般来讲,这个-ist 表示"具有某种信仰或笃信某种原则的人",recyclist 就是地地道道的环保主义者。

(7)我越界了。I'm overstepping the boundary.

这句话主要用于涉及了别人的隐私的语境中,中英文基本上按字面意思走的,比较好理解。还有更简单的说法,"我越界了。/I overstepped."和"你越界了。/You cross the line."

(8)意外情况 unforeseen circumstances

何为"意外"? 就是"没有预见到的",可以用 unexpected 来表达,而 unforeseen 更有趣,简单分析一下:"see/看见"是词根,已变成过去分词,表形容词,加上前缀"fore- /之前,先,在……前面",再加上否定前缀 un-,整体意思为"在之前为看到或预见到的",有趣的加法游戏。再举个例子:"前戏/ foreplay"。

(9)我哑口无言。I was speechless.

"哑口无言"就是"闭上嘴,无话可说"的意思,记忆窍门:大家知道 e 是一个比较活跃的字母,字形也像一个张开的嘴,后面的两个 s 就像两个别针,将 e 这个没有闭上的嘴封住。

(10)特大号 oversized

前面讲过 over-这个前缀,这里的 over-放在 size 前,表明这个尺码不是一般的大。当然,这个表达有点吓人,委婉一点可以这样表达:queen sized 或 king sized。

(11)你疯了吗? Are you insane?

sane 是"心智健全的,神智正常的"的意思,前面加上否定前缀 in-就变成了否定意思,类似于"out of one's mind/脑子进水"的意思。记忆窍门:否定前缀 in-本身这个单词就是"在……里面",想象成"脑子进水"。

(12)同父异母兄弟 half-brother

"同……异……"不就是只有"一半的血统"吗? 所以这个表达还可以这样讲"half-blooded/同父异母的,同母异父的;混血的"。再看看这些词:"half-life/半衰期","half-mast/表示哀悼或遇险下的半旗","half-baked/半熟的"。

(13)流产 miscarriage

mis-否定前缀,使用该前缀的单词有:misspelling, misunderstand, mislead 等。记忆窍门:mis-与 miss 相近,理解为"错过了,没有了",所以 miscarriage 就是"孩子没有了"。

(14)大房子 a roomy house

这里的 room 不是指"房间",而是指"空间",所以加上后缀-y 就是"宽敞的"的意思。那么大家知道"教学楼"怎么表达吗? 可以用 classroom building 搞定。

(15)傲慢苛求的父亲 an overbearing, hypercritical father

中国人明白一个道理:做什么事都不要过分,所以"过分的/over-"都不是什么好事,"overbearing/专横的",也可以说 bossy。而 hyper-这个前缀表示"高于,超过,过度"的意思,比如"hyperactive/过分活跃的","hypercritical/ 吹毛求疵的,苛评的"。看个例子,"请不要激动。/ Please don't get too hyper."

(16)欢迎加入母亲行列。Welcome to motherhood.

后缀-hood 表示"时期、状态、团体等"。比如"childhood/童年时期","adulthood /成人,成人期","likelihood/可能性","knighthood/ 骑士身份"……

(17)你还嘴硬。You are a denier.

"嘴硬"就是"拒不承认","denier /否认者"。这个句子是词缀帮助解决难题的典型例子。

(18)始作俑者 original initiator

initiator 是"开始、创始、发起"的意思,这里的难题是,很多人搞不清楚表示"人",后缀用-er,-or 还是-ist? 记忆窍门:先看看这个单词"房产商/ realtor",再看看这个单词"教育者/ educator",不管是"始作俑者"还是"房产商",还是"教育家"干的都是费脑子的活,所以要计划周详,"-or"中的"o"就是一个圆圈,代表"周详"的意思。

(19)私生子 an illegitimate son

"私生子"也叫"非婚生子",不受法律保护,legitimate 是"合法的,正当的"的意思,另外,以"l"开头的单词的否定前缀是 il-,比如:"illegal/非法的","illiterate/文盲"等。不过,"私生子"还有一种委婉的说法:"love child"。

(20)历史性的一刻 monumental occasion

说到"历史性的,重大的"我们还学过一个单词 historic,两者的侧重点可以通过词根进行判断:historic 强调"历史上重大的",而 monumental 突出"值得纪念的"的这个意思。再介绍一个同根词:"纪念品,值得纪念的事物/memorabilia"。

(21)无精打采,没良心,冷漠的 soulless

"soulless/没有精神,失魂落魄"。记忆窍门:利用画面感来记忆这个词:soul 就是"灵魂",

后面的否定后缀-less 中的两个“ss”像不像灵魂出窍，从头顶冒出来了，灵魂都出窍了是不是就“无精打采的”了呢？

(22)整容 face-lift

整容手术最热门的莫过于“拉皮”，就是提拉面部皮肤，消除皱纹。而-lift 就是“举起，提升，升起”的意思。“振奋精神”怎么表达？“spirit-lift”。

(23)兄弟情谊 bro-mance

这个单词的构成是 brother 的前半部 bro-和 romance 的后半部-mance 结合而成，是一个情谊浓浓的单词。

(24)花花公子 a womanizer

什么是“花花公子”？从字面就能做出较好的理解 playboy 强调“吃喝玩乐”，而 womanizer 侧重于“玩弄女性，沉溺于女色之中”。

(25)放开我！Unhand me！

记忆窍门：unhand 中的否定前缀是 un-，而 un-中的 u 就好像松了一个口子，就是放手的意思。“把绳解开/ untie the rope”。

(26)印在人们心上 to imprint everyone's heart

记忆窍门：动词前缀 im-中的“m”可以想象成两个“n”：原件 1 个，复印 1 个，把原物反映在心上，所以就是“印在……心上”的意思。

(27)多给点好处 to sweeten the deal

英语中，形容词后面跟上-en 变成动词，比如：“养肥某人/to fatten sb. up”，“调节或缓和气氛/to lighten the moo”。

(28)嗨，懒虫 Hi, sleepy！

口语中常见的用法，本来“sleep +-y”构成形容词，但这个句子中转成名词，是一种对孩子或恋人亲昵的表示方法。在汉语中现在有一非常时髦的打招呼的方法，不论长幼对女士一律称呼：“嗨，美女！”，英文就用“Hi, beauty！”

(29)不请自来 unannounced visit

记忆窍门：如果把 announce 中的“nn”看成用两个盖子遮住某人，那么否定前缀 un-就看成是翻开盖子，也就是走漏了风声的意思。延展一下词汇：“未预约的人/ unscheduled guest”，那“重新安排”呢？“reschedule”。

(30)超自然现象 paranormal activity

para- 在这儿做前缀表示“超越”的意思，其实这个前缀还有“并行”，比如：“paragon/典范”，“para- + gon 角”→“旁边顶尖人物”→“典范”。

(31)性骚扰 sexual misconduct

misconduct 是否定前缀 mis- + 中心词 conduct。记忆窍门：把 mis-看成是 miss：“对小姐不礼貌的行为”。

(32)读书更能干的人，理论知识比较扎实的人 book-smarter

个人认为，这个表达十分有创意，也极具启发性，那“实干家”就不止 doer 这个表达，还可以说 activity-smarter。那“聪慧过人”呢？super smart。

(33)大器晚成的人 a late bloomer

这个表达生动形象，late bloomer 是指“开花晚的植物”用它来喻指“智力发展晚的人、后知后觉者”。那“学得很快的人”呢？“fast learner”。

(34)视觉骚扰 visual harassment

前不久,在江苏省泰州市有个小学生写信给市长,状告林志玲,称其广告中深深的乳沟在他脑海中挥散不去,令其时常自读,这让他无心学习,恳求市长帮帮他。在这儿我们不去管谁的对错,利用这则新闻记单词倒是挺好的:-ment 中的 m 可以想象成"乳沟"就不会搞不清楚 harass 的名词后缀是什么。希望你不会受到 mental harassment。

(35)有权势的人;具有号召力的人 a mover and shaker

什么是"有权势的人"? 他们一说话,没有人敢不听从并付之行动。什么是"具有号召力的人"? 他们一开口,没有人不为之震撼。延展词汇:"搬运工/mover"。

(36)阴谋家 a schemer

我们以这个单词来复习一下后缀"-er"的用法:首先,表"……人":"阴谋家/framer","爱情杀手/ heartbreaker","真舍得花钱的人/big spender","枪手、带枪的歹徒 /gunslinger","流浪汉/drifter","阴险小人/backstabber","分裂家庭的人/home wrecker","newcomer /新生,新来的"。其次,表"……的物":"传单/flyer","屏保/screen saver","午休,午餐期间从事的活动/nooner","使人窒息的事情/ smotherer","干洗店(商)/cleaner","抹杀一切乐趣的事/ fun killer"。

(37)他们总是碍手碍脚。They always get underfoot.

这里的 underfoot 是副词,意为"在脚下;脚下面"。记忆窍门:感觉什么东西在脚"foot"下"under-",所以绊手绊脚的。

(38)他把某人狠狠揍了一顿。He flattened sb.

记忆窍门:大家知道 flat 是"平的,扁的"意思,形容词后面-en 构成动词,意为"把某人揍扁","揍扁——狠狠揍一顿"。

(39)幼稚的 immature

记忆窍门:否定前缀 im-里的 m 与 mature 的 m 都是中文字"毛"的第一个声母,中国人不是说"嘴上无毛办事不牢"嘛,这样就记住了前缀 im-。

(40)微表情 micro-expression

听上去像个时髦词汇,其实就是指"皱眉、抬嘴角、眨眼"等面部细微表情,建议大家看看美国电视剧"*Lie To Me*",看看心理学家怎样研究微表情。

三、实战演练

(1)这个故事不吸引人。This story is not readable.

"不吸引人"就是"没有可读性"。"可读性的":read + -able = readable。记忆窍门:readable 里的"-ada-"很像鼻子两旁瞪大的双眼,当阅读材料很吸引人、很有可读性,这种反应是很正常的。

例如:这是一本研究深刻、可读性强的书。This is a well researched and very readable book.

(2)我穿得太正式了吗? Am I overdressed?

表达"太正式"这个词,如果通过字面理解用"very, too..."肯定让人莫名其妙,"over-"这个前缀表示"过分、过于"的意思,比如:"饮酒过度的/over-drunk","高估的/overestimated","过分强调的/overemphasized"等。那"等会儿,我没穿好衣服。"这句话又怎么表达呢?"Wait a second, I' m underdressed."这真是"一通百通":"低估的/ underestimated","未达到法定年龄的/ underage”,“不太高兴的/ under-enthusiastic”。

例如:宴会上女人永远是焦点,不要着装太随便。Women are supposed to be the center of attention at party, and should not be underdressed.

(3)他不能白白牺牲。Losing him should not be meaningless.

“白白牺牲”就是“没有意义的做法”,吃透了意义,采用灵活简单的词缀方式,让表达变得很容易。记忆窍门:-less 中-es-的发音是不是很像中文中“意思”的发音呢?

例如:罚款对于能挣几百万的人来说是不重要的。Fines are meaningless to guys earning millions.

(4)你真是以自我为中心。How self-involved are you?

对于 self-这个前缀,大家都很熟悉,“self-criticism/自我批评”,“self-sacrifice/ 自我牺牲”,“self-estimation /自我评估”,“自拍/elfie”等,所以词缀的使用可以让我们的词汇量大大扩展,口语表达的信心倍增。

例如:别再沉浸在自我怜悯中了。Stop wallowing in self-pity!

(5)无痛 pain-free

-free 是“无……的”或“免除……的”的意思,记忆窍门:从痛苦中解脱出来。

例如:这是一个无痛的门诊手术。It was a pain-free, outpatient operation.

(6)这地方容不下我。I' ve outgrown this place.

前缀 out-表示“向外,出外;超过;外部”等意思。比如:“超越某人/outshine sb.”,“非法的/outlawed”等。

例如: 我待得太久了。But I' ve outstayed my welcome.

(7)婚前协议 a pre-marital agreement

“在……之前”可以用前缀 pre-来表示,也可以这样说 pre-nuptial agreement。举一反三,“预热”怎样表达?“preheat”。“事先安排的 /pre-arranged”,“事先录制好的/pre-recorded”,“学前教育的/ pre-school”。

例如:目前大学生对婚前性行为和同居有自己的看法。Nowadays, college students have their own idea over pre-marital sex and cohabitation.

(8)我经营一个七口之家,这是一个没有工资、无人喝彩的工作。I have run a household of seven. It's an unpaid, unappreciated job.

两个否定前缀将句子结构简化,符合口语特征。记忆窍门:两个 un-可以将 u 理解为圆圈有缺口,表示遗憾。

例如:无报酬的义务劳动非常有意义。Unpaid voluntary labor is very meaningful.

(9)防孩子的 childproof

后缀-proof 是“防……的;不透……的;耐……的;不受……影响的”意思,比如:“不透水的/waterproof”,“防锈的/ rustproof”,“防火的/ fireproof”,“耐热的/ heatproof”,“保值的/ inflation-proof”。

例如:选用有防小儿开启的安全瓶盖的咳嗽与感冒成药,并且放置在小孩无法拿取的地方。Select OTC cough and cold products with childproof safety caps and keep them out of reach of children.

(10)是人甩我,不是我甩人。I was the dumpee, not the dumper.

英语中的“施动者”用后缀-er 或-or,而“受动者”用-ee 以示区分,比如“教练员/ trainer”,

“受训员 trainee”,“老板 employer”,“员工 employee”,“发件人 addressor(-er)”,“收件人 addressee”,“否决者 rejecter”,“遭拒者 rejectee”等。

例如:收信人不在,原件退回。Original mail returned in the absence of the addressee.

(11)骗子,爱情不专一的人 a two-timer

记忆窍门:首先说说“骗子”这个词,还记得“狼来了”的故事吗?那孩子一而再,再而三地欺骗众人,所以是个 two-timer。其次,“爱情不专一的人”:同时与两个人保持关系,算不算 two-timer 呢?另外,two-time 还可以做形容词“有过两次的”以及动词“欺骗,对爱情不忠”。“two-time somebody/一脚踏两船的人”。再延展考大家一个单词:“第一次的人/first-timer”。

例如:她对丈夫不忠。She two-timed her husband.

(12)我赚钱养家。I am a provider.

这句话的英语表达利用词根 provide 加后缀-er 的方式,简洁易懂,那如果就用 provide 的动词形式,这个意义怎么表达呢?I have a big family to provide for. 再看看这个词组“养家糊口的人/ breadwinner”,所以掌握好词根词缀,句子的表达会变得“丰俭由人”。

例如:他有两个孩子要抚养。He has two children to provide for.

(13)急性子的人 a hothead

中国人讲一个人“头脑发热/hothead”就是“一时冲动,控制不了自己”,这个词汉英有相同的内涵。考考大家与“head”搭配的单词:“轻率的人愚蠢的人/featherhead”,“傻的/soft-headed”,“金钱至上的人/breadhead”。当然,“急性子的人”还可以这样说“hot-tempered guy”。

例如:这个年轻人性情急躁,总是急着下结论。The young guy is a hothead and always jumps a conclusion.

(14)看错了某人 to mischarge one's character

charge 是个活跃词汇,意义也比较多,使用起来非常灵活,所以我们对这个词的掌握需要花功夫。mischarge 原意为“记错账目,错定罪名”,在这儿引申为“对……做出了错误的判断”。扩充一下表达:“电话充电器/phone charger”,“出院/discharge”,“乱收费/illegal charges”等。

例如:除了解雇之外,你觉得什么还有助于改进员工中产生的问题?Besides discharge, what do you think can solve the problems among employees?

(15)没有约束力的条约 a non-binding political treaty

non-为“非;不;无”的意思,比如“没商量的/non-negotiable”。记忆窍门:non-中的两个 n,像不像手挽手的两个人,表示决心坚定。也可以这样记忆,两个 n 就像连说两个“no,no…”,表明不可以。延展词汇:“有约束力的承诺/ binding pledge”。

例如:由于讲演人未到,听众显得有些不耐烦。Some impatience was exhibited owing to the non-arrival of the speaker.

(16)任性的孩子 willful children

willful 就是“由着性子来,想怎样就怎样”。记忆诀窍:“will + ful”,-ful 就是“充满,多”的意思,willful 就是自己的意愿太多。

例如:当孩子胡闹时,如果你能克制,你就可以分辨出是任性的胡闹还是对压力的反应。If you are under control when the child is misbehaving, you will be able to distinguish between willful misbehavior or reaction to stress.

(17)草药疗法 herbal remedies

herb 是名词“草药”的意思,加上-al 构成形容词。“草药/herbal medicine”,“花草茶/herbal tea”。延展词汇:“热疗法/thermotherapy”。

例如:草药疗法并不适合所有人。Herbal treatments are not suitable for everyone.

(18)我足智多谋。I'm pretty resourceful.

“足智多谋”就是“富有智慧,善于谋划。形容人善于料事和用计”。“智慧多”就是“resourceful”。

例如:他极具创造力又足智多谋,在我的职业生涯中起了重要的作用。He was amazingly inventive and resourceful, and played a major role in my career.

(19)让我先梳洗一番。Let me freshen up first.

“梳洗”的目的就是让人“焕然一新”,所以用单词“fresh/新鲜的”+后缀-en 构成动词。你肯定知道这些词组和句子怎样表达了:“这使人精神焕发。/That's refreshing.”,“帮某人回忆一下/ refresh sb.'s memory”,“神清气爽/ refreshed”。

例如:润肤液使皮肤凉爽清新。The lotion cools and refreshes the skin.

(20)误会某人 misjudge sb.

misjudge 就是“做出错误的评判”。记忆诀窍:否定前缀 mis-的 m 就像架在鼻子上的眼镜,我们把它想象成“有色眼镜”,戴“有色眼镜”看人,不就是“对人有偏见”的意思。延展词汇:“有偏见的/ judgmental”。

例如:我想我看错他了。I think I've misjudged him.

四、巩固练习

1. 请根据词缀或词根提示完成下列词和词组的英语表达。

(1)虚度(否定前缀)

(2)销声匿迹的(否定前缀)

(3)能适应环境的人(前缀)

(4)驱逐出境(否定前缀)

(5)国籍(后缀)

(6)羞辱(否定前缀)

(7)无人陪伴的孩童(否定前缀)

(8)失败者、输家(否定前缀)

(9)自以为是的(前缀)

(10)分租(前缀)

(11)如胶似漆的(否定前缀+形容词后缀)

(12)难以忍受的(否定前缀+形容词后缀)

(13)低调的(前缀)

(14)多话的(后缀)

(15)无足轻重的(后缀)

(16)狡猾的(后缀)

(17)不可原谅的(否定前缀+后缀)

(18)使陷入困境(前缀)
(19)不知为什么(否定前缀)
(20)臭名昭著的(否定前缀)
(21)股东(后缀)
(22)猛男(后缀)
(23)把某人大卸八块(否定前缀+后缀)
(24)无条件地(否定前缀+后缀)
(25)脾气坏的暴躁的(后缀)
(26)某人重打招牌(前缀)
(27)没邀请某人(否定前缀)
(28)联合署名(前缀)
(29)中年危机(前缀)
(30)离奇失踪(后缀)
(31)忘恩负义(否定前缀)
(32)做出不顾后果的行为(否定后缀)
(33)下流动作(后缀)
(34)有信誉的(后缀)
(35)公众形象(后缀)
(36)再赛一次(前缀)
(37)富有教育意义的(后缀)
(38)先知(前缀)
(39)马屁精(后缀)
(40)围观者(前缀+后缀)
(41)操劳过度(前缀)
(42)活动筹划人(后缀)
(43)运动员风范(后缀)
(44)订婚戒指(后缀)
(45)忽视你的教养(前缀)
(46)世界无烟日(否定前缀)
(47)古怪念头(否定前缀)
(48)卧底警察(前缀)
(49)挑剔的口吻(后缀)
(50)说真的(后缀)
(51)受打击的朋友(后缀)
(52)严格的人;厉行纪律的人(后缀)
(53)不退押金的(否定前缀+后缀)
(54)机器故障(否定前缀)
(55)可笑的(后缀)
(56)令人沮丧的;使人气馁的(否定前缀)
(57)威胁信(后缀)

(58)命案调查科(后缀)

2. 请根据词缀或词根提示完成下列句子的英语表达。

(1)她无能为力。(否定后缀)
(2)这块地毯没有污点了。(否定后缀)
(3)我完全低估了你们。(否定前缀)
(4)太奇怪了!(否定前缀)
(5)我不是没心没肺。(否定后缀)
(6)我们的关系密不可分。(否定前缀)
(7)你太不爱惜你的生命了。(否定后缀)
(8)做好事得付出代价。(否定前缀)
(9)你就必须得反思你的教育方式。(前缀)
(10)你太冷酷无情了。(否定前缀)
(11)你在怀疑我的穿衣品味?(否定前缀)
(12)别人会认为这是不尊敬长辈的表现。(否定前缀)
(13)也许是我误读了某些暗示。(否定前缀)

3. 熟悉并背诵下列词组和句子,体会词缀和词根的魅力。

(1)内讧 infighting
(2)不高兴 moody/ discontented
(3)双黄蛋 a double yolker
(4)出言不逊 unkind words
(5)攀高枝的人 social climber
(6)玷污某人 to deflower sb.
(7)反季淘 off-season shopping
(8)太挤了 super-crowded
(9)交流时间 fellowship hour
(10)手无寸铁的人 an unarmed man
(11)误解 a misguided idea
(12)助消化 to quicken digestion
(13)洗心革面 to rebuild one's life
(14)难看的伤疤 unsightly scarring
(15)双层玻璃 double-paned window
(16)主动提供的意见 an unsolicited opinion
(17)让一个女人回心转意 to reclaim the heart of a woman
(18)有个性的 classy (优等的;上等的;漂亮的)
(19)门诊病人 (前缀)outpatient (住院病人 inpatient)
(20)冷漠的 detached (反义词:attached)
(21)对某人不恰当的表扬 unearned good opinion of sb.
(22)做贼心虚 a guilty conscience

(23)洗去心中歉疚的痛楚 to cleanse the pain of a guilty conscience

(24)熟悉潮流的人 a trend-watcher（潮流的跟随者 a trend-follower）

(25)抛弃了我国最珍贵的传统 to blow off our most beloved tradition

(26)撒谎面不改色心不跳 unwavering commitment to the lie（unwavering a. 坚定的，不动摇的）

(27)有可疑的举动 to make some questionable movement

(28)愕然发现 to make an unwelcome discovery

(29)我那六亲不认的儿子 my son who disowns me（disown vt. 否认；脱离关系）

(30)我心知肚明。I am mindful.

(31)他被冤枉的。He was wrongly accused.

(32)他还挺招人喜欢的。He seems agreeable enough.

(33)事情变得复杂了。The plot thickens.

(34)别像个失败主义者似的。Don't be a defeatist.

(35)你搞错了。You're misinformed.

(36)我正在搬家。I'm relocating

(37)掩盖不完美 to conceal imperfection

(38)对某人指手画脚 to criticize sb.

(39)我这会儿不舒服。I'm currently indisposed.

(40)时间都凝固了。Time goes slower.

(41)我想我死定了。I thought I was a goner.（goner n. 无望的人，无法挽救的人）

(42)你的意见与此无关。Your opinion is irrelevant.

(43)我们双方力量似乎很悬殊。Looks like we're outnumbered now.

(44)她轻描淡写这事。She downplayed it.

(45)"骗"真是个难听的词。"Lie" is so unmusical a word.

(46)你肯定说了什么让他误会的话。You must've said something he misinterpreted.

(47)恐怕测试结果还不能做出定论。I'm afraid the test was inconclusive.

(48)事情容人误解吗？Is there room for misinterpretation?

(49)我希望离开时别被人看到。I rather hope to escape unobserved.

(50)所有的快感都激发出来了。Every sense was heightened.

(51)她已经解释清楚了。She straightened it out.（直截了当的回答/a straight answer）

(52)要死要活的做法打动不了我。Desperation is so unappealing to me.

(53)他在吃的方面很挑剔。He's kind of a picky eater.

(54)你有时候真是出奇地铁石心肠。Sometimes you can be curiously unfeeling.

(55)你怎么这么晚还在干呢？Why on earth are you doing that at this ungodly hour?

(56)这会让母子二人陷入极大的危险。It would expose both mother and child to untold danger.

(57)甲：我一定得面对这一劫吗？乙：你很坚强。你是最有担当的。A：So I must brave the storm? B：You're strong. A storm-braver if ever I saw one.

4. 用本单元所学的知识造句。

(1)孩子们发现《哈利波特》是本吸引人的书。
(2)教育的重要性如何强调也不为过。
(3)他们没有时间和精力去做无意义的破事。
(4)人有时候就是只想到自己。
(5)在中学的出色成绩让他免费进入了纽约的大学。
(6)这不是什么过分的问题。
(7)非常抱歉,我事先有个约会,恐怕不能参加你的讲座。
(8)尽管乡村教师的工作是无人知道无人赏识,但他们的献身精神却是最伟大的。
(9)银行为吸引顾客开展了各种业务,利率保值是其中一项。
(10)请不要这么严厉地要求孩子,你太吹毛求疵了。
(11)我是来应聘见习推销员的。
(12)骗人没有好下场。
(13)修读该课程是免费的,但你要自备课本。
(14)长期以来,在众人心目中,父亲的角色一直是挣钱养家的人。
(15)信不信由你,感情用事的炒股人士往往能做出更好的决定。
(16)身体语言是一种非语言交流形式。
(17)就是这种任性和不可理喻的行为导致了她的婚姻破裂。
(18)许多草药茶使用上口的名称和包装以提高它们的吸引力。
(19)我常常惊讶贫穷家庭和社区的人们是何等足智多谋。
(20)他醒来感觉精神完全恢复了。
(21)现在轮到他低估自己的对手了。

5. 你能找到更多词缀词根帮助表达的例证吗?请与大家共同分享本章的学习体会。

Chapter 7　Common Collocations

固定搭配

一、思路讲解

什么是固定搭配？网络有道字典的解释是：In linguistics, collocation is the way that some words occur regularly whenever another word is used. 不过，个人认为，A collocation is a pair or group of words that are often used together. 固定搭配就是两个或一组经常在一起使用的单词。这些单词的结合对母语使用者来讲是十分自然的，但对英语学习者来讲却要下大工夫去记去背，因为仅从字面上是很难把握其意义和用法的，比如：fast cars（而不是 quick cars），fast food（而不是 quick food）；a quick glance（而不是 a fast glance），a quick meal（而不是 a fast meal）。

但我们不得不承认，对英语口语表达来讲，使用固定搭配是开口说英语的一个捷径，不需要自己费事去组织语言。掌握好英语的固定搭配，可以让你的表达更加自然地道，比如：Smoking is strictly forbidden. 就比 Smoking is strongly forbidden. 显得更地道些。固定搭配还能给你多一个选择，让你的表达更多彩、更精确，避免重复。比如：It was very cold and very dark. 这句话我们还可以这样讲，It was bitterly cold and pitch dark. 最后，熟练掌握口语中的固定搭配，可以改进我们的口语表达风格。

另外，大家要清楚口语表达中的固定搭配与书面语中的搭配是有差异的，所谓"口语"，按照《现代汉语词典》[8]的解释就是指"谈话时使用的语言，区别于'书面语'，即用文字写出来的语言"。口语中的固定搭配充分体现了口语的特点：简单、浅显、生动和易记，有助于口语交流。比如："不必为孩子牺牲。"这句话里的"牺牲"在书面语中的表达可能就要求助于 sacrifice 这个单词，但口语中有一个非常简单的固定搭配结构：lose oneself for，所以这句话在口语中可以这样表达：You don't have to lose yourself for children. 大家还要了解的是口语交流十分依赖语境，利用语境，可以让表达变得更简单、轻松。比如："相互照应"，书面语的表达可能就会是 take care of，但在口语交流中，这句话如果是在商量旅途中的注意事项，就可以表达为 keep each other safe。

不过，辩证法让我们清楚地知道，有幸福就有痛苦，要享受轻松表达的前提是接触尽量多的语料，下苦功夫背诵搭配，这一切都要从平时开始，积少成多，利用真实语境来实践、强化和内化我们掌握的固定搭配。

二、案例分析

下面我们用更多的例子来帮助大家理解、体会、记忆英语口语表达中的固定搭配，为提高口语表达能力提供大量的鲜活的典型案例，通过这些语料，大家要学会分析、归纳和总结，比如：搭配中的小品词最容易弄混淆，怎样才能记得多和记得牢？这都需要大家多想办法，灵活学习，善于学习。

(1)他会完成任务的。He'll get the job done.

说到"完成",第一反应是 finish,但口语中可以用 to get sth. done 这个搭配。

(2)站起来 be on one's feet

be on one's feet 这个搭配是较为生动,极具画面感的表达,其反义结构为 be off one's feet,利用这种联想记忆让我们轻松完成两个固定搭配的记忆。

(3)我的生活七零八落。My life is falling apart.

这句话里又是七又是八,怎么弄呢?"七零八落"也可以说"乱七八糟",这个搭配 to fall apart 是"瓦解,破碎"的意思,理解为"散落成一块块的"。

(4)跑题了 to go off the track

track 是"轨道、小道"的意思,off the track 就是"不在小道或路上",就是"跑题"。口语对话中,跑题的人回神过来的第一句话通常是 Where am I ? 这儿的语境理解应为"我讲到哪儿了?"而不是理解为"我在哪儿?"。

(5)做鬼脸 to make faces

为什么"做鬼脸"是 to make faces? faces 为什么用复数? 记忆窍门:笔者理解这个词组时,联想到了川剧中的"变脸"绝活,在短短的几秒钟,不同的脸谱变幻,所以"做鬼脸"就理解为不同脸部表情变化,所以"faces"用复数。

(6)感谢你看得起我。I've appreciated you looking me up.

"看得起"的英文搭配词组是 to look up,其实这个搭配在记忆上没有太大的难度,想想,"看得起"就是"看得上","向上"英文不就是 up 吗? 拓展搭配:第一类:"看得上某人 to have eyes on sb.","瞧见、看见/ to set eyes on";第二类:"吹捧某人/ to talk sb. up","写文章赞扬、详细记载;补写/ to write up","让某人振奋/ to cheer sb. up"。

(7)训某人 to snap at sb.

to snap at sb. 表示"声色俱厉地训斥某人"。记忆窍门:在大多数情况下,与 at 搭配的词组多半没有好事:"to laugh at sb./嘲笑某人","to throw at sb./用……掷某人"," to stare at sb./怒视某人"," to shout at sb./朝某人大吼大叫"。

(8)收买某人 to buy sb. off

记忆窍门:to buy sb. off 中的 off 理解为"断掉、摆脱"。所以这个搭配理解为"收买;出钱以摆脱"。

(9)向某人伸出援手 to reach out to sb. in trouble

这里要提醒大家的是,利用词组就能防止逐字翻译的发生,比如这个例子,"伸手"就是 to reach out,理解 to reach out 的内涵,使表达更地道。

(10)商谈细节 to hash out details

如果了解这个搭配的内涵,你会发现这个例子表达十分生动。to harsh out 意为"消除,经过长时间讨论解决一个问题",简单的两个英文单词的搭配解决了中文较长的内涵表达,这就是口语特点的绝佳体现。

(11)昂首翘尾;活跃起来;振作精神 to perk up

perk 做名词是"小费,额外收入"的意思。当别人给我们小费时,我们是不是精神为之一振,觉得自己的劳动得到承认,从名词到动词,逻辑关系顺理成章。拓展搭配:"振作精神/to boost sb.'s spirits"。

(12)放手、后退、放弃 to back off

to back off 中的 back 不是常用的形容词和副词的用法，而是动词，显得十分生动：back 是"向后"，off 理解为"断掉、切断"。

(13) 使劲加价 to jack up the price

大家可能都知道 jack 有"千斤顶"的意思，这里的 jack 转成了动词，十分形象地表达出"提升、提高"这个意思。拓展知识："英国国旗/the Union Jack"。

(14) 从头开始做某事 to do sth. from scratch

还记得"白手起家/to start from the scratch"这个词组吗？该固定词组意为："If you do something from scratch, you do it without making use of anything that has been done before. 从零开始"。

(15) 生活富裕 be well fixed

记忆窍门：fix 有"修理"的意思，be well fixed 表示该弄好的都弄好了，用重庆话来讲就是"生活弄巴适了"，就是"生活富裕"的意思。

(16) 我们谈正事吧。Let's get down to business.

to get down 可以理解为"从跑题的状态又回来，定下(down)心来"。

(17) 扫某人的兴 to spoil sb.'s fun

"扫兴"就是"原有的兴致因某种干扰而低落"。"扫兴"就是"扫走兴致"，"破坏兴致"的意思。spoil 就有"破坏、糟蹋"的意思。

(18) 支持；维护 to stick up for

注意 to stick up for 和 to stick up to 的区别，前者后面所连接的名词或代词常表示人、权利、正义及信仰等概念，而后者则表示"抵抗、追求"的意思，其后所连接的名词或代词常指人或动物等，切勿混淆。

(19) 多嘴！Big mouth！

英文的名词转为中文的动词，词性虽变，但意义上中英文十分相似，"大嘴巴"指"某人喜欢散布不可靠的消息或者是传播别人隐私"，这种人是否是不是很"多嘴"呢？

(20) 为什么……？How come…？

英语里的"为什么"除了大家耳熟能详的 why 之外，也常会听到 how come，这两个单词还可以放在句首，但是注意不用倒装语序。

三、实战演练

(1) 坚持你的信念 to hold on your faith

关于"坚持"，我们在书上学过 insist，persist 等，它们的小品词搭配常把我们弄得晕头转向，那不妨试试简单点的 to hold on。延展记忆："to hold up/挺住，坚持住"，这个词组的内涵是："If something such as a type of business holds up in difficult conditions, it stays in a reasonably good state.（在逆境中）保持良好状况"。记忆窍门：to hold on 中的 on 理解为："站稳脚跟，一定要站在……上"，而 to hold up 中的 up 理解为"陷入困境中，挣扎着要出来。"

例如： 在经济衰退期间，童装是持续销售良好的一个领域。Children's wear is one area that is holding up well in the recession.

(2) 不要和你妈妈顶嘴。Don't talk back to your mother.

"to talk back to sb./跟某人顶嘴"，to talk back 本指"说回去"，意思就是"顶嘴"。

例如:你怎么敢这样和我顶嘴！How dare you talk back to me like that！

(3)小孩有时候不听话。Children sometimes get out of control.

对家长来讲,小孩不乖的表现就是不听大人的话,不在大人的掌控之中。所以"不在掌控之中/be out of control"。那"在掌控之中"呢？就是"be under control"！拓展搭配:"控制……/to keep sth. in check"。

例如:我已经掌控着一切。I've got everything under control.

(4)我希望很快能学会。I hope that I can learn it in no time.

"快"的英文表达太多了,quickly,fast,immediately 等,但固定搭配 in no time 却十分形象,字面记忆为"不需要很多时间",这不是很快?

例如:通过正确的饮食和营养摄入,你会很快从流感中恢复。With the right food and nutrition, you'll rebound from the flu in no time.

(5)隐瞒某人 to keep sth. secret from sb.

"隐瞒某人"就是"不让某人知道这个秘密"。还可以这样讲"隐瞒某人/to keep sth. from sb."。

例如:我啥事都瞒不过你。I can keep nothing secret from you.

(6)保持清醒 to keep one's head

中文中形容一个人犯糊涂常用:"你脑子进水了?","你的脑子让门夹了?","你有没有脑子?"。我们喜见英语中对"脑子/head"的重要性与汉语有同等认识。扩展搭配:"让我理顺一下头脑/to get my head straight","你疯了吗？/Are you out of senses?","保持镇定,不慌不忙/to keep a level head"。

例如:现在最重要的便是保持清醒和思想集中,把我们的工作做好。The important thing now is to keep our head and concentrate on doing our job well.

(7)我被设计了。I was set up.

虽然是简单的一个 to set up,但意思很多,比如"设计陷害某人;给某人介绍对象"等,"给某人介绍对象/to set sb. up"。扩展搭配:"撮合/to fix sb. up with sb. else"。

例如:我是清白的,有人在设计陷害我。I'm innocent and somebody is setting me up.

(8)你想玩狠的。You wanna play rough.

to play rough 这个词组搭配来自赛场上,指"比赛时做粗野动作"。我们不得不承认,运动场上激烈的碰撞,放狠话,更增添了运动的吸引力。扩展搭配:"合作;参与/to play along"。

例如:我非常高兴你决定参与进来。I am so glad you've decided to play along.

(9)我吓死了。I am freaking out.

to freak out 有"极度兴奋、崩溃"等意思。这里要提醒大家的是一个固定搭配词组经常有很多意义,大家一定要通过语境去琢磨它的内涵。扩展搭配:"我快把自己逼疯了。/I'm starting to freak myself out.","别激动！/Don't freak out！"

例如:你最好坐下,这个消息会使你晕倒的。You'd better sit down, this news will freak you out.

(10)昏迷 to black out

这个词组搭配尤显生动:两眼一抹黑不就是昏过去了吗？那 black 后面的小品词 out 怎么才能记得牢呢？记忆窍门:把 out 中的 u 看成是人的身体,而"o"就像人脑袋,昏过去的时候,脑袋就耷拉下来了。延展搭配:“to pass out/昏迷”。

例如:当你“黑掉/black out”,就是说你暂时失去了知觉。When you “black out”, you temporarily lose consciousness.

(11)我很少在人背后弄些小动作。I don't normally do plots against people.

大家要了解 plot 做名词表示“情节、图谋”,做动词“密谋、策划”,所以 to do plots against sb. 就是“暗算别人,背后弄些小动作”的意思。我们提倡有什么,当着面讲,“当着我的面说。/Say it in my face.”。

例如:不要对信任你的邻居起歹心。Do not do plots against your neighbor, who lives trustfully near you.

(12)流行;明白 to catch on

由于 catch 是个活跃词汇,与之相搭配的小品词特别多,记忆方法就尤为重要。记忆窍门:首先说“流行”这个意思,可以将 on 看成是 be on 表示这种趋势正在进行之中,接着说“明白”,on 看成是“跟得上”,因为 on 本身就有“在……上”的意思。

例如:请把你的话再说一遍,我没十分听明白。Please repeat what you said, I didn't quite catch on.

(13)我们可以叙叙旧。We can catch up then.

记忆窍门:to catch up 中的 up 可以理解为“把过去的事回想起来”,“起来”就是 up。拓展搭配:“关注最新新闻/to catch up on the latest news”,“发现某人的错误/to catch sb. out”,“我最近一直在忙。/I got so caught up in everything.”

例如:The ladies spent some time catching up on each other's health and families. 女士们花了些时间聊聊彼此的健康和家庭情况。

(14)使……平静 to sort oneself out

大家都知道 to sort out 有“整理”的意思,但 to sort oneself out 却是“平静下来,冷静高效处理事情”的意思。拓展搭配:“to sort this out/解决这个问题”。

例如:我们这儿处于一片混乱之中,我需要一些时间让自己平静下来。We're in a state of complete chaos here and I need a little time to sort myself out.

(15)我把事情都想清楚了。I have thought everything through.

记忆窍门:to think sth. through 中的 through 即为“通透”的意思。

例如:一旦你提出了一个很好的方案,先要花些时间去好好考虑下。Once you have come up with a great idea, take a little time to think it through.

(16)心情好 in good mood

不管是口语还是书面语表达,这都算是个比较常见的表达,mood 是“情绪、心情”的意思。拓展搭配:“有心情做某事/be in the mood to do sth.”,“没有心情做某事/be in no mood to do sth.”。

例如:别来惹我!我没有心情和你讨论这件事。Leave me alone! I am not in the mood to discuss this issue with you.

(17)在恍惚中,茫然;眼花缭乱;不知所措 in a daze

“daze”是“眩晕”的意思,“If someone is in a daze, they are feeling confused and unable to think clearly, often because they have had a shock or surprise. 迷惑”。记忆窍门:不管是“daze/眩晕”还是“haze/霾,薄雾”,都好像有“模糊不清的、晕头转向”的意思,而字形上-aze 中印刷

体的 a 有点像颠倒过来的 e,是不是有点晕呢?

例如:我神思恍惚地向教室走去。I made my way to the classroom in a daze.

(18)留宿某人 to put sb. up

记忆窍门:to put up 可理解为"为无家可归的人撑起帐篷",所以引申为"收留某人,为某人提供膳宿"。这个搭配后可接介词 at,for 或 with。拓展搭配:"我们需要忍气吞声吗? /Do we need to put up with it?"

例如:恐怕我不能给你们提供膳宿。I'm afraid I can't put you up.

(19)别再踏进大楼半步。Never set foot in the building again.

"涉足、踏进/to set foot in"这个搭配记忆方面问题不大,但要记住,这个搭配常用于否定结构。

例如:踏进教室的那一刻,我感到迷茫和恐惧。I felt lost and terrified when I set foot in the classroom.

(20)对付某人 to get around sb.

这个词组注意内涵的理解,"If you get around someone, you persuade them to allow you to do or have something by pleasing or flattering them. 通过取悦或谄媚说服"。拓展搭配:"希望大家都聚过来。——I need you all to get around."

例如:麦克斯总能说服她。Max could always get around her.

(21)看某人不顺眼(生某人的气)to piss off at sb.

2014 年澳网公开赛,李娜在战胜马卡洛娃挺进八强后接受澳大利亚记者采访时调侃地说,当自己表现不好时,教练会"piss her/朝她吐口水",也就是"严厉批评她"的意思,所以利用一切机会拓展自己词汇量,可以帮助我们理解和深化并最终掌握英语表达有着很大的帮助。

例如:不想被炒鱿鱼的话,不要把老板惹毛才是明智之举。Unless you wish to be fired, it is wise not to piss off at your boss.

(22)我会亲自要求人们得对你有点尊重。I'll personally see to it that people start treating you with a little more respect.

"to see [to it] that"是"务必,必定;设想使;确保"等意思,这个搭配更多的是在书面语中使用。

例如:你务必保证上班别再迟到。See to it that you're not late for work again!

(23)饶恕她 to lay off her

to lay off 的本意是"解雇;休息;停止工作",引申为"饶恕"。

例如:她心情不好,别再烦她了,行不行? She is in a mood. Lay off her, will you?

(24)领先一步 to beat sb. to sth./a place

beat 就是"在……方面战胜某人","战胜某人"不就是比别人"领先一步","捷足先登"吗?

例如:她比我先到山顶。She beat me to the top of the hill.

(25)这事你处理得好。You got a good handle on this.

handle 做动词就是"处理"的意思,但这个词组中的 handle 转为名词。拓展搭配:"她有办法解决那事。/She knows how to get around that."。

例如:用一段时间后,你会掌握好它们的。After using them for a time, you will get a good handle on them.

(26)倾全力 to buckle down

大家经常用 to try one's best 来表示"尽全力",但这里我们学一个新的用法表达同样的意思:to buckle down。记忆窍门:buckle 的原意是"皮带扣,带扣", to buckle down 理解为:扣好皮带,做好一切准备,全力以赴。

例如:你必须真正努力从事这项新工作。You must just buckle down to the new job.

(27)你不觉得你俩该重修旧好了吗? Isn't it time you two patched things up?

patch 是名词"补丁",动词"打补丁"。电脑中的"打补丁"就是"软件有缺陷时,完善程序"的意思。夫妻之间有问题就应该马上修补,绝不能让问题扩大,"修补"就是 to patch up。

例如:我们决定消除我们之间的分歧,言归于好。We decided to patch up our differences and become friends again.

(28)在酒吧与人搭讪 to pick up sb. in a bar

pick 是一个非常活跃的单词,比如"to pick sth. over sth. else/选什么而不选什么","炒股/to pick stock","炒股高手/the greatest stock-picker","挑剔的/be picky","我肯定一学就会。/I could pick up in a trice.","在车站接人/to pick up sb. at a station","获取信息/to pick up information"。

例如:她在哪里找到这个同伴的? Where did she pick up this companion?

(29)疏远对方 to drift away from each other

这个搭配利用内涵的理解也容易记忆:drift 就是"漂流、漂移"的意思, to drift away 表示"渐渐疏远,慢慢散去",因此,"疏远对方"用这个 to drift away from each other 十分贴切。拓展搭配:"离题/ to drift away from a subject","疏远某人 / to shove sb. away","不跟某人交往/ to push sb. away"。

例如:如果你只考虑自己,你的朋友将会离你而去。Your friends will drift away from you if you are too self-centered.

(30)被记忆包围着 to wrap oneself up in all memories

to wrap up 本意就是"包裹起来",这里利用原意,形象地表达了词意,非常具有画面感。延展词意: to wrap up 还有"最后达成、解决","掩饰、遮盖","别吵、安静","全神贯注"等意思。

例如:在北京人们冬天必须穿得暖和些。In Beijing, one has to be wrapped up in warm clothes in winter.

(31)玛丽在为他尽地主之谊。Mary's settling him in.

"尽地主之谊"就是"指尽本地主人应尽的义务,指招待外地来客。"这里就是使用了 to settle in 的引申含义。to settle in 本义有"使迁入、使安顿","使适应、使习惯","坏天气持续下去、无变化"等。

例如:你还习惯吗? How are you settling in?

(32)我膝盖疼。My knees played up.

在很多时候,我们需要通过不同的角度去思考表达的方法和方式,让交流变得更加活跃。以这个句子为例:平时我们说"……地方很疼"通常用"…hurts."或"…is killing me."而这里的"膝盖疼"采用的是"to play up/调皮捣蛋,制造麻烦"这个词组,意思是"我的膝盖又给我找麻烦了。"

例如:别让小学生们淘气! Don't let the pupils play up!

(33)就给我们写封信。Just drop us a line.

"to drop a line to sb. /写信给某人",记忆窍门:发明这个词组的时候,人们用鹅毛笔蘸墨水写字,墨水不是"一滴滴/drop"地留在纸上的吗?

例如:我得给你姐姐写封信,感谢她给我们的帮助。I must drop a line to your sister to thank her for helping us.

(34)复习;温习;重温 to brush up on sth.

中国人讲"复习"有另一种说法"重新梳理一遍",而英文中的 brush 做名词就有"刷子"的意思。

例如:考试前再复习一下你还不了解或不懂的概念。Brush up on the concepts you still don't know or understand before examinations.

(35)冷静下来,缓和情绪;放松 to chill out

chill 就有"使感到冷"的意思,不过这儿引申为"精神或头脑的冷静"而不是"身体感到寒冷"。out 理解为"头脑冷静了,把不理智的情绪赶出去。"

例如:是不是他热衷于朋友间的聚会而她宁愿待在家里放松休息? Does he have lots of energy for activities with friends while she'd rather rest and chill out at home?

(36)说出,讲出 to breathe a word

请大家注意,这个词组搭配常用于否定句中。记忆窍门:"breathe"是动词,"呼吸"的意思,你想想,"呼吸"是轻轻的,无意识的,悄悄进行的,所以这个词组笔者更倾向于理解为"透露"。

例如:这件事你不能泄露只言片语。You mustn't breathe a word of it.

(37)掌握了线索 to have a clue

clue 译为"线索","to have a clue/掌握了线索"就等于"对某事有了头绪,知道了某事"。拓展搭配:"to have no clue at all/毫无线索","to have a vital clue /有了重要线索"。

例如:Did you have a clue? Not at all. 您知道这事吗? 完全不知道。

(38)可能发生的 be in the cards

记忆窍门:西方人喜欢用扑克牌算命,认为命运都有扑克牌决定,所以这个搭配还有"命中注定"的意思。拓展搭配:"掌控整个局势/to hold all the cards"。

例如:对于他而言,赢得这次比赛已胜券在我。It's in the cards for him to win the competition.

(39)问候 to ask after

注意"to ask after"和"to ask about"之间的区别,前者指出于礼貌或一般关心对第三者表示间接问候或问及,而不是为了获得某个特定的信息;而后者则是指为了获得有关第三者的信息而询问。

例如:我昨天碰到琳达,她问你好。I met Linda yesterday, and she was asking after you.

(40)遇到(困难);遭到(反对)to come up against

这个搭配后常接 difficulty, problem , opposition 之类的词。另请注意,该短语不可用于被动语态。

例如:你可能会碰到些困难。You may come up against some difficulties.

四、巩固练习

1. 从固定搭配的角度说说下面中文词组或句子的英语表达。

(1)筹钱
(2)溺爱
(3)许愿
(4)同意
(5)视觉帮助
(6)诸如此类
(7)经受考验
(8)断绝往来
(9)排斥某人
(10)全面管理
(11)不论好歹
(12)下午休息
(13)承担后果
(14)搞得一团糟
(15)有点幽默感
(16)偷偷溜出去
(17)偶然碰到某人
(18)赢得某人的心
(19)选 A 而不是 B
(20)有勇气做什么
(21)破坏别人的家庭
(22)为某人挺身而出
(23)积极参加社会活动
(24)看看情况怎么发展
(25)在命运的掌握之中
(26)一心想着……专注于……
(27)我马上来。
(28)别指望我!
(29)我想自首。
(30)别让我失望!
(31)我们合不来。
(32)别让我碍了事!
(33)你一个人来吗?
(34)我正想弄明白。
(35)让你们好好叙叙旧。

(36)你打算怎么处置我们?
(37)我受够了假装彬彬有礼了。
(38)难道没看到我正玩得高兴吗?
(39)在聚会上派发简历有点俗气。
(40)我恐怕不怎么精通家族史。
(41)比赛十分精彩,令他兴奋不已。

2. 从固定搭配角度说说下面英文词组或句子的中文表达。

(1)to take a vote
(2)to shake up
(3)to stress out
(4)to make a pact
(5)to put on an act
(6)to call the shots
(7)a rabbit in heat
(8)to screw over sb.
(9)to end up there
(10)to pull one's weight
(11)to save one's breath to
(12)too hard on sth.
(13)to write up a resume
(14)to be full of oneself
(15)to run an errand
(16)to burst straight into
(17)to act out in anger
(18)to fall out with friends
(19)to jump to hasty conclusions
(20)to flip out about other things
(21)to prevail on one's good nature
(22)to go to some extraordinary lengths
(23)to take a toll (take a heavy toll)
(24)I like travelling by nature.
(25)You caught me off guard.
(26)Her marriage hit the rocks.
(27)She pulled out on the spot.
(28)He took the blame for me.
(29)Further research will have to sort this out more completely.
(30)But some teachers have begun to catch on to the American model.
(31)I'm so sick of everybody looking at the glass half-full.

3. 熟读并背诵下列句子，理解口语中词组搭配的精妙使用。

(1)尽公民的义务 to perform one's civic duty

(2)为某人对公益事业所做出的杰出贡献颁奖 to present sb. with an award for outstanding public service

(3)转眼就睡着了。to fall asleep in a trice (in a trice 立即，马上)

(4)我如痴如狂。I am in the grip of madness. (in the grip of 受……控制)

(5)别把大家说烦了。We don't need to wear everyone out. (wear sb. out 使人筋疲力尽)

(6)你是哪根筋搭错了? Have you taken leave of your senses? (taken leave of one's senses 举止若狂)

(7)我只是最近有些心事。I've just got a lot on my mind.

(8)可能他们会打听到消息。They can dig sth. up. (dig up 找出，查出，发现)

(9)快请进。您一定旅途劳顿。Come on in. You must be worn out.

(10)他现在已经够焦头烂额了。He's got a lot on his plate right now. [on his plate(英国口语) 在面前，待处理，待考虑]

(11)中国政府对日本提出强烈的反对。The Chinese government raises opposition against Japan. (raise opposition against 向……提出强烈反对)

(12)我不太确定他能否胜任。I'm not entirely sure that he will prove equal to the task. (胜任……工作)

(13)凡是读过我的信件的律师，都是一惊一乍。The lawyers I write to only huff and puff. (huff and puff v. 蒸汽吞吐;咆哮)

(14)打电子游戏会耗尽你的精力，让你对其他事情都不感兴趣。Playing computer games consumes you and blots out everything else. (to blot out 完全清除思想、记忆等;遮盖)

(15)这种关头我们就应该齐心协力。It's hours like these we must all pull together.

(16)在体制让他失望的时候，他努力把握自己的是非观。He tries to hang on to his sense of right and wrong when the system fails him.

(17)他其实比我想象的要善良的。There's more true kindness in him than I give him credit for. (to give sb. credit for 为……而称赞某人)

(18)比尔身体非常好，他健康饮食，注重运动。Bill is in the best of health. He eats well and exercises.

(19)她从美国旅游回来后看来特别精神。When she came back from her trip to the United States, she was in fine fettle. (be in fine fettle 精神振奋、身体强壮;be in fine good fettle 身强力壮)

(20)我开了很长时间的车，但是只要喝杯茶，我就立刻又精神抖擞了。It's been a long drive but give me a cup of tea and I'll soon feel fresh as a daisy. (as fresh as a daisy 精力充沛、精力饱满、像雏菊一样新鲜)

(21)即便是对于可以依靠存款或配偶的收入生活的中产阶级，工作生涯突然结束，安稳的退休生活遭受挑战也无疑是个打击。But even middle-class people who might skate by on saving or a spouse's income are jarred by an abrupt end to working life and to a secure retirement. (to stake by on 依靠)

4. 用本单元所学的固定搭配造句。

(1)作为她的老师真的让我很为她开心,希望她可以一直这样坚持信念,健康的成长,完成她的梦想。

(2)当愤怒失去控制的时候,它将会成为梦魇。

(3)你不用担心,你的身材很快就会恢复的。

(4)假如不想让你的敌人得知你的秘密,就不要把秘密告诉你的朋友。

(5)发生火灾时,要保持冷静,打电话给消防队。

(6)他愤怒地声称有人设计陷害他。

(7)有时候,表现粗暴是停止威胁的唯一方式。

(8)我感冒了,我都快疯了,因为我知道感冒一来就得难受三个星期。

(9)她听到这噩耗后晕了过去。

(10)有人曾当面告诉我说我的工作方式是难以忍受的。

(11)这个观点由来已久,但一直未风行。

(12)你跟某人聊得挺热乎的。

(13)或许会自然得到解决吧。

(14)当你选择了看似最好的解决方案,再花几分钟时间考虑一遍。

(15)我茫然地走了一个小时。

(16)记得有位哲人说,人不能两次踏进同一条河流。

(17)你要是方法得当是能够说服你们的顾客的。

(18)我们要确保这个国家的每个孩子都受到良好的教育。

(19)我正要拿那最后一块饼,却给他抢先一步。

(20)我们要完成计划的唯一办法是全力以赴,继续工作。

(21)他帮忙调解玛丽和母亲之间的关系。

(22)他从不掩饰自己的观点。

(23)他们两人都需要适应一下新婚生活。

(24)给久未联系的朋友写封信,传个短信或发个邮件。

(25)既然你决定去美国念书,最好多温习你的英文。

(26)我不想扫了他们的兴。

(27)如果你生活在压力之中,通过工作之余与朋友的放松来使自己冷静下来。

(28)那你为什么要疏远我?

(29)我试图向母亲做最后的告别,但说不出一个字来。

(30)我感觉自己好像是房间里唯一没有一点头绪的人。

(31)昨天碰到琳达时她问起你的情况。

(32)他碰到了一系列的问题。

5. 你能找到更多口语中固定搭配的例证吗?请与大家共同分享本章的学习体会。

Chapter 8　Free Transition

词性转换

一、思路讲解

在前面几章中，我们通过采用“内涵理解”、“固定搭配”、“增添词缀”等方式迅速找到了解决口语交流中暂时性“失语症”的对策，让说话者在遇到交流障碍时能尽快再次融入口语交流中。在本章中，我们将通过“自由的词性转换”这一更为简单的手段来确保口语交流达到更为通畅的目的。值得一提的是，本章的“词性转换”不是通过平时采用的通过派生词缀或曲折词缀的方法来完成的，而是通过以下几种方式实现的：第一种方式——英语单词的常用词性转化为非常用词性。比如：winter 在英语中是名词，表示“冬天”的意思，但你听听这段对话：

A. How's your winter vacation?

B. I wintered at the tropical seashore, Phuket Island.

第二句话中的 winter 转化为动词使用，“度过冬天”，这就是“词形不变，词性转变”的典型例子。第二种方式为中文的某个单词的词性在用英语表达出来时转变成另一词性的同义或近义的英文单词。比如：“他擅长倾听。/He's a good listener.”。汉语中的“擅长”（动词）变成了英语中的“good”（形容词），“倾听”汉语中是名词，而英语中虽仍是名词，但却成了“倾听者”（listener）。第三种方式是不仅中英文的单词词性相互发生了变化，甚至使用的单词或句型结构都不同，但内涵意义是完全一致的。使用这种方式最大的优势在于，分别利用了英汉各自表达的最方便、贴切和简洁的方式。比如这句话：“你在想什么？/Where is your head?”当然，这句话在特定的语境里含有极大的抱怨情绪。

这些方法在使用过程中要注意以下几点：

（1）口语中这种词类转化不要在正式文体中经常使用，因为这毕竟是口语的用法，大家可能已经发现，这些用法在我们平时的书面学习中很少见到，比如：You wrong everything./你把所有的事情都弄糟了。

（2）既然在书面语中不常遇到，我们在生活中累积语料时就要花大力气，下苦功夫，平时做个“有心人”，多观察，多留心，多收集，多使用，毕竟语言是交流的工具。

（3）一定要在语境中去理解发生了词性和表达方式变化的单词和语句。比如：It is not easy to bone the fish, for it has hard plates. 这个句子里的 bone 就是名词转成动词“剔除……的骨头”，整句话的意思是：要想剔除这条的鱼的骨头不容易，因为它有很硬的鱼尾板。

英语就是这样广泛、巧妙地通过更多的转化，使某一词的词性增加，使语言更加简练生动，幽默亲切，新鲜有趣。英语词类的转换主要在动词、名词和形容词三大词类之间进行，而数量最多的是其他词类转化为动词和转化为名词。

二、案例分析

(1)怎么不在大学里找个女朋友呢? Why not google yourself a girl friend in college?

google 是全球知名的搜索引擎,这里是名词转为动词。

(2)请在 QQ 中加我为好友。Please friend me in your QQ.

“加某人为好友”的汉语在英语表达中利用了 friend 这个大家熟悉的单词,不过常用的名词词性转为了动词。

(3)雾霾污染了空气。Haze has dirtied the air.

雾霾对空气的污染越来越严重,关心空气质量的朋友请留心这句话,其中,动词“污染”是用 dirty 表达的,由形容词转为动词。

(4)我是过来人。I have been through this.

汉语中的“过来人”,名词,在英语句子中被 be through this 化解。

(5)有人正在等你。Somebody is ready for you.

本来 be ready for sb. 是“为某人做好准备”的意思,这不正是“专等某人”吗?

(6)我还忘不了你。I' m still not over you.

“忘不了”,动词,“be not over sb.”;“over”,“结束,越过”,介词。

(7)我改变了对……主意。I have second thoughts about…

“改变”,动词,变成了英文的“have second thoughts about…/对……有了另一种想法”,此处的 second 为序数词。

(8)支持某人的计划 to back sb. 's plan

“支持”,动词,英文中 back 常作名词、形容词或副词,但在此作了动词。拓展记忆:“支持某人/ be behind sb.; be by sb. 's side; be there for sb.”。

(9)我俩都知道彼此在逢场作戏。We both know we' ve been faking it.

fake 常用的词性是形容词,这里是动词用法,“作假”,人与人“彼此逢场作戏”就是“作假”。

(10)站一边去 to park oneself

此处的 park 用得十分精妙,park 平时最常见的用法是名词,但此处转为动词,本意指“车停到一边去”,这里指人“哪儿凉快哪儿待着去”。

(11)可以告诉我这次旅行的真正原因吗? So are you ever gonna tell me what exactly prompted this trip?

“原因”,名词,被 prompt 这个动词替换了。

(12)他刚刚组建家庭。He has a young family.

“刚组建家庭”的动词结构被 a young family,名词结构转换,非常生动形象,且结构简单。试试理解一下这句话:“The night is still young!/还早着呢!”

(13)记住我说过的话。Mark my words.

“记住”就是要在脑海里“留下印迹/mark”,“mark”由平时常用的名词形式“标志、记号、分数”等转为动词“留下记号”。

(14)提示某人 to jar sb. 's memory

jar 平时知道“罐子、广口瓶”等意思,名词。这里转为动词,“震动、刺激”,“刺激一下记忆/to jar one's memory",就是"提示某人"的意思。

(15)收集证据 to bag evidence

bag 做成了动词,表示"用包收集"的意思,太有意思了。

(16)除掉这些人 to thin this herd

"除掉"就是"减少",只不过有些贬义,这儿的人群也用了一个表示"畜群"的单词。thin 由形容词转为了动词。

(17)我真懦弱。I'm a pushover.

"懦弱",形容词,而名词"pushover"是指"易于征服或控制的人;容易打败的对手"。

(18)我是个超级说客。I can be pretty persuasive.

"说客"就是要极具说服力,打动别人。名词"说客"在英语里变成了形容词"有说服的"。

(19)激发某人灵感 to tip sb. off

tip 作为名词有"窍门"的意思,转为动词后理解为"给……窍门",也就是"激发……"的意思。

(20)你又发呆了?You stoned again.(↗)

"发呆"就是像一块石头似的,一动也不动,所以这里的 stone 从名词"石头"转为动词"像石头一样",这句话词性发生了变化。中文句子结构是问句,而英文采用的是陈述句加升调的方法搞定,说这句话时,句末要用升调。

(21)你们俩又和好了。You guys back together.

"和好"就是"回心转意","回"首先想到的是 back,但这儿 back 不是常用的形容词或副词的用法,而是转为动词。

(22)搞三捻四 to whore around

首先,我们弄清"搞三捻四"的中文含义:指男女私生活混乱。这个词在方言里说得比较多。whore 常作名词表示"娼妓、淫妇"的意思,这里采用它的动词意义。举一反三,那"和某人鬼混,一天到晚无所事事"怎么说呢?"fool around with sb."。

(23)我要狠狠教训他一顿!I'll fix him good.

这句话怎么看怎么像中英文的逐字表达,看来"文化相通"的威力不可小觑。"教训某人"按方言的说法就是"好好修理某人"。这里的词性转换重点放在 good 这个词上,平时这个词用形容词形式比较多,而这儿用做副词,有"充分地"意思。

(24)分好组!Team up!

这个结构再一次生动地反映了口语的特点,简洁实用。team 从名词"小组"转为了动词"分组"。那"(两个人一组)分组!"怎么说?对!"Pair up!"。

(25)这是我灵机一动想出的瘦身法。It's my thin - spiration.

这个结构比较生动,中文动词"鼓励"在英文中转为了名词 inspiration,而且还巧妙地使用了单词裁剪法/clipping,利用 thin 的后半部的 in 结合 - spiration。

(26)把……转移到…… to channel sth. into sth. else

如果单理解"转移",有很多的表达方式:shift, move, change, transfer, transform 等。但这里用的 channel 却将内涵表达得十分清楚,强调通过某种渠道转移。channel 常用名词形式,"渠道,通道"。

(27)给我们说个大概。Give us the approximate.

像这种表达形式,还真只有在口语中才能出现。名词"大概"在英文中利用了 approximate

这个常作动词的单词的形容词形式,加上 the,转成名词。

(28)我就暂不透露了。I will make no pronouncement of the stage.

动词"透露"在句中用名词"pronouncement/声明、公告"替换,另外副词"暂时"由名词结构"of the stage"替换。

(29)特色菜 special

正式的餐厅学会不定期推出"special/特色菜或特餐",通常会比较便宜。"中午特餐"是 lunch(eon) special,和中国不同的是,美国的特餐不会附在套餐里面,都是要另外点的。需要大家留心的是 special 常作形容词,这儿作名词用。

(30)我一定守口如瓶。My lips are sealed.

"My lips are sealed.",嘴都被封上了,当然"守口如瓶"了。seal 从名词"图章、印章"转为动词"封印"。

三、实战演练

(1)我赞成这个提议。I second the motion.

平时 second 常作名词或序数词,表示"秒;瞬间;第二"等意思,但这儿转成了动词,表示"赞成"。

例如:联合国秘书长支持这项和平呼吁。The UN secretary-general seconded the appeal for peace.

(2)我对你管教很严。I have been hard on you.

又是"管"又是"教"的动词构成,再加上"很严"的副词结构,被"be hard on/对……苛刻,对……要求严格"中的 hard,形容词,给轻易搞定。

例如:别为难自己。Don't be hard on yourself.

(3)我呼吸困难。I have trouble breathing.

"呼吸困难",动词结构,在英语中利用 have trouble (in) doing sth. 替换,变成了名词结构。

例如:由于语法不好,我参加了一个英语学习班。Having trouble in using grammar, I attend an English class.

(4)如果我记得不错的话…… If memory serves…

实际上这是一个相对来讲比较固定的结构,在这个结构中"记",动词,被 memory 名词代替,该结构适合做整体记忆,不要拆开。

例如:要是没记错的话,今天是你的生日吧! If memory serves, today is your birthday!

(5)某人是对的。Somebody has a point.

"对的"是形容词,"to have a point/正确、中肯、很有道理",动词词组形式。

例如:我们不得不承认在那个问题上他是对的。We had to admit that he had a point on that issue.

(6)他总是把老婆呼来唤去。He's always bossing his wife about.

这是一个典型的英文中把名词转为动词的用法,很生动。boss 就是"老板",是"发出命令、做出安排的人、指挥别人做事的人",所以"把某人呼来唤去/to boss sb. around"。

例如:别把我使唤来使唤去的! 你当我是什么? Don't boss me around! What do you take me for?

(7)抱歉这么急通知你。Sorry about the short notice.

中文中的动词“这么急通知”变成了英文的名词“short notice/临时通知”。

例如:虽然我已经被邀请参加开幕式,但是时间这么仓促还是没能去成。Although I had been invited to the opening ceremony, I was unable to attend on such short notice.

(8)你的表现可圈可点。You behave honorably.

“可圈可点”就是“做得好,值得表扬”的意思,这个动词结构被副词“honorably/体面地,值得尊敬地”代替。

例如:记住,真诚地采取行动是第一要务。Remember, taking action sincerely/honestly should always be the first order of business.

(9)别教训我。Don't lawyer me.

还记得 to boss sb. around/about 吗?这里拿 lawyer 说事,lawyer 在维护当事人合法权利时候,据理力争:摆事实、讲道理,呵,那架势!直至说得对方哑口无言。基于此特点,英语 lawyer,名词转成了动词。

例如:别总是教训你儿子!经常交流也许是更有助于改善你俩的关系。Don't always lawyer your son! If you want to improve your relationship between you and your son, constant communication may be a better way.

(10)振作起来 to man up

man 由名词转为具有名词特性的动词:“做得像个男人样”,“别像懦夫,像个真正的男人!”,“雄起!”。

例如:所以振作起来,别再愧疚了。So man up and dump the guilt.

(11)他就那样大摇大摆地插队?He just waltzes in and cuts in line?

先说说 waltz,本意为名词“华尔兹舞曲”,动词“跳华尔兹”,如果看过国标舞比赛,大家都为华尔兹舞者的优雅、从容、舒展、优美而倾倒。这里的“大摇大摆地”,副词结构,在英语中以动词 waltz 出现,部分利用了 waltz 的本意,带有贬义。

例如:她轻而易举地获得了数学和科学奖。She waltzed off with the school prizes for math and science.

(12)你怎能看着她的家被毁而幸灾乐祸呢?How could you dance around her burning house?

这句的里的 dance 的使用与上一句有异曲同工之妙。

例如:我站得更加平直,脸上略带微笑,怀着纯粹的好奇,我的目光跳跃在大厅里。I stood up straighter, put a small smile on my face, and let my eyes dance around the large room in pure wonder.

(13)他逼我的。He cornered me.

这里的用法是 corner 由平时常用的名词“角落”转化成了动词“被逼到角落”,那“被逼到角落”不就是“走投无路,陷入绝境中”吗?

例如:逃犯最后走投无路了。The escaped prisoner was cornered at last.

(14)我的愤怒需要宣泄。My rage needs an outlet.

中文中的动词“宣泄”被英文里的名词“outlet/出口,出路”转换,引申为“感情、精力等发泄的途径和手段。”

例如:有些人需要用交流来宣泄不满。Communication is needed for some people as an outlet for their dissatisfaction.

(15)我会把他们踢出门外的。I'll give them the boot.

"踢出"这个汉语句子里的动词,在英语中转为同义的名词。

例如:他父亲将他踢出家门。His father booted him out of the house.

(16)到处宣传某事 to trumpet sth.

trumpet 是名词"喇叭"的意思,以此意进行延伸,可做动词"到处宣传、大声宣布"的意思。

例如:我们把我们的胜利向全校大声宣布。We trumpeted our triumph all over the school.

(17)磨炼我的抗失望能力 to steel myself for disappointment

"磨炼能力"的目的就是要让自己坚强,所以有"钢铁意志"的说法。"steel/钢铁"名词,在此处转为了动词,意为"使……更坚强"。

例如:然而迈克应该在沮丧的新闻面前更加坚强些。Mike, however, should steel himself for disappointing news.

(18)增添某人的怀疑 to fuel sb.'s suspicions

fuel 从名词"燃料"变成了动词"添加燃料",生动地表达出"增添"的意思。

例如:他那番挑衅的话语只是激化了争论。His provocative words only fuelled the argument further.

(19)精心照料某人直至康复 to nurse sb. back to health

把"护士/nurse",名词。做成动词,就是要体现"照顾得很好的,像护士一样精心照顾"的意思。

例如:他坚持不睡觉来护理这个女孩。He insisted on staying up to nurse the girl.

(20)我抽出时间过来帮帮忙。So I freed up some time in my schedule to help.

free 形容词,表示"自由的",在此转为动词,"to free up/空出来,开放"。

例如:我们制定了开放市场和扩大竞争的政策。We have made policies for freeing up markets and extending competition.

(21)打扮得漂漂亮亮或花枝招展 to doll up sb./oneself

说到 doll,不由得让人想到"芭比娃娃",这款风靡全球的洋娃娃经久不衰的最大魅力在于,孩子们可以根据自己的喜好对自己心爱的娃娃进行打扮,这就不难理解从名词转换成动词的 doll 在词组 doll up 中表示"打扮得花枝招展"的意思。

例如:打扮得这么漂亮是要去哪里啊?Where are you going all dolled up?

(22)筹划、安排 to map sth. out

map 由名词转为动词,表示"在地图上标出或筹划或安排"的意思。

例如:我喜欢预先安排好一个月的工作。I like to map out the whole month in advance.

(23)他被跟踪了。He's been tailed.

"跟踪"还有一种说法是"尾随",所以这里名词"tail/尾巴"转为动词表示"跟踪"的意思一点也不奇怪。

例如:他们跟踪那个嫌疑犯。They tailed after the suspect.

(24)我们完全搞定了。We totally nailed it!

要让一个单词从常用的词性转为不常用的词性的关键在于抓住这个单词的基本词意,比如:nail 名词的意思为"钉子",那大家想想"钉子"有什么基本特征?这里就是"使固定"的意思。

例如:你为什么要死盯我不放呢?Why (you) nail me?

(25)拼凑信息 to piece together information

"拼凑"这个词让人联想到拼图游戏,将散乱的小块拼凑成一幅完整的画。不过 piece 从名词转为了动词。

例如：在朋友宴会上，大家都在回忆过去的美好时光。At the friend reunion party, all of them pieced together their happy old memories.

(26)我也需要人陪陪。I could use the company.

这次的词性转换是从中文的动词转为英文的名词。company 作名词有“陪伴、同伴、一群人”的意思，比如“keep company with/与……交往，与……做朋友”。

例如：我担心，她需要更多正常人的陪伴。I worried she needed the company of more normal people.

(27)我都等不及看你准备了什么菜了。I can't wait to see what you dish up.

“什么菜”，仔细想想还真不能找到个中英文完全匹配的单词，当然不能用“菜/vegetable”这样逐字逐句的表达方式，因为这种方式完全不顾文字所传递的内涵。这里的解决办法是中文的“什么菜”，名词，转为了英文的动词“dish up/上菜”。

例如：我请她帮忙把晚餐的菜肴分别盛到大家的盘子里。I asked her to help me dish up dinner for people.

(28)为某人加油；支持、赞助 to root for sb.

root 是名词“根”的意思，在这里用成了动词。记忆窍门：root 就是“根”，就可以想象成“脚”的意思，再延伸理解为“跺脚加油”。

例如：他们来到棒球场为他们的校队鼓劲。They came to the baseball field to root for their school team.

(29)我当那人为偶像。I idolize that man.

从中文的名词“偶像”转换到英文的动词“把……当偶像崇拜”。

例如：大多数孩子崇拜明星，不管是电影明星，摇滚乐队还是足球运动员。Most kids idolize celebrities whether it be movie stars, rock bands or soccer players.

(30)对某事牢骚满腹 to beef about sth.

beef 用得最多的词性是名词“牛肉”，这里转为了动词，表示“抱怨、发牢骚”。

例如：你都在发什么牢骚？What are you beefing about now?

(31)令人恶心 to gross (sb.) out

gross 本指“粗劣的；粗大的，总共的”。俚语中则常表示“恶心的”，类似 disgusting 的用法。此处转为动词，就是“to disgust sb./ 令某人恶心”。名词是 gross-out，表“令人恶心的事物”。“gross”这个单词通常出现在小孩子的对话中，并时常单独使用，表“恶心死了”！

例如：如果你继续像那样说话，就会引起人们的反感。You are going to gross out people if you continue talking like that.

(32)她无法忍受他的粗鲁。She cannot stomach his poor manners.

记忆窍门：通常人吃到不好的东西都会直接反应吐出来，但是如果已经到了胃部了，就表示这份食物是可以被身体所“接受的、忍受的”，因此名词 stomach 在俚语中可表示“忍受、忍耐”，通常用在负面情形。

例如：工友们发现鲍勃的态度难以忍受。The workers found Bob's attitude hard to stomach.

(33)寻找某物 be on the lookout for sth.

be on the lookout for sth. 表示“留意寻找某事物”。lookout 是名词，当动词用时为 to look out，可用同为动词化的 to watch out 来代替。中文中的动词“寻找”变成了英语中名词的 lookout。

例如:你最好留意找辆新车,我想你那辆修过的旧车撑不多久了。You'd better be on the lookout for a new car. I don't think the repairs you did to the old one are going to last for long.

(34)休息片刻 to take a breather

breather 在口语中表示“短时间的休息”,所以这个短语表示“休息片刻”,不过中文的动词“休息”变成了英语的名词“短时间的休息”。

例如:我们已经是练习了 3 个小时了,休息一下。We've already practiced for three hours. Let's take a breather.

(35)狼吞虎咽 to wolf down

wolf down 一般形容狼吃东西的样子,意思是“贪婪地吃食物,即“狼吞虎咽”。“狼吞虎咽”是动词,wolf 由名词转为了动词。

例如:我还以为能剩下些饼干,但是他们都吃光了。I thought there would be some biscuits left but they've wolfed down the whole lot!

(36)丢掉,赶走 to eighty-six

这是一个有趣的俚语表达,eight-six 在俚语中是“丢弃、丢掉”的意思,这个单词是当“动词”用,可直接写为“86”。

例如:我不再需要这个了。你可以把它扔了。I don't need it anymore. You can eighty-six it.

(37)尾随 to dog sb.

想象这样一个画面:忠实的小狗摇着尾巴,跟随着主人,亦步亦趋。名词 dog 变成了动词。

例如:无论我上哪儿,小弟总是尾随着。Wherever I go, my little brother dogs my footsteps.

四、巩固练习

1. 从词性转换的角度说说下面中文词组或句子的英语表达。

(1)冲动
(2)逃避
(3)正直
(4)样本
(5)修补
(6)重组
(7)找房子
(8)随便挑
(9)诋毁某人
(10)国际追捕
(11)陷害某人
(12)折磨我们
(13)内部消息
(14)面对现实
(15)正式开战

(16)融入他们
(17)自吹自擂
(18)权衡利弊
(19)聊了几句
(20)例外一次
(21)到旁边来说话
(22)有品位且高雅
(23)好好看着某人
(24)下定决心做某事
(25)暗中监视那个女人
(26)浑水摸鱼,趁火打劫
(27)一个有心灵创伤的人
(28)善待对方
(29)我生气了。
(30)激发兴趣
(31)弥合代沟
(32)这样做好吗?
(33)我要透透气。
(34)你真有天赋。
(35)我决不怀疑。
(36)不许探视了。
(37)恃强凌弱
(38)你充满魅力。
(39)场面很骚动。
(40)这语言很难学。
(41)我是自不量力。
(42)我帮你接杯水。
(43)某人人生坎坷。
(44)他越来越抑郁了。
(45)别把事情搞砸了。
(46)别把我的证件弄乱。
(47)让某人疏远某人
(48)如果你结束这件事……
(49)我是一个有信仰的人。
(50)他每天乘公交上班。
(51)偶尔过来喝喝咖啡。
(52)吃东西不要狼吞虎咽。
(53)某人的健康状况急转直下。
(54)他提出了一个草案让老板过目。
(55)他不得不肩负起养家糊口的责任。

2. 从词性转换的角度说说下面英文词组或句子的中文表达。

(1) payback
(2) be full bodied
(3) water boy
(4) to caution sb.
(5) get-together
(6) backup plan
(7) poor mouthing
(8) celebration night
(9) to peel an apple
(10) to pencil the eyebrows
(11) to cover my shift
(12) career suicide
(13) conflict interest
(14) to take first watch
(15) profit participation
(16) immediately effective
(17) to crack sb.'s knuckles
(18) the pull of sth.
(19) to make a full recovery
(20) to trade places with somebody
(21) the vocalization of emotion
(22) to thumb through the dictionary
(23) to make a reckless mistake
(24) to lay down some ground rules
(25) crossing-examination
(26) to give sb. a spare napkin
(27) We are so in luck.
(28) I'm reasonable.
(29) Make your move!
(30) You are so into it!
(31) The decision is yours.
(32) I'd like to surprise her.
(33) Can I give you a ride?
(34) He is red with anger.
(35) She's sick of listening.
(36) Don't baby your child.
(37) This is a good finish.
(38) This is your screw-up.

(39) You couldn't fool me.
(40) We sense this isolation.
(41) I minored in modern dance.
(42) Father's hair begins to grey.
(43) Shall I sugar the milk for you?
(44) You must pressure him to do it.
(45) Will you write under your own name?
(46) He had blacked his face with soot.
(47) He went out to water the plants.
(48) They elbowed their way through the crowd.
(49) The child was eyeing the chocolate cake.
(50) Mr. Smith has authored a book on AIDS.
(51) I could really use a change of scenery.
(52) You want him nursing that kind of grudge.
(53) I didn't mean for you to go to all this trouble.
(54) You do not need to contradict me with all your contradictions.

3. 熟读并背诵下列句子并体会词性转换的精妙使用。

(1) 阵仗之大！Quite a turnout！
(2) 尽量别长大。Stay kids for as long as possible.
(3) 你在笑什么？What's that smile about?
(4) 别跟我耍手段！Do not fox me！
(5) 别让我妨碍你！Don't ever let me be a nuisance！
(6) 决定权不在我。That's not for me to say.
(7) 别那么输不起。No need to be a bad loser.
(8) 我们要叙叙旧。We have so much catching-up.（catch-up 朋友小聚）
(9) 但是你可别累着。But don't tire yourself out.
(10) 我想和你说清楚。I just want to be really clear with you.
(11) 我不把你当外人。I'm not trying to exclude.
(12) 你们合伙对付我啊。You're ganging up on me.
(13) 你又更上一层楼了。You top yourself.
(14) 他模仿他的父亲。He patterns himself upon his father.
(15) 你怎样弹这曲子？How do you finger this piece?
(16) 别乱动我的电视机。Don't monkey with my television.
(17) 他一直被厄运缠身。He has been dogged by the bad luck.
(18) 某人对你赞不绝口。Somebody is full of your praise.
(19) 武汉每天早上都堵车。The car wormed on the way every morning in Wuhan.
(20) 可我们都和他们约好了。But we gave them the date.
(21) 她强作镇定唯恐失态。She willed herself into not reacting.
(22) 他们的薪水少得可怜。They're paid a pittance.（pittance n. 少量；小额施舍）

(23)你们正好赶上吃晚饭。You are just in time for breakfast.

(24)我知道你们对我有成见。I see how you guys are eyeing me.

(25)可爱的年轻姑娘现在很幸福。A lovely young woman is at the height of her happiness.

(26)每天晚上开舞会,真累。I am really burned-out on partying every night.(burn out 表示使疲惫不堪;使精力不济)

(27)你得密切关注股市的变化。You have to eye every change in the stock market.

(28)我们就画上一个圆满的句号。Let's end on a happy note.

(29)他的拒绝浇灭了我们的热情。His refusal iced our enthusiasm.

(30)男孩都跑去救火,迈克却退缩了。All the boys ran to put out the fire, but Mike chickened out.

(31)我不是在拐弯抹角地让你邀请我们。I wasn't fishing for an invitation.

(32)这个谜已经在我心中郁结了好多年。I've wondered about this for years.

(33)他们把农场管理得井井有条。They have husbanded their farms very well.

(34)这次阴谋是由迈克策划的。This plot was engineered by Mike.

(35)在中国,人们非常注重讲礼貌。In China, there is a lot of emphasis on politeness.

(36)他放下斧头,坐在树桩上休息。He downed his ax and sat on a stump to rest.

(37)某些工业特别容易受季节性不景气的影响。Certain industries are subject to seasonal downs.

(38)这或许影响到了我生育后代。It may have limited my chances of fathering a child.

(39)他对未来提出来一些不错的计划。He was outlining some interesting plans for the future.

(40)不要自找麻烦,除非麻烦来找你。Don't trouble troubles till trouble troubles you!

(41)我刚与布莱克先生达成一笔交易。I've just closed a deal with Mr. Black.

(42)招拢这大群人,我有很多事要做。I've got too much to do, rounding this lot up.(round…up聚拢)

(43)下班之后,我们都匆匆忙忙去喝点什么。After work we all beetled off for a drink.

(44)不应该让退休的人感到自己是个闲人。A retired person cannot be made to feel he's on the shelf.(be on the shelf 被搁置不理;无人问津)

(45)我只是坐享先人的劳动苦心打造成就的家业。My fortune is the work of others who labored to build a great dynasty.

(46)科学家们都深信,所有的物质都是不灭的。Scientists are confident that all matter is indestructible.

(47)旅馆都客满了,我们只得在旧棚子里对付一晚。The hotels were all full so we had to pig it in an old hut for the night.(pig 为动词,"在肮脏处挤或睡在一块儿"。)

(48)列车开始弯弯曲曲地急速前行之后,餐车便开始左右摇晃起来。Since the train was snaking along at a brisk clip, the diner swayed from side to side.

(49)国际影院本星期的新片是一部不可不看的片子。The new show at the International Theatre this week is an absolute must.

(50)我学会用柔和的声音来使自己的吐字圆润。I learned to use a soft voice to oil my words.

(51)长城从渤海边的山海关到甘肃的嘉峪关向西蜿蜒延伸了 6700 公里。The Great Wall

snakes about 6700 kilometers westward from Shanhaiguan on the Bohai Bay to Jiayuguan in Gansu Province.

4. 用本单元所学的知识造句。

(1)我赞成他提议成立一个特别委员会来研究这个问题。
(2)即使别人亏待了你,你的人生不会亏待你。
(3)如果我没记错的话,我们第一次相遇是在图书馆。
(4)她喜欢把她的孩子们呼来喝去。
(5)这么迟才通知我,我没有办法做出一顿饭来的!
(6)这名士兵光荣退伍了。
(7)他必须像个男子汉那样说出事情的真相。
(8)所有的这些都揭示了最主要的事实,我们想要快乐。
(9)这个问题把我难住了。
(10)弹奏摇滚乐可以发泄精力。
(11)他们以他不工作为由把他开除出公司。
(12)他到处吹嘘他儿子的智商高。
(13)我是一个乐观的,自信的,坚强和自我激发的人。
(14)要维持爱情,需要不断地为它增添“养分”。
(15)你能不能抽出时间锻炼一下。
(16)他们为参加聚会着意打扮了一番。
(17)他们所要做的就是挑拨离间,浑水摸鱼。
(18)我们必须逐步制定我们的规划。
(19)在咖啡馆,重点不在于食物和饮料,而在于有大家陪伴的那份轻松愉快。
(20)史蒂文返回厨房准备上菜。
(21)学院的全体学生都支持新院长的计划。
(22)不要对涨价没完没了地发牢骚了。
(23)皮特无法忍受那部电影的暴力镜头。
(24)但当火气开始冒头时,退下来歇口气。
(25)那个饥饿的人狼吞虎咽地吃完了食物。

5. 你能找到更多词性转换的例证吗?请与大家共同分享本章的学习体会。

Chapter 9　Brief Expressions
简洁表达

一、思路讲解

口语表达的特点之一就是简洁。所谓“简洁”，在这里不仅指句子结构方面，也指用词方面。口语中使用简洁的表达，原因如下：第一，在交流语境的帮助下，不需要使用完整的句子或复杂的句型结构，否则会显得十分别扭。比如：“你被录取了。/You got it.”；“你完了。/You're out.”；“我不干了。/I am out.”。第二，简洁的表达会使信息传递更流畅，更凝练，更突出，更高效。“好点了吗？/Does that help?”（询问对方生病吃药后的感受）“我不知弹到哪里。/I keep losing my place.”（弹钢琴走神后，询问别人自己弹到哪儿了）。第三，简洁的表达，让对话留有思考和回旋的余地，或隐晦表达交流双方都心知肚明不便于讲得太明显的人或事，让对话更有意思。比如“他算是免受坐牢之苦。/He would be spared.”。

口语表达要做到简洁，要注意以下原则：

（1）语言不累赘，能用词组不用句子，使用句子时，结构要简单，在简单的句子结构中，说出重点关键的单词，使对话更有效率，节省时间，用最少单词的句子传递最大的信息量。比如：“你（们）干嘛慌慌张张的？/Why the rush?”。

（2）对话内容切题，一针见血，点到为止。比如：在餐馆按照菜单点菜，但服务员对你讲你点的菜都没有时，你可能会满怀怨气地告诉他随便上什么菜，这时候这个“随便”怎么说呢？“Surprise me！/随便！”仔细感受一下这里的“Surprise me！”二字，真是用得太妙了！

（3）复杂且不常用的单词用比较简单、更容易理解的方式表达。比如：“荒郊野外/ a place without anyone”，“看你多有出息！/Look how well you turned out！”。

（4）为了更突出单词的简洁，有的单词采用缩略形式。比如：“有空吗？/Got a sec(second)?”，“那样大家能自在吗？/Would that make everyone comfy (comfortable)?”

下面请大家利用鲜活的语料和上述思路讲解，感受口语中简洁表达的魅力，通过消化吸收实践，让我们的口语表达更言简意赅。

二、案例分析

（1）敬咱自个！ Here's to us!

这个结构用在酒宴上，省去了 toast，或 propose the toast 这些单词，仅用 Here's... 这个简单的结构搞定。

（2）（这主意）不好，还有呢？ Not tempting. Next?

充分利用了语境，省去了交流双方都知道的主语，从对话的语气已知现在说话者很着急，所以简洁的语句体现了这种心情。

（3）出城开会 an out-of-town conference

完整的对话模式是:“某某在吗?”“某某出城开会去了。”这句话前面省略了“某某”这个主语,从句子变成了词组,让表达更轻松。

(4)我赢官司的可能性很大。I have a good case.

“赢官司”,“可能性很大”都被逐一化简为一个简单的句子 I have a good case.

(5)让他老实一点。Make him behave.

从句义上理解,说话人是很生气的,所以用了省略主语的祈使句形式,加强语气。“让某人老实点。”就是“让某人行为规矩点”,所以句子里采用了 behave 这个单词。

(6)太多的衣服要洗 so much laundry

其实要将这个表达说得简洁,就是要充分理解 laundry 这个单词,laundry 有“洗衣店,洗衣房;要洗的衣服;洗熨;洗好的衣服。”

(7)你们之间有什么纠葛?What did you get between you two/yourselves?

这里的“纠葛”就用了隐晦的方式,省略了体现这个意义的单词,用整体简单的结构完成了这个表达。

(8)我说错了什么吗?Did I say something?

这里的 something 是指交流双方都明白的“让人感到误会或在此处不适宜的事情”。

(9)什么?Sorry?(↗)

此处的“sorry”要用升调,表示“不明白,没听懂,没听清”的意思。类似的一、两个词的简略形式我们看看:“出去! Out!”,“什么事? Yes.(↗)”,“快点! Move!”,“太好了! Super!”,“真的? Serious?(↗)”,“你好! Howdy?”,“好极了! Bingo!”,“放箭! Loose!”,“省省吧! Drop it!”,“算了! Skip it!”,“天啊! Oh, man!”,“嘿,哥们! Hey, man!”,“不行! No way!”,“退下! Leave us!”,“进攻! Full attack!”等等。

(10)你一定如释重负。You must be so relieved.

汉语的“如释重负”这个动词词组,用一个形容词“relieved”就轻松搞定。再比如“松了一口气。/That's a relief.”

(11)你疯了?You've lost.(↗)

中文的问句改成了英文中的陈述句,相对问句来讲,陈述句的结构更符合思维惯式,更简单,唯一要注意的是这句话结尾要用升调。

(12)废话连篇。This is such lame bullshit.

在此句中,说话人怒气十足,所以英文句子不仅将句子结构便简单,而且加上了语气更重的两个单词“lame/蹩脚的,没有说服力的”和“bullshit/胡说八道”。

(13)我从没有想过我有多了不起。I never thought I was gonna amount to much.

amount to much 这个结构常用于否定句中,表示“有重要性,了不起”。

(14)假如失败的话,…… If it goes out…

这里的 go out 来自“熄灭”这个意思,“火或者光熄掉,”不就是“没有希望,没有成功”的意思吗?

(15)方便吗?Is this bad time?

如果没有语境,这句话肯定在表达上会产生歧义,但有了语境:打搅别人时说的话,这个表达就会让人觉得是简洁表达的最佳的例子之一。

(16)我很理解你。I feel for you.

中文里不是“感同身受”这句话吗?英文表达就很有点这个意思,所以引申为“我很理解你”。

(17)小苏珊 Susan q.

口语中经常用昵称呼喊对方,Susan 的昵称是 Susie,而 Susan q. 是 Susan Cute 的缩略形式,意为“可爱的苏珊”。

(18)让我来给你讲解这道难题。Let me talk you through this difficult problem.

“讲解”就是要“讲清楚、讲透彻”,而英文词组 talk sb. through…就能表述这个意思。

(19)名师出高徒。I' ve learned from the best.

“名师出高徒”是中国人的说法,通过内涵理解,英文表达简化用词和结构。

(20)没必要了。There is no point.

“没有必要”就是“没有意义”,而 point 就是“要点、意义”。

(21)别再说了。Say no more.

这是一个常用的简洁表达,无须赘言。

(22)金玉良言。It' s a good motto.

“金玉良言”比喻非常宝贵的劝告和教诲,而 motto 是“格言、警句”的意思,起到规劝和教育的作用。所以这个中文成语和英文表达可以算是较好的对应表达,也算是一种“金玉良缘”。

(23)真不错。That was something.

这就是英语中典型的隐晦说法,从字面上讲“就是那么回事。”也就是“不错”的意思。

(24)我们应白头偕老。We should be growing together.

“白头偕老”是中国人的说法,中国人有首歌的歌词是这样的“我知道最浪漫的事,就是和你一起慢慢变老”,这句话倒是“应了”英文表达的“这个景”。

(25)我脑子进水了。Where is my brain?

“脑子进水”是最近几年才流行的一种说法,形容一个人“不会用大脑思考,是个白痴。”这是句骂人的话,而英语中没有这种说法,但类似意思的表达,口语中有个很简单的说法 Where is my brain?

(26)我做了坏事,坐了牢。I did my dirt. Served my time.

用隐晦的方式简洁表达的又一个例子,句子结构也明显具有口语特征。

(27)如果你这么说…… If you say so…

这个结构一般用于不同意对方的意见的婉转说法,口语中可单独使用,也可后接句子。

(28)别误会! Don' t get me wrong!

对于“误会”这个词的英文表达,大家记得最牢的莫过于 misunderstand,但口语中有更简洁的表达方法:get sb. wrong。延展记忆:“别误解! /Don' t take this the wrong way.”

(29)你说了算。It' s your call.

该约定俗成一说还可以理解为“决定权在你。”当然表达同样意义的英文表达还很多,比如“You have the last word.”,“You have the final say.”“You are the boss.”等等,这个相对来讲还比较简单。

(30)客气话别说了,喝酒。Less thanking, more drinking.

这是口语表达中典型的不顾句子结构,只突出要表达意义的重点单词的形式,大家掌握这个方法会让口语表达变得轻松容易。

(31)真是一刻不得闲啊。No rest for the wicked.

这句话出自《圣经》,是“There is no rest for the wicked.”的省略形式,原意是“恶人总有坏事要做,永远也没有足够的时间把坏事做完"。现在引用此句是抱怨工作太多的一种幽默说法:这么多事情,何时能做得完?

(32)Nothing for me? 没有我的吗? Afraid not. 恐怕没有。

这轮对话是典型的在语境下采用省略的简洁方式,只强调表意的那几个单词。

(33)典型的老奶奶 a classic granny

老奶奶的典型行为是什么? 特别关爱孙子,言语啰唆等。那 classic student, classic housewife, classic parents 呢?

(34)有话直说!(别兜圈子,我听不懂)In English, please!

这个说法也挺有趣的,在两个人交流中,认为对方讲了自己听不懂的话,就幽默地用"In English, please!"来要求对方不要绕圈子,当然这里的语境是两个人都在说英语。与此类似的搞笑的说法有"You are speaking Chinese? /说什么? 听不懂。"

(35)但你袭警就得入狱/进去。But when you hit an officer, you go in.

没有语境 go in 就不好理解,但前面有"袭警",所以后面的 go in 是"入狱,进去"就顺理成章了。

(36)玛丽没来? No Mary? (↗)

这就是典型的口语的省略形式,利用语境省略了句子结构,用两个单词搞定意义。

(37)全部都完成了。All done.

done 是 do 的过去分词,表示"做好了"。用在食物上,则指煮熟的,如 well - done 表示全熟的。此处为省略的常用说法,即"All has been done. /全部做好了"。

(38)随时;不客气。Anytime.

当别人向你表示感谢时,回答的表达方式有很多:You are welcome! 等,"Anytime." 算是最简单的。

(39)不知道。Dunno.

这是 don't know 的口语说法,也是照着发音直接书写下来的。通常使用这个单词时会省略 I,多半用在当我们对某事很震惊,而不知该说什么事时候。

(40)一定是开玩笑。Got to be kidding.

gotta 是口语用法,等于 have/has got to,"You gotta be kidding. /你一定是开玩笑。"亦可代换为 You've got to be kidding. 或 You must be kidding.

(41)如果顺利的话。Hopefully so.

当我们想要表达肯定的回应,但又不完全确定时,我们可以说这句话,来表达如我所愿的话;如果一切顺利的话。

(42)我是……(name) here.

打电话除了一开始的"hello",接下来通常就会报出自己的姓名。最完全的说法是"This is (name) speaking.",中间加上姓名。亦可化为 This is (name)."或"...(name) speaking."。此外也可直接说"…(name) here.",尤其是在办公室接电话时。

三、实战演练

(1)这只是例行公事,不针对个人。It's business. Nothing personal.

"例行公事"和"不针对个人"都采用了简洁的方式,前者省去了"例行",后者省去了"针对”,采用了词组而不是句子,表达变得干练。

例如:我没有针对你个人的意思,但我不同意你的观点。Nothing personal, but I don't agree with your opinion.

(2)我有个条件。Here's a deal!

中国学生一看见“条件”,很自然的条件反射就是书本里学过的那个单词 condition。这里的英文表达不仅省掉了主语“我”,而且“条件”也成了口语中常用 的“deal/交易”这个单词,句子结构也做了简化。延展记忆:“一言为定/ Deal!”,“我们有约定。/We had a deal.”。

例如:说好了,这事就交给你了。Here's a deal! You're responsible for this issue.

(3)亲爱的,别担心! Honey, relaxed.

“别担心!”的另一种说法就是“放轻松!”。在安慰别人时,尽量用简洁有力的话语,别在那儿用啰唆的语句给别人添堵。

例如:别担心! 你有超人的智慧和缜密的思维,我看好你。Relaxed! You have extraordinary wit and thoughtful mind. I back you!

(4)我们的订婚取消了。Our engagement is off.

“取消”这个动词被 be off 轻松简化,有一种干脆利落的痛快。

例如:因为天气原因,原计划被取消了。The original plan is off due to the bad weather.

(5)我们快成功了! We are almost there!

“almost there/快到那儿了”,“快到哪儿了?”对话者双方都明白的目标,这儿的简洁表达充分利用了语境。

例如:如果你改掉之前的坏习惯,你就离成功不远了。You're almost there, if you correct the previous bad habits!

(6)你的话太多了。You get chatty.

汉语中的“话”怎么表达? 是 word 还是 talk? 一个 chatty 搞定所有的问题, 另外用 chatty 这个单词从语境上讲含有“饶舌的,爱讲闲话的”的意思。

例如:我忍受不了那个人了,他话太多了。I can't stand that man, he is so chatty.

(7)你不交便不及格。You don't do it, you flunk.

像这种句子结构在正式语法中不能算正确的句子,但在口语中确实可以接受的。另外还要弄清 flunk 这个单词的内涵,“未通过考试或课程”。

例如:学生中流传这样一种说法:挂柯南,挂科难。You-Paste-Up-Conan-You-Won't-Flunk is popular among students. 注:“柯南”是日本动画片《名侦探柯南》里的主角,这里是利用了谐音。

(8)你应该分清轻重缓急。You have to make priorities.

“分清轻重缓急”就是要知道哪些重要,应该先做。priority 就是“优先要做的事情”的意思。

例如:你在我心中是第一。You're my priority.

(9)别让我失望。Don't fail me!

这里的动词“失望/disappoint”换成了更简单的动词“fail/失望、辜负”。

例如:我对这个队很有信心,我相信他们不会使我们失望的。I've got a lot of faith in the team; I'm sure they won't fail us.

(10)闭嘴! Hold your tongue!

“闭嘴!”就是不要再发出声响的意思,这里的重点是放在了 tongue 这个单词上,表达尤显生动,中国人常讲“巧舌如簧”、“三寸不烂之舌”,类似 hold your tongue 的生动表达有 shut up, zip one's mouth 等。

例如:我建议你当老板说话时保持沉默。I suggest you hold your tongue when the boss is talking.

(11)他要求很高。He is demanding.

中文中四个字的“要求很高”,换成了英文中的一个单词“demanding/苛求的,要求高的”。

例如:是你的老板要求太高? Is your boss too demanding?

(12)是件费工夫的事。It's a long shot.

long shot 的意思是:If you describe something as a long shot, you mean that it is unlikely to succeed, but is worth trying. 胜算不大的尝试。

例如:这宗交易不太可能成功,但他没什么可损失的。The deal was a long shot, but he had little to lose.

(13)事情不如你愿。You don't get your way.

“事情不如你愿。”就是指“诸事不是按照你的套路在进行。”to get one's way 就是“为所欲为,随心所欲”的意思。

例如:事情总不会都如人愿,所以不要做这样的期望。不要期待着一切都完美。You are not always going to get your way, so don't expect to. Don't plan on everything to come out of perfect.

(14)有消息称,至少有 1/3 的破解程序专家失败了。Sources say at least one – third of deprogrammers fail.

“有消息称”用 sources say 表达,其意义跟 It is said that…类似。

例如:有消息称,他上次工作的那家公司最近倒闭了。Sources say the last firm he worked for closed down recently.

(15)上下班车流高峰让我不堪。I can't beat the commute.

commute 是“通勤”的意思,也就是指“从家中往返工作地点的过程,即相对‘出勤’和‘退勤’而来。”一个 commute 就轻松表达出“上下班”这个意思。beat 是“战胜”的意思,如你不能战胜某物,那某物就一定会给你带来痛苦。

例如:不管你用什么方式上下班,你总是可以有效利用你的时间。No matter how you commute, you can always take advantage of the time you have.

(16)就等你决定了。Just give me the word.

因为是对话中的句子,所以英语表达中省略了主语,to give me the word 意为“给我个话”,什么“话”?当然是“最后的决定”。

例如:说出你的决定,我们就走。Give me the word, and we'll go.

(17)我们可以低价买入。We can get it for a song.

for a song 就是副词“非常便宜地,廉价地”的意思,常与动词 sell、buy 和 get 连用,利用这个词组可以让表达变得既简洁又生动。

例如:他们廉价地买下那幢房子。They bought that house for a song.

(18)别管我,先考虑他吧。Put her feeling ahead of mine.

“优先考虑”就有前有后,“把……放在……之前/put …ahead of …”

例如：他把老百姓的利益放到自己利益之先。He put the benefit of civilians ahead of his.

(19)我们千辛万苦换来成功。Our success came at a price.

俗话说得好，"天下没有白吃的午餐。"做任何事情都要付出代价，at a price 就是"以较高的价格，以很高的代价"的意思。

例如：这一慷慨举动并非毫无代价。This largesse comes at a price.

(20)他是一个少言寡语的人。He is a person of few words.

"沉默寡言"用英语一个非常简单的表达说出来 a person of few words。

例如：他不爱多说话，但常常笑容可掬；那微笑是自然而友好的。He was a man of few words, but of all smiles. His smile was natural and friendly.

(21)请讲具体点。Please be specific.

这里省略了交流双方都知道的那个动词"讲"，用形容词 specific 解决问题。

例如：将它写下来 ，而且要写得具体。Write it down, and be specific.

(22)我们分头行动。Let's split up.

"分头行动"就是"大家分开，朝不同方向去"。to split up 正好体现了这个意义，用两个字简洁地表达了中文四个字表达的意思。

例如：这个家让此事使弄得四分五裂。This situation has split up the family.

(23)我是不是把这事想得太复杂了？Am I making too much of this?

事实上"to make too much of"是一个意思表达较为灵活的词组，可以根据语境理解为"想得太多"，"看得太重"，"太较真"等意思。

例如：经济学家警告不要把那些报告看得太重。Economists warned us not to make too much of those reports.

(24)事已至此。It is what is it.

It is what is it. 还有"就是这样"、"该什么就是什么"等意思。另外这个简单的表达很有特点，反过来倒过去的单词都是一样的，便于记忆。

例如：这可能不是我们喜欢的方式，但是这就是它存在的方式。It may not be the way we like, but it is what is it.

(25)这谁说得准。Could be anything.

在对话过程中，对"不确定之事"的回答可以采用这个省略结构。

例如：高兴可以是任何事，从欣赏歌剧到朋友聚会。Happiness could be anything ranging from the appreciation of the opera to the get – together of friends.

(26)少说风凉话。Ditch the sarcasm.

"风凉话"就是"打消别人积极性的嘲讽话。以及不负责任的冷言冷语"。ditch 作动词，有"丢弃、抛弃、摆脱"的意思，sarcasm 是"挖苦、讽刺、嘲笑"的意思。

例如：少说风凉话。多鼓励！Ditch the sarcasm. More courage!

(27)别对我大吼大叫！Don't raise your voice to me!

"大吼大叫"就是加大音量说话，有在气势上要压倒别人的作用，"吼"和"叫"用 yell 还是 shout 呢？本句将这两个词简化为 raise one's voice。延展记忆："to raise one's voice against sb. /发表针对某人的批评"。

例如：他不是那种需要用提高嗓门来说明某一观点的人。He's not one of these guys that needs to raise his voice to make a point.

(28)别抬杠！Don't catch me out!

“抬杠”就是“是一种凭借机伶巧诈的嘴上工夫指责别人”。而“catch sb. out”意为“发现某人有错”。“别抬杠！”就是“别老挑我的错。”

例如：你随便问吧，决问不倒我。Ask me anything you like ——you won't catch me out.

(29)Much more and we shall all burst into tears. 再说下去我们就都要哭了。

这里要根据语境来理解“much more”——“再喝下去”，“再学下去”，“再练下去”等，这里就是利用了语境，进行了省略。

例如：别再逼孩子练钢琴了，你再逼下去，她会永远放弃弹钢琴。Don't push her to play piano. Much more and she will give it up forever.

(30)他陷入困境了。He is in a proper fix.

在美式俚语中，in a fix 表示“陷入困境”。

例如：天呀！我们真是进退两难。Bless my heart! We are in a fix.

(31)您怎么现在念叨起这个了来？Why dwell on that now?

dwell on 是“细想、详述”的意思，而中文的“念叨”就是“碎碎念”，略带贬义，但基本意义匹配。

例如：你为什么一直在喋喋不休地讲那个问题？Why do you keep dwelling upon that matter?

四、巩固练习

1.从简洁表达的角度说说下面中文词组的英语表达。

(1)明白了

(2)没必要

(3)要好好的

(4)个人表演

(5)重新做人

(6)时机未到

(7)废话太多

(8)完美的人

(9)抓紧时间

(10)新来的人

(11)不吃不喝

(12)挪用公款

(13)控股公司

(14)信号不好

(15)无论如何

(16)谢谢提醒

(17)小心说话

(18)把话讲清楚

(19)竭诚为您服务

(20)有道理，说得对

(21)每况愈下的健康状况
(22)“欢迎回家”庆祝会
(23)大家都知道的秘密(公开记录)

2.从简洁表达的角度说说下面中文句子的英语表达,尤其注意画线部分。

(1)不必问。
(2)别伤心。
(3)别多事!
(4)别得意。
(5)省省吧。
(6)别插队!
(7)我活该!
(8)明白了吗?
(9)你没打中。
(10)马上回来。
(11)我说完了。
(12)他是家人。
(13)太夸张了。
(14)搞定了吗?
(15)直说就行。
(16)不能回头了。
(17)就这么定了。
(18)别大事化小。
(19)请你吃火锅。
(20)他真抬举我。
(21)有什么事吗?
(22)(敲门)谁啊?
(23)不关我们的事。
(24)欢迎自由参观。
(25)某事意义重大。
(26)我都等不及了。
(27)我看到了希望。
(28)决赛要开始了。
(29)已经准备妥当。
(30)午餐准备好了。
(31)注意你的语调。
(32)全都是你功劳。
(33)我和她分手了。
(34)我真是太感动了。
(35)很快就有小孩。

(36)我不想来这儿。
(37)那也无济于事。
(38)我们来收拾他。
(39)惨到无以言表。
(40)(占座)有人了。
(41)立即闭嘴,先生。
(42)我是上了真人秀。
(43)我不配拥有这个。
(44)我们已经很熟了。
(45)我要单身一辈子。
(46)我们的需求量很大。
(47)你现在被指控谋杀。
(48)请让他马上提出来。
(49)你跟她不是有一腿吗?
(50)我们终于能在一起了。
(51)现在回头已来不及了。
(52)我知道我的职责所在。
(53)你觉得她值得信任吗?
(54)他肌肉发达。/他很强壮。
(55)家人对她寄予巨大的希望。
(56)你认为这个女孩适合我吗?
(57)你甩了他?我们彼此甩了对方。
(58)而她,根本不会知道这个秘密。

3.熟读并背诵下列句子。

(1)休会。Meeting adjourned.
(2)我就办。I'm on it.
(3)瞧瞧你。Check you out.
(4)真方便。That's handy.
(5)敬请赐教。I'm listening.
(6)有话直说!Come to the point!
(7)与你何干?What's it to you?
(8)即将开幕!Coming soon!
(9)别纠缠了!Stop badgering!
(10)爱莫能助。Wish I could have helped.
(11)别管闲事。Butt out.
(12)我很难过。I was hurt.
(13)随你的便。Do as you will.
(14)你难住我了。You've got me.
(15)有人来过?Did you have company?

(16)会让你紧张？(↗) Gets you all jittery and nervous？(jittery 神经过敏的)
(17)别板着个脸！Stop pouting！(pout n. & v. 撅嘴、生气)
(18)少来这一套！Save it！
(19)没事，别慌。No fuss.
(20)我都看到了。I see enough.
(21)我想说两句。I just need a word.
(22)别管他！Leave him be.
(23)最近怎么样？What's rocking？
(24)收到，重复。Copy that.
(25)(下棋)将军！King me！
(26)我谁也不帮。I'm not taking anybody's side.
(27)你和我分居。You moving out on me.
(28)她在用电脑。She's on the computer.
(29)老师正忙呢？Teacher is engaged.
(30)我一定要做吗？Do I have to？
(31)已造成了损失？Is the damage done？
(32)那该怎么分工？Who's doing what for that？
(33)真是太失败了！What a loser！
(34)你对他动心了？You hit on him. (↗)
(35)有消息通知你。I'll keep you informed.
(36)你把我弄糊涂。You lost me.
(37)不知怎么开始？How to start this？
(38)听听你的口气。Listen to yourself.
(39)都说些什么呀！What a thing to say！
(40)下辈子投个好胎。On the way to a better life.
(41)我对食物感兴趣。I'm great in food.
(42)你的行装真简便。You pack light.
(43)该我的就是我的。What's mine is mine.
(44)我只是略尽绵力。It's the least I could do.
(45)这是某人在捣鬼。This is somebody's doing.
(46)别跟我来这一套。Don't give me that！
(47)你想怎样就怎样。You can do as much or as little as you want.
(48)谢谢你为我说话。Thank you for your standing up for me.
(49)还没有……消息？Still no word from…？
(50)他越界了，犯规了。He crossed the line.
(51)还没有遇到特别的人？Still no - one special？
(52)你知道那些人的德行。You know how people can be.
(53)现在经济这么不景气。But with the economy being the way it is.
(54)那么你们是未尽全力。Your best is not good enough.
(55)听上去你受了不少罪。Sounds like you went through a lot.

(56)我知道你经历了许多。I know that you've been through a lot.

(57)让我来关心你、珍视你。Let me take you into my heart. Make you special.

(58)不要怕做错,先斩后奏。And for forgiveness, not for permission.

(59)谢谢你挤出时间来陪我。Thank you for your time.

(60)你的循序渐进没什么用。Your subtle approach got us nowhere.

(61)我们怎么会落到这步田地? I wonder how we got that way?

(62)你们家今天发生了许多事。It's a quite day for your family.

(63)我知道这个要求有点过分。I know it's a lot to ask.

(64)这可不是离家独立生活。This is not leaving the nest.

(65)我的替班来了,我下班了。My replacement showed up. I'm done.

(66)亨利人呢?(看见亨利了吗?) Any sign of Henry?

(67)你必须作好最坏的准备。You must prepare for the worst.

(68)这么短的时间,学这么多东西。So much to learn, so little time.

(69)民族风服装真漂亮啊! What a delightful ethnic ensemble! (ensemble 全套的服装)

(70)他们先念完新闻,通报一下交通情况。So they'll finish with news, do a quick traffic update.

(71)在我们最不盼望的时候,那一刻就来了。When we least expect it, the moment comes.

(72)恕我直言,我认为你无法打开他的心结。No offense, but I don't think you gonna get through to him.

(73)现在讲究男女平等,所以让一个粗壮的小气的女孩得到教训是可以的。If feminism means anything, it's okay for a big, mean girl to get her butt kicked.

4.用本单元所学的知识造句。

(1)没有针对你个人,但我从来没有跟我的客户有私人社交。

(2)放轻松! 不过就是个小测试。

(3)救援的黄金72小时已过去,所以取消了该项救援。

(4)别放弃! 你看你已经完成了不少了! 就要成功了。

(5)别唠唠叨叨了! 你话太多了。

(6)做母亲是她的头等大事。

(7)我们可以指望他,他不会使我们失望的。

(8)在长者面前管好你的舌头。

(9)我想放弃这个要求很高的工作。

(10)如果没有得到自己想要的也不要感到失望。

(11)据相关媒体报道,这对皇家新婚夫妇正在塞舌尔群岛享受一个为期十天的旅行。

(12)他低价买进了那些股票。

(13)要把学生是综合能力而不是学习成绩放在第一位。

(14)但灵活性是要付出代价的。

(15)他是个不多话的人,但我们都喜欢他。

(16)详细的说明你在哪,还有你能看见什么。

(17)研究显示,父母离异的孩子更有可能在中学辍学。

(18)我们提醒读者不要对这些发现太较真。

(19)从个人层次的角度来看,这样似乎并不公平,但事情本身就是这样。

(20)真的任何事都行:出门结交新的朋友,学一门陌生的语言,甚至可以是一次蹦极。

(21)挖苦和贬损的言语不应用来教育子女。

(22)他很少提高嗓门和别人说话。

(23)他们想挑你的毛病,所以你要把所有的回答都准备好。

(24)别喝那么多酒。再喝,你的身体会扛不住的。

(25)他犯难了不知哪个是最好的答案。

5. 你能找到更多英语中简洁表达的例证吗?请与大家共同分享本章的学习体会。

(1)动作角色扮演 LARP = Live Action Role - Playing

(2)(喝醉的,极度兴奋的)酒后驾驶 DWI = Driving While Intoxicated

(3)我们的小临时工 our little temp

(4)特别告诉你 F. Y. I. (for you in particular)

(5)Pro 行家;专家:Pro 是 professional 的简称,意思是行家、专家、专业人员,反之则为 amateur 业余爱好者。当我们欲赞美某人水准媲美行家时便可以说他是 pro. 例如:If you want to improve your game, go talk to Brad . He's quite the tennis pro. 假如你想打得更好,去请教布莱德。他是个网球专家。

Chapter 10　Dramatized Expressions

生动表达

一、思路讲解

生动传神的表达,可使谈话变得十分有趣,交流者参与欲望变得更强,交流变得更顺畅、更活泼、更幽默。由于生动传神的表达语言轻巧,画面感极强,对该语言的学习者而言,更容易理解记忆使用。

要做到生动传神的表达,注意遵循以下原则:

(1)用词简单,可入木三分地表达出意境。比如:“浪费时间”,平时我们可以用 waste time 来表达,但请大家看看这个说法“to burn time/烧时间”,既强调了对时间的浪费,也再现出对时间一去不复返的遗憾。

(2)要注意英语国家的历史渊源、文化背景、思维习惯和审美习惯。刚开始学习这种技巧时,要多细心观察,积累语料,使自己的表达不仅生动,还能符合英语的表达习惯,也就是说在具体的语境中,你的表达应该使用什么样的单词,不应该使用什么单词,要做到心中有数,因为并不是所有的你认为可行的表达都能让英语国家的人明白。比如:“闻起来很臭。”这个句子,我们如果要表达生动,可采用比喻的方式“闻起来像臭豆腐一样”,但老外可能理解起来就有点费劲,如果改成“to smell like a cockroach/闻起来像蟑螂”,就容易接受了。中国人说“小可怜虫”,你可不要以为 a little poor worm 这一比喻是个生动传神的表达,此说其实是个 Chinglish, 英文的说法应是 little poor。

(3)多用比喻、夸张、借喻、拟人等修辞手段。“他太野蛮了。/He is such an animal.”,“我被你的美貌俘获。/I'm arrested by your beauty.”, “我又胡说八道了。/My mouth runs away from me again.”。

(4)用生动的方式解决隐晦的内涵。“我见过嘉丽,她跟丈夫分居了。/I just saw Carrie and she's separated.”,“热吻/ big kiss”,“他说了一大段话。/He spoke a quite story.(很明显,该表达的内涵有编故事的嫌疑)”。

(5)对内涵进行更生动的挖掘。“你们两个很相配。/You deserve each other.(值得拥有对方)”,“彻底分手/to clean break(干干净净地了断,没有藕断丝连)”,“强颜欢笑/an artificial smile/a plastic smile(强颜欢笑不就是假笑嘛)”。

(6)英语是一种包容性极强的语言,每年都有时髦的最新的外来语进入英语,如果偶尔能使用该表达来源国的语言,将会让其变得更生动。“友谊地久天长/Auld Lang Syne(苏格兰文)”,“茶点/dim sum(闽粤语)”,“和服/kimono(日语)”,“比萨/pizza(意大利语)”等。

二、案例分析

下面我们用更多的例子来帮助大家理解英语中的生动传神表达,在身临其境的感觉中体会语言描述的魅力,为大家提高口语表达能力提供一些较为鲜活的语料。

(1) an aha moment 顿悟阶段

当我们经过冥思苦想,最终有了好念头时,我们会睁大双眼,面带胜利的微笑,口中惊呼"Aha",然后奔走相告"I got it!I got it!/我知道了!我知道!"。最令人称奇的是不管是中文还是英文,顿悟的一刹那都发出同样的"Aha!"之音。

(2) lip singing 假唱

掏钱买票看演唱会,最令人气愤的就是歌手的"假唱"行为,什么是假唱,就是和着音乐带只动嘴唇,这是"红果果"的抢钱!

(3) take-home pay 实得工资

"实得工资"就是扣除税收、房贷、水电气费等,你最终揣进腰包的钱,也就是你"拿回家"的钱。

(4) Where's the fire? 发生什么事了?

从字面上直译是"哪里发生火灾了?",当别人十万火急地大呼大叫,而我们认为没理由这么急的时候,就可以用这句俏皮话来挖苦对方,事实上并且不是真的发生火灾了。

(5) How are your honeydew melons today? 你们今天的哈密瓜如何?

这句话并不是在问"你们的哈密瓜今天过得好不好?",而是问今天的哈密瓜品质如何。

到菜市场去买菜,总会和老板聊两句,看看今天的果蔬质量如何。

(6) I'm losing you. 我听不见你讲话。

现在很多人都有手机。用手机通话时常因为信号不好就听不见对方的声音了。在这种时刻,你就可以说"I'm losing you./我听不到你的声音了。"

(7) to have the ball at one's feet 通向成功的有利条件

这个表达肯定是喜欢运动的人士发明的,ball 就是"球",该词组直译为"球在某人脚上",球都在里的脚边了,不就是喻指"机会来了",或"通向成功的有利条件"。

(8) to cram 临阵磨枪

学生最大的烦恼及挑战,无非就是一堆考试,"为了考试",英文叫"cram";"为了某个考试猛看书"的词组是"to cram for"。各种考试的说法:"quiz/小考";"pop quiz/临时考、随堂考";"test/测验";"exam/大考";"midterm/期中考";"final/期末考";"entrance exam/入学考"。

(9) to dash the cup from sb.'s lips 夺走某人的所属之物

字面意思为"夺走某人嘴里的杯子",比喻"使某人不能获得快到手的东西"或"使某人的希望或意图落空"。

(10) He's got love handle. 他有爱把手。(腰部有赘肉)

love handle 直译是"爱把手",指腰间赘肉。当男士拥抱女士的时候,双手会自然落在女士的腰际。就是说,男人拥抱自己所爱的人的时候,都会用手搂住爱人的软腰。倘若女人太瘦,那就不盈一握——男士摸到的尽是骨头。虽则骨感美人是现如今的时尚,但那只是给人以视觉享受。所以,女士还是要适当有点脂肪,以便给爱人更好的手感。再看看"spare tire/腰部多余的肉;游泳圈",此外,spare tire 还可以用来形容"多余的人,工作无效率的人"。而中文的

"啤酒肚",美国俚语是用 beer belly 或 beer gut 来形容。

(11)Boys will be boys! 本性难移!

直译就是"男孩就是男孩!",意为"男孩就是这样,本性难移!"

(12)My cell phone battery's dead. 我的手机没电了。

"没电了"不就是"电池死掉了,电池没有了。"

(13)I am up to my ears. 吃得太饱了。

be up to my ears 就是指食物涨到了耳朵了,是不是"吃得太饱了"呢?

(14)It was nothing more than a boneheaded mistake. 那不过是个低级错误而已。

bone head 是"笨蛋、傻瓜"的意思,所以 boneheaded mistake 就是"低级错误"。

(15)It's not just a case of a marriage gone sour. 那可不仅仅是感情出问题的事儿。

中国人说"感情出了问题"也说"感情变味了",所以这个的 go sour 就很形象了。

(16)I'll right by your side. 我绝对全力支持你。

有时候哪怕就是有个人坐在身边,什么也不说,什么也不做,这也是一种安慰和支持。"我来帮你。/I got your back."也就是"背后鼎力相助"。

(17)You gave me a big speech. 你给我上了一课。

这儿的"上课"不是一般意义的上课,而是通过"晓之以理,动之以情"的方式让人明白道理,故请注意其内涵。

(18)to do a little courting 献点殷勤

courting 是"求婚"的意思,"求婚"不是得说好听的来打动对方,所以你会觉得这个表达很有意思。

(19)a sudden burst of courage 突然想逞强

"burst/突然发作","a sudden burst of courage"就是"逞一时之勇"。延展记忆:"一时冲动/a sudden burst of passion"。

(20)The evidence is mounting. 证据越来越多。

说到"越来越多",大家最熟悉用得最多的就是 more and more,这儿介绍一个形象的表达:mount 是动词,"增加、上升"的意思,该句用正在进行时,将这个意思表达得更生动。

(21)"Let's be friends" speech 友好宣言

大家仔细体会这个表达方式,你会发现这个方法会让表达更生动更简单。再试试:"典型的事不关己态度/ typical "not in my backyard" attitude。

(22)You can take your mind off Janice. 你会忘记珍妮丝的。

"take one's mind off sb."就是"心思不在某人身上",当心思不在某人身上,不就是"忘记"吗? 延展记忆:"你在想什么? 有啥心思? /Something on your mind?","你在想什么? /What did have in your mind?","他有很多心事。/He had so much on his mind.","我会考虑的。/I'll keep it in mind."。

(23)一大串问题 a bunch of questions

a bunch of 表示"一束、一堆、一群",用它来修饰 questions,让人一下有了画面感,再比如"一堆专业术语/a bunch of buzzwords"。延展记忆:"花哨的术语/ fancy lingo","滔滔不绝地说一些术语/to spout off a bunch of terms","一大群长颈鹿/a journey of giraffes"。

(24)随叫随到 be always on call

有部名为《On Call 36 小时》香港电视连续剧,讲的是 36 小时随时待命的医生的工作和生活，也许对你记忆这个词组有帮助。

（25）a million times 很多次

中国人强调说了很多遍，一般是“我都跟你说了一百遍了”，看来还不够，英国人强调得更厉害：百万遍。

（26）She does have the PHD in tending to kids. 她照顾一群孩子很有一套。

to have the PHD in tending to kids 意为“在照顾孩子方面拿过博士学位”，这句话虽有些夸张，但却不乏幽默。

（27）We're on the same page. 我们一条心。

be on the same page 直译为“在同一页面上”，意为“齐心协力”。延展记忆：“很高兴又齐心协力了。/It's nice to be back on the same page.”，“我们意见一致。/We're on the same page.”。

（28）It's like déjà vu. 感觉似曾相识。

“déjà vu”是法语，意为“见到过”。

（29）I just slipped it out. 我说漏嘴了。

“说漏嘴”就是“没注意说出了不该说的事”。而 to slip out 指“悄悄溜出去”。这里就是利用了 to slip out 强调“悄悄地，不被察觉地”意思。延展记忆：“口误/a slip of tongue”，笔误/a slip of pen，“我忘记了。/It slipped my mind.”。

（30）mouthwatering food 垂涎欲滴的美食

一看 mouthwatering 这词就十分有感觉，这东西太让人有食欲了。再复习一下“手抓食物/finger food”。

（31）to play girlfriend card 打女朋友这张牌，说有女朋友

也就是说拿某事来做幌子，逃避其不想做的事。比如：“打学习这张牌，逃避做家务 /play study card to avoid housework”。

（32）I'm in the middle of the thing. 我正忙着呢。

be in the middle of sth. 的字面意思为：“正处于某事之中”，那就表示“正忙着……事情”。延展记忆：“让某人左右为难/to put sb. in the middle of sth.”。

（33）housewarming present(s)乔迁小礼物

housewarming 从字面意思讲就是让家温馨起来，housewarming present(s) 这样的礼物特别贴心。延展记忆“喧闹打斗/roughhousing”。

（34）zero relationship 没有关系

知道这些时髦的词吗？“零容忍”、“零距离”等，所以“zero”这里生动地表达这种强烈的意愿。延展记忆：“绝不姑息/zero tolerance”，“没有联系/zero contact”。

（35）It's foggy to me now. 我记不清楚了。

“记不清”也就是一切都是模模糊糊的，就好像雾的感觉。

（36）the next to impossible 很难的事

the next to impossible 仅次于不可能的程度，不就是“很难”吗？

（37）I think of you as the man with all the answers. 我总觉得你无所不知。

with all the answers 这就是典型的“天上知一半，地上全知”的状态。

（38）He is in the wind. 还未联系上他。

“还未联系上某人”用“sb. is in the wind.”来表达，生动描写出“这人”行踪不定，不知在

哪儿飘荡着。

(39) My mind plays tricks on me. 我出现了幻觉。

"one's mind plays tricks on sb."思维跟某人开玩笑或捉弄某人,不就是"出现幻觉"。

(40) a woman of loose morals 水性杨花

这里最关键是 loose 用得好,该词是指"宽松的;散漫的;不牢固的;不精确的",比如"不准确的描述/loose description","一分一秒都浪费不起。/There's not a minute to loose."。

(41) trophy wife 花瓶一样的老婆

这里的"花瓶"怎么理解?摆在那儿好看不中用的东西。那么"吃软饭的老公"呢?对!trophy husband。

(42) Housing market's in the toilet. 房地产市场太糟了。

这句用是很形象,但怎么都觉得有点"过",恐怕也只有口语表达中才能使用。

(43) a mama's boy 听话的孩子

乖孩子的标准是什么?就是要听大人的话,尤其是妈妈的话。

(44) She's behind this. 她捣的鬼。

有人捣鬼,那他一定是在背后使坏,所以这句话的表达简单生动。

(45) to swallow pride 放下尊严(架子)

不管这个"pride/尊严"是吞掉也好,放在兜里也好,扔掉也好,都形象地表达了"不端架子"这个概念。

(46) I'm an open book. 我是一个坦率的人。

坦率的人就像本翻开的书,让人一目了然。

(47) You look like a million bucks before taxes. 你看起来真是满面春风。

中国人有句话:"见钱眼开",我们姑且不去理会这个词的深层含义,单凭字面的描述就知道,见到钱,人的心情是愉快的,尤其是没有扣税之前的钱,那钱叫一个多呀!咋能不高兴呢?

(48) Your naiveté is adorable. 你真是天真到家了。

这句话明显带有宠溺的语气,其字面意思就是"你天真得可爱",可以对子女或亲朋好友说这句话。

(49) Dump this to you. 向你发泄。

dump 有"倒垃圾"的意思,某人向你吐苦水,用 dump 是十分贴切的。

(50) The first chick lands with a thud. 出师不利啊。

thud 是指"砰"的一声,这句话字面意思是说小鸟第一次学飞行失败,"砰"的一声掉在了地上。

(51) You're full of ideas. 你想法很多。

我们形容一个人"想法很多",就说"你满脑子都是……的想法",也就是脑子里"充满"了各种"奇思妙想"。

(52) be over the rainbow 高兴极了

据说看见彩虹的人会幸福,那"彩虹之上"不得幸福死啊!

(53) Let's not play sad-life poker. 大家别装可怜了。

to play poker 就是"打牌"的意思,中国人也说"打感情牌"之类的话。

(54) Your eyes look a little glassy. 眼睛也有点泛泪光。

这句话不仅表达生动,也体现了说话人善于观察生活:当人悲伤想哭时,眼眶里的泪水闪着玻璃一样的光亮。

(55) a doormat 门垫;受气包

“门垫”千人踩,万人踏,不是“受气包”又是什么?

(56) to nip sth. in the bud 消灭某物在萌芽期

这里的“nip”是“剪断”的意思,在“bud/花蕾”时就消灭掉,正是消灭某物在萌芽状态中。

(57) Stop sniffing each other. 别再相互试探了。

sniff 是指狗用鼻子到处嗅,这里利用这个单词生动地描写了双方试探的动作,极具画面感。

(58) I won't burden you with something. 我不让你操心。

“操心”就是让你为某事背上心理负担。

(59) I've a mountain to get through. 我简直应接不暇了。

I've a mountain to get through. 意为“我还有一座山要翻越”,表明还有“山”一样多的事要做。

(60) to spread vicious gossip 传毒舌八卦

“毒舌”就是指“用词恶毒阴辣”,与“vicious/恶毒”如出一辙。延展记忆:“劲爆八卦/ delicious gossip”。

三、实战演练

(1) be like taking a candy from a baby 很容易做的事

虽然此方法不值得提倡,但不可否认表达十分形象。注意中国人形容“做某事容易”,喜欢用“囊中取物”。

例如: Winning that bet with him was like taking a candy from a baby. 要赢得和他打的那个赌很容易。

(2) high and low 到处

试想想,你找东西是不是上下左右全方位搜索?这个词组常与 search, hunt 和 look 等表示“寻找”的动词连用。

例如: We searched high and low but we couldn't find it anywhere. 我们到处找,可就是找不到。

(3) to hit the ceiling 大发脾气

这个短语很形象,表示“怒气恨不能把屋顶捅个窟窿”。比喻大发雷霆。

例如: When my father finds out that I flunked math again, he's going to hit the ceiling. 当父亲知道我数学又没有考及格时,他会气得吐血。

(4) to ring a bell 唤起一点记忆

当我们想到一个好主意时,通常脑袋上方就出现一个灯泡或是响一声铃声,意思就类似中文所说的灵光一闪,灵光乍现,因为一闪而逝的想法,所以可能只是片断的模糊回忆。因而“ring a bell”这个短语是指人“想到……;似曾相识;有点熟悉”的意思。

例如: That name doesn't ring a bell. 我记不起那个名字。

(5) on a shoestring (budget) 低成本

shoestring 意思是指“鞋带”,其特点是小而细,后来用来表示“节俭,节省”。

例如: Frank Miller originally started his business on only a shoestring. 弗兰克·米勒是以小资本创业的。

(6)to read sb. like a book 彻底了解某人

这个词组直译为"看某人就像看一本书一样清清楚楚",即"对某人非常了解",包括其动机和思想等。

例如: Clothes or no clothes, I can read you like a book. 不管你怎样伪装,我都能看透你。

(7)to push the panic button 恐慌

button 是指"操纵门铃、机器开关等的按钮",push the button 就是"按动按钮"。panic 意思是"恐慌;惊惶"。push the panic button 直译是"按动了恐慌的按钮",引申意思是"恐慌;极度紧张"。

例如: When she discovered that the house was on fire, Mary pushed the panic button. 当发现这栋房子起火后,玛丽非常惊慌。

(8)be up to one's ears 深深卷入;深陷

我们可以想象这样的画面:一个人深陷沼泽,最后只剩下耳朵露在外面,所以该词组用来形容"深深卷入",非常形象。

例如: He was up to his ears in the conspiracy. 他参与密谋。

(9)My brain's too fried for that. 我用脑过度。

fried 是 fry 的过去式及过去分词,当形容词可表"油煎的;油炸的";也用来形容"人过度疲劳;累过头了"。

例如: My brain's too fried for anything. I'm just going to bed. 我的脑袋已经累到无法思考了。我只想上床睡觉。

(10)be on the blink /fritz 故障

blink 是"眨眼"的意思是。试想,如果眼睛眨个不停,视线自然不清楚,看不到东西,就是好像是眼睛出现故障一般,因此,on the blink 或 on the fritz 就表示有"毛病;出问题了"。

例如: My stereo is on the blink. 我的音响出故障了。

(11)to scream at the top of one's lungs 竭尽某人的力气大叫;声嘶力竭的呼叫

at the top of one's lungs 是指"用尽所有的肺活量",scream at the top of one's lungs 则表示"拼了命地大叫"该词组中的 lungs 也可替换为 voice。

例如: Why is he screaming at the top of his lungs? What happened? 他干嘛在拼命地大叫?发生了什么事了?

(12)to drive sb. up a wall 把某人逼上绝路

车是不能开到墙上去的,那么谁能 drive you up a wall 无疑是个"惹你讨厌的人"!

例如: My mom is driving me up a wall! She won't ever let me stay out late. 母亲不让我在外面待得晚,让我感到非常讨厌。

(13)to wake up and smell the coffee 认清现实

这个短语非常形象。wake up 表示"醒来",to smell the coffee 表示"闻咖啡的香味",本来就"醒过来了",再加上"闻到提神醒脑的咖啡味道",不就是"完全清醒"的意思吗?

例如:A: Tom can still become a better man. B: Wake up and smell the coffee. He's never going to change. A: 汤姆会变好的。B: 醒醒吧,他永远都那样。

(14)to itch for sth. 想得到某物

itch 是"发痒"的意思,这里可不是"皮肤痒"而是"心痒痒",也就是"渴望得到某物"的意思。

例如:Joan's been itching for a cat. Let's get her one. 琼想要一只猫,我们给她弄一只吧。

(15)be in the dark 不知、蒙在鼓里

in the dark 就是"黑暗中",黑灯瞎火,啥都看不清,啥都不知道。该词组一般与 keep, leave, 或 be 等动词连用,其后接 about sth. ,或 concerning sth. 。比如:"活得稀里糊涂/live in the dark"。

例如:Don't keep me in the dark next time. 下次可不要再瞒我了。

(16)be older than dirt 非常陈旧

dirt 表示"污垢;灰尘",所以这个短语说"比灰尘还陈旧",说明有很久没有人打扫了,已经非常陈旧了。

例如:That building is older than dirt. It's been here a long time. 那幢楼非常老旧,它已经矗立在这儿很长时间了。

(17)to get cracking 加速赶工;开始工作

crack 是"鞭打的声音",如果你鞭打马儿,它就会跑得更快,因此引申为"加速赶工"。另外,crack 也可表"打开",因此 get cracking 亦常用来形容开始工作。

例如:I'd better get cracking on my work, or I'll be here all night. 我最好快马加鞭完成我的工作,不然就得整晚待在这里了。

(18)to beat the pants off sb. 完全打败某人;使某人一败涂地

beat 是"打败",pants 是"裤子",当人们打赌却没有赌注时,便会用自身的服装来当作赌本,如果可以让对方输到全身衣服脱个精光,就是"完全打败对方"了。所以这个短语就是用来称赞在游戏中把"某人打得一败涂地"。

例如: He must be a champ or something. He beat the pants off me without even trying. 他一定是冠军之类的。他不费吹灰之力就让我一败涂地。

(19)be on the rocks 没有希望了,无法挽救了,完蛋了。看到这个词组,就会想到船触礁,无法开动的画面。

例如:Within a year their marriage was on the rocks, because his wife had unfaithful intentions. 不到一年,他们夫妻关系就濒于破裂,因为他妻子有了外心。

(20)a hardliner 持强硬路线者

hard line 的意思是"强硬路线"。hardliner 则表示"采取强硬路线者;不肯妥协的人"。这个单词常用来形容在社会上有权有势的人,表示其立场绝不轻易改变,作风相当强势。

例如:The new mayor is a hardliner on the issue of public safety. 这位新市长在公共安全方面态度十分强硬。

(21)a yes-man 唯唯诺诺的人

顾名思义就是"只懂得说 yes,而没有主见的人"。

例如:Jack had served as a yes-man for so long that he was incapable of making any management decisions by himself. 杰克长久以来都是唯唯诺诺的人,因此,他无法自己决定事情。

(22)from hand to mouth 现挣现吃的;仅够糊口的

常与动词 live 连用,其中的 from 可省略。另外,from hand to hand 与其形式相近,表示"从一人之手转到另一人之手"或"经转手",切勿混淆。

例如:Being out of a job, he lived from hand to mouth. 他因失业而勉强度日。

(23) kit and caboodle 全部

kit 表示"衣物和装备",而 caboodle 意思是"全部事物",两个合在一起表示"全部事物"。

例如:Henry, that man over there wants to buy everything we are selling in the yard sale. What do you think the whole kit and caboodle should go for? 亨利,那边的那个人要买我们工厂正贱卖的每样东西。你认为所有这些东西值多少钱?

(24) to handle a situation with kid gloves 用温和或圆通的手段处理某事

kid gloves 是"小山羊皮手套"的意思,小山羊皮的特点是:皮板轻薄,手感柔软,光滑而细腻。带上这种优质皮做的手套一定是轻柔、温和地处理黄金珠宝文物等高级的物质。

例如:The boss is angry now. You' d better handle the situation with kid gloves. 老板现在正在气头上,你可要小心行事。

(25) You must wean yourself from smoking. 你一定要戒烟。

英文中"断奶"是 wean,比如 to wean a baby from the breast,指的是"给婴儿断奶",这里引申为"戒除恶习"。

例如:但当你的信心增强后,他就会让你摆脱这些依赖。But as you grow in faith, he will wean you from these dependencies.

(26) The doctor says I am the picture of good health. 医生说我的身体状况非常好。

picture 表示"图画",在这里是指"事情的眉目,大概情况"。picture 也是个活跃词汇,请看,"put sb. in the picture /了解;使某人了解实情;把现在的情况以图像的形式展示给某人,使他明白真相","Are you in the picture now? /你现在知道咋回事了吗?","我只是从大局出发。/I' m just thinking about the whole picture. ","get the picture/了解某事"。

例如:A: There aren' t enough parking places here. B: I get the picture. I' ll park across the street. A:这里没有足够的停车位置。B:知道了,我会把车停到对面。

(27) motor mouth 长舌妇;多嘴男

直译为"马达嘴",这无疑能再现出"说话滔滔不绝,没完没了"的意味。

例如:Dick is a nice guy, but he' s such a motor mouth that people avoid talking to him. 迪克是个好人,但他那张滔滔不绝的嘴让人们对他敬而远之。

(28) to get a flying start 开门红

a flying start 意为"迅速起步,迅速发展"。

例如:Our company got a flying start when it opened to business: we got three big orders during the first week of opening. 开业时我们公司取得了开门红,第一周便获得了三大笔订单。

(29) a big baby 幼稚的人

baby 是指"婴儿",比如:"婴儿肥/baby fat","乳牙/baby teeth"等。big baby 是指身体成熟但心智不成熟的人。

例如:He certainly was being a big baby when he threw things around the room just because he didn' t get what he wanted. 因为得不到想要的东西,就在房里乱扔东西,他这种举动实在很幼稚。

(30) You are out of options. 你别无选择。

out of options 就是"没得选,没有选项了,黔驴技穷了"。

例如:We' re running out of options! 我们无计可施了。

(31) be rock solid 非常充分

怎样才能生动表达出"非常充分"之意? rock 是"岩石",坚如磐石,表明坚实,引申为"十分充分”。延展记忆:“充分理由/solid reason”。

例如: My case is rock solid. 我铁证如山。

(32)Put this behind us. 让我们忘记这件事。

“忘记某事”就是把“某事抛到脑后/to put sth. behind sb.”。

例如: Happiness will return so that eventually all of those sad and painful memories maybe put behind you. 幸福会回来的,你们也终将忘掉所有悲伤和痛苦的记忆。

(33)to have the last word 强辩到底,有决定权,最后说一句

在争辩之中,有些人总是不服输,老要说最后那句话,就像一只好斗的公鸡一般。

例如:I don't appreciate people who always have to have the last word on everything. 我不欣赏啥事上都要去拍板的人。

(34)to rub sb.'s nose into it 不断地提醒某人

“rub /揉、搓、摩擦”,rub sb.'s nose into sth. 指“不断地提醒某人曾犯的过错”,有小题大做之意。延展记忆:“rub your success in our faces /向我们好一番炫耀你的成功”。

例如: She rubbed my nose into it so much, I couldn't forget. 她不断地提醒我这事,我想忘都难。

(35)You don't have to be Shakespeare. 没有让你当大文豪。

“大文豪”用 Shakespeare 代替,既生动又容易理解。

例如: Don't push yourself. You don't have to be Liu Xiang. 别逼自己。没有让你当运动健将。

四、巩固练习

1. 下面这些词组表达生动有趣,请试着说出其中文意思。

(1)joyride
(2)ass dial
(3)air kick
(4)to blow in
(5)to aim high
(6)busybody
(7)caveman
(8)sleepyhead
(9)stage fright
(10)born leader
(11)fast money
(12)angry note
(13)a born liar
(14)ghost town
(15)girls' time
(16)in one's book

(17) to eat the cost
(18) off the clock
(19) in plain sight
(20) to pick up pace
(21) lucky escape
(22) criminal record
(23) breaking news
(24) tight schedule
(25) shallow people
(26) top of the list
(27) to roll one's eyes
(28) Mr. Popularity
(29) long-suffering
(30) broken system
(31) a sneak preview
(32) reading glasses
(33) to get a clear head
(34) a little rounder
(35) to have a hand in sth.
(36) to take your bow
(37) suggestion box
(38) full cooperation
(39) promising start
(40) be on store shelf
(41) to ruin one's game
(42) to take a wild guess
(43) a model employee
(44) be out of the hole
(45) altitude sickness
(46) a baby whisperer
(47) all-round genius
(48) her-and-his sinks
(49) perfect timing
(50) to waste sb.'s heart
(51) be history-sensitive
(52) words on the yard
(53) a face like thunder
(54) to uproot a family
(55) depressing talking
(56) to divide and conquer

(57) be dead on one's feet
(58) last-minute decision
(59) rough neighborhood
(60) aggressive stranger
(61) in one's twisted mind
(62) be under magic power
(63) be open to suggestions
(64) be under house arrest
(65) to give sb. free pass on sth.
(66) mother & daughter talk
(67) to make a mountain out of sth.
(68) be back by popular demand
(69) be on one's best behavior
(70) to save oneself to marriage
(71) to build one's better nature
(72) glowing recommendation
(73) to stick to sb. like glue
(74) after much soul-searching
(75) When all is said and done…
(76) far-reaching consequence
(77) a life of hiding and running
(78) to open one's mouth about sth.
(79) to get the bottom of the thing
(80) to come off with flying colors
(81) to thaw one's chilly relationship
(82) a couple in romantic embrace
(83) to put himself through the college

2. 试体会下面句子中画线部分的生动表达，并说出句子的中文意思。

(1) I am on top of it.
(2) She is appealing.
(3) You asked for it.
(4) You froze me out.
(5) to give sb. a full story.
(6) I drop the attitude.
(7) You canceled on me.
(8) You are in the soup.
(9) Keep up your energy!
(10) Love is not my friend.
(11) You are disappearing.

(12) You are so tight-lipped.
(13) This is one-in-a-million.
(14) Everything was cooked.
(15) He always plays by rules.
(16) I am a man of no service.
(17) I have the deciding voice.
(18) You saw me for who I was.
(19) You are worth everything.
(20) I'm not playing your game.
(21) I'd look on the sunny side.
(22) What a charming surprise!
(23) My patience is wearing thin.
(24) I really can't spare the time.
(25) You are not pushing yourself.
(26) You make my life a living hell.
(27) But I think he's in a deep hole.
(28) He never completely let me in.
(29) What a night for people to feed off.
(30) Maybe you married the wrong woman.
(31) Clearly, we have to be diplomatic and crafty.
(32) I gave you the Bible in your own tongue.
(33) Cell phones are lifelines to kids nowadays.
(34) Men have always thrown themselves at you.
(35) I thought you gave him his marching orders.
(36) Everyone was dying to meet her new boyfriend.
(37) If you lie to your teacher, you will be in the hot seat.
(38) My brother is ill-tempered, and always stirs up trouble.
(39) She seems to be very good at dancing attendances on her superiors.
(40) Sam decided to cut class and spend the afternoon swimming at the lake.
(41) After Lisa moved to a new house, she made friends with her neighbors in no time.
(42) First he had that accident and then he went bankrupt. He had certainly been down on his luck lately.

3. 熟读并背诵下列句子，体会生动表达的精妙。

(1) I'll see you out. 我送你出去。
(2) It's by the book. 按章行事。
(3) I'm running late. 我还有事。
(4) It's heart-stopping. 令人叹为观止。
(5) Issue's on the table. 事情已经说开了。
(6) I don't have all day. 我没时间了。

(7)I gave him my word. 我答应了他。

(8)She's such a martyr. 她很有牺牲精神。(martyr n. 烈士:为正义事业而牺牲的人)

(9)They twist your words. 他们曲解你的话。

(10)How screwed are you? 你们有多惨?

(11)Who picked up pieces? 谁来收拾这个烂摊子?

(12)I am in back and forth. 我很矛盾。

(13)Let me enjoy my denial. 就让我自欺欺人一会儿吧。

(14)That's really a last minute. 真的很急。

(15)I'm such a muddle head. 我真糊涂。

(16)He's up to the ears in debt. 他债台高筑。

(17)That's my pleasure reading. 这是我的课外读物。

(18)My mother hijacked my day. 我母亲霸占了我一天。

(19)Did he have a mask and a gun? 这不是明抢吗?

(20)Our skills are second to none. 我们的水平可谓是举世无双。

(21)I know this issue up and down. 我知道怎么做。

(22)It's like being right on the field. 颇有身临其境之感。

(23)I put you in an awful situation. 我让你难堪了。

(24)Our boss is a hard nut to crack. 我们的老板是个难缠的人。

(25)Forgive me if I'm casting a gloom. 请原谅我扫了兴。

(26)There's nothing that can be done. 为时已晚。

(27)I fed the flames of your little spat. 我火上浇油了。

(28)If I stay here, I keep the story alive. 只要我在这里,流言就不会消失。

(29)It's a snatched moment of happiness. 这是偷得浮生半日闲。(snatched vt. 夺得;抽空做)

(30)Time to take the lid off the cookie jar. 是该揭秘的时候了。

(31)Aren't we getting ahead of ourselves? 咱们是不是有点操之过急?

(32)But I don't want the wedding to sink her. 但我不想让婚礼累垮她。

(33)He's making a problem where none exists. 他真是太小题大做了。

(34)Thanks for letting me get that off my chest. 谢谢你听我吐苦水。

(35)Everybody's trying to throw him curve balls. 大家都对他旁敲侧击。

(36)I picked the man I love over you——my friend. 我只能重色轻友了。

(37)We have an agreement to keep things casual. 我们说好要随缘的。

(38)You seem to have been slaving away for hours. 你已经埋头苦干了几个小时了。

(39)Do you think I should sell the sizzle or the steak? 我该卖牛皮的滋滋声还是牛排呢?(外在风格还是内在风格)

(40)Don't be a man who will bite the hand that feeds you. 别做恩将仇报之人。

(41)The war's reaching its long fingers into this village. 战争的魔爪伸到了这个村庄。

(42)She has an hourglass figure./She's got a curvy figure. 她的身材玲珑有致。/她曲线玲珑。

(43)Even at this sad hour, your words are music to my ears. 即使在这伤心的时刻,您的话也

十分入耳。

(44) Then please don't spread the word of my incompetence. 那就拜托别跟其他人提起我这糟糕的枪法。

(45) She was off work for a while, but now she's back on her feet. 她请了几天假,现在已经恢复了。

(46) The letter was passed from hand to hand until all had read it. 那封信几经传阅,大家都读过了。

(47) Clearly, I have been managed and steered by an expert hand. 我显然一直被幕后高手操纵着。

4. 用本单元所学的知识造句。

(1)他这人就是外向,交朋友对他来讲是轻松容易的事。

(2)我们到处寻找一个居住条件好的地方,但最后还是留在了老房子里。

(3)妻子可能会因为丈夫忘了他们的结婚纪念日而勃然大怒。

(4)我记不得叫这个名字的人了,可又好像能隐约回忆起来。

(5)不用担心,他会教你三招如何用低预算过高水准生活。

(6)别紧张,时间多的是。

(7)会计部门的电脑总是出故障,导致账单不能及时支付。

(8)参加这样的会议我简直觉得无聊。

(9)许多事已经改变许多,你最好能看清事实。

(10)大多数人渴望令人激动的事。

(11)她还被蒙在鼓里,这件事她一点都不知道。

(12)我们没有时间可浪费了,让我们赶快行动吧。

(13)自从互联网泡沫爆破了以后,这公司就一直困难重重。

(14)不用问他的意见。他是个没有主心骨的人。

(15)她只有一份临时工,只能勉强糊口。

(16)中午以前,我要你把你所有的东西从这搬出去。

(17)她害羞敏感,请你善待她。

(18)杰克真能说,我根本插不上嘴。

(19)我们的假期一开始十分顺利:天气晴朗,火车准点。

(20)你只有在不得已的情况下才能用致命武力。

(21)在任何争论中总是得他最后说了算。

(22)过去一年的苦难和失败已被抛在脑后。

(23)你一直都有信心,这是个板上钉钉的事情吗?

5. 你能找到更多生动表达的例证吗?请与大家共同分享本章的学习体会。

Chapter 11　Regular Expressions
常用表达

一、思路讲解

“常用表达”是指“常用口头语”，或简称为“口头惯用语”，也可叫作像 money 一样使用频繁的“口头禅”。什么是“口头惯用语”？就是说话时经常不自觉地说出来的词句。你最常说的英语口头语是什么？如果不提这个问题，估计很多人都不会觉得自己说英语有固定的口头用语：有的人在表示惊讶时，常说“Oh, my God!”，或“Oh, my boy!”，还有更简单的“Oh, my!”；也有的人教养好，经常用礼貌的话语回应别人，“Thank you!”，“It's my pleasure!”等不离嘴；还有的人甚至连 Language Filler 也有常用的表达，比如“Let me think.”，“OK, OK.”，“How to say?”等。

“口头惯用语”是一种司空见惯却又别具一格的语言现象，具有高频复现和脱口而出的特点，频率是促使语言发生变化的神奇推手，在高频输出并成为口头惯用语的过程中，有些话语的语义得到强化。“口头惯用语”最大的好处是对话语表达过程中衔接与连贯的期待，是开启或转换话题，控制或流转话语的需要。

本章所探讨的英语口头惯用语，我们更愿意把其内涵理解得更广泛些，只要是人们在交流过程中经常使用到的，脱口而出的，结构相对固定的词、词组或句子，我们统统归入此类。虽然是常用口头语，但对于英语学习者来讲，还是需要积累、分析、消化、吸收、实践，有些特点还得牢记。常用的口头语依据说话人身份、性别、年龄、职业，交流语境，交流话题等不同会略有差异，但大致是一样的，还应注意英语常用口头语的以下特点：

(1)结构简单，朗朗上口，有些甚至只有一两个单词，比如：“Bingo!”，“Sure thing.”。

(2)结构和形式约定俗成，已经相对固定，不要拆开分析，要整体记忆。比如：“You bet!”。

(3)常用口语表达依据语境也要做出相应的调整，比如：“太美了！太好了！”，一般情况下可使用“Great!”，但对高质量的文艺演出，观众一般会欢呼“Bravo!”，而看到美女，却使用“Gorgeous!”，对美景，人们惊叹“Marvelous!”。

(4)因身份、性别、职业、年龄、情景等不同，常用表达也会发生变化，比如：说食物好吃，小孩可说“Yummy!”，而成年人说这个词就会显得十分别扭。

二、案例分析

下面我们用更多具体的例子来帮助大家理解英语中的常用口语表达，在案例分析中，我们会对大家理解和记忆这些语料提供建议，同时也适时提供该表达使用语境，让学习者少走弯路。记住，下面的语料都是常用表达的例子，这点在分析中就勿用赘言了。

(1) This is not the point. 这不是问题的关键。

“关键、要点”如果你想用 key point 表达，就变成了中文式英语，因为 point 本身就有“要点的"意思,另外,这也是固定结构。延展记忆:"你想说什么? /What's your point?","他的主意真不错! /He does make a good point! ","说重点。/ Just make the point. ","你什么意思? / What's your point?"。

(2)What's that worth? 有什么意义?

worth 表示"价值",也就是说"做这事价值何在?"。一般用在提醒对方不要做傻事,万事多加思考。

(3)I'm done with him. 我和他分手了。

be done with 表示"完全结束","与……不再有关系"的意思。表示"某人与某人分手"这个结构比较简单,也常被使用。延展记忆:"已经结束了。/That's done. "。

(4)You are sweet. 你真关心人;你很讨人喜欢。

这句"甜言蜜语"在美式英语中的出现率之高,据"个人经验",仅次于 I love you。人家说"礼多人不怪",经常赞美别人,你也会有很多意外的惊喜。

(5)Don't trouble yourself! 别自寻烦恼!

替别人分忧解难的时候,这句话很管用。

(6)Dinner is served. 开始上菜了。(餐点开始供应了)

说这句话时,就是招呼宾朋就座的意思。也可用在提醒餐饮供应的时候。

(7)Do you have an appointment? 有预约吗?

当你有事上律师事务所,或身染小恙上医院时,或因业务要见公司主管等情况时,常被问到这句话,你的回答一般是"Yes. I'm…. I have an appointment with sb. at…",因为"无事不登三宝殿"嘛。

(8)What's up with you? 你怎么了?

当发现有人不舒服或脸色不对时,表现你关心的第一句话就是 What's up? 或 What's up with you? 这时也可说 What's happening ? 或 What's going on ? 这个结构也可以用来表示对别人做的事或表现不满意。What's up? 若用于一般见面问候时,可表示"有什么新鲜事?"。

(9)May all be seated! 各位请坐!

招呼大家落座的比较简洁的说法。

(10)You did the best you would. 你尽力了。

当别人对所做的事情为达到预期的效果而深感遗憾是,这是最好的让别人从此事中抽身出来的劝慰方式。

(11)Are you enjoying yourself? 玩得愉快吗?

如果有最常用口语表达排行榜,这句话也是上榜的句子。延展记忆:"祝你吃得愉快! / Enjoy your dinner!"。

(12)I have no idea. 我找不到头绪。(我不知道。)

这句话比 I don't know. 说的时间还多,那是因为它比 I don't know. 显得委婉一些,而且总说 I don't know. 似乎也太土了些,还可以说 I have no idea. 或者 I don't have a clue…延展记忆:"I have no idea what you have said. /不知道你说了什么。""I don't have the slightest idea…/我一点也不知道……"等。

(13)What's that about? 怎么回事?

发现问题后说出的第一句话还有"What's up/ the matter/ wrong?"等。

(14)It's a long story. 说来话长(一言难尽)。

当别人向你打听某事,你可以用这句话拒绝回答,或用 Don't let me started. 当然,也不排除说这句的人想让听者有心理准备,弄清事情的来龙去脉得花时间和耐心。延展记忆:"另当别论。/That's another story."。

(15) Be careful! 小心点!

这个结构单用时,一定是情况十分紧急,用惊呼的方式提醒对方注意危险。如果放在句子中使用时,就是平时规劝对方什么事不该做,谨慎行事。

(16) Good decision! 好主意!

这是对别人想出好办法的一种肯定和支持。

(17) Let go! 放手!

这个词组单用就是字面意思,在于别人争抢某物时常用。但当这个词组应用到 let go of…的时候,就对其内涵进行了延伸,有人说,"放手"是一种睿智,学会放手的人才会走得更远,才会拥有更光明的未来。纠结过去的人或事都是不明智的做法。

(18) Not me! 我例外!

当你想撇清某种关系或不想参与到某事之中时,这句话很管用。

(19) One more thing. 还有件事。

当你还有事情要提醒对方注意时,这句话起到很好的提示作用。

(20) Don't panic! /Don't be panicked! 别慌张!

当某人因某事吓得不行或紧张到不行时,这个表达可以起到安抚作用。

(21) Who's that? 是谁?

这句话常用来询问某人的身份。

(22) This can't work. 这个不行。

要知道 work 在口语中是一个很好用的单词,这里是指"起作用"的意思。比如:"一切都能顺利进行吗? /Is everything working as it should?"。

(23) I got it. 我明白了。

让我们清楚某事时,常回答"I got it. /我明白了。"这可是个"出勤率"较高的表达。延展记忆:"我们都清楚了吗? /Are we clear?","明白了吗? (生气)/Do I make something clear?","把话说清楚。/Get one thing straight.","我知道了,我接受你的意见。/Point taken."等。

(24) What's the deal? 到底怎么回事?

询问事情的原委,这句话是常用的"口头禅"。

(25) I appreciated that. 谢谢!

这个"感激"与 Thank you! 相比,更强调对别人做法的一种欣赏。

(26) I'm just saying. 我只是说说而已。

当别人对你说的话提出质疑,你也觉得理亏或心虚时,可采用此句。

(27) Ask whatever you want. 想问啥就问呗。

这种"知无不言、言无不尽"的态度尽管少见,但听到这句话,你会感到信任在交流双方之间的建立。

(28) Safe journey! 一路平安!

送行时说的最后一句话。延展记忆:"一路顺风。/Have a safe trip.","路上小心。/Safe journey.","一路平安! /Safe travel!"等。

(29) Safe drive. 路上小心。

由于现在汽车普及,“路上小心。”都变成了“小心驾驶!”。

(30)Do you mean that? 你当真?

对别人说话的真实性提出质疑时,可采用这句常用表达。延展记忆:“我不是故意的。/I don't mean it.”,“我是当真的。/I mean it. = I am serious”,“我说真的。/I mean that.”等。

(31)Nothing more to say? 再没说的了?

在对方叽里呱啦说完一大堆之后,用这句话表示一种轻微的讥讽味道,意指对方话太多,终于“山穷水尽”的地步。

(32)That's very generous of you. 你太大方了。

对于别人的善举,这句话是很好的赞美。

(33)I'm flattered. 过奖了。

别人对自己的褒奖,我们除了说 Thank you! 之外,还可以用这句略显幽默的话回答,“我被拍马屁了;我受宠若惊。”,当然,将 Thank you! 和这句话合在一块用也是可以接受的。

(34)Have a nice day! 祝你今天愉快!

和别人分手时,除了 Bye-bye! 之外,加上这句话,表达良好的祝愿。也可以说 I bid you all a good day! 或 Good day! 等。

(35)This is what you deserve. 这是你应得的。

这个表达既可指好事“应得的报答、报酬”,也可指坏事“罪有应得”。

(36)What brings you down here? 什么风把你吹到这儿来了?

这个表达经常在朋友和熟人之间使用。延展记忆:“有何贵干? /What brings you here?”

(37)That's fine to me. 我没什么。

由于客观条件所迫,某人将他都认为十分不妥的事情想让你来做时,出于礼貌你就会这样说。

(38)Time is losing. 没时间了。

做某件有时间规定的事情时,就应该注意时间要求。时间快到时,可用此句话做提醒。延展记忆:Time is running out.

(39)So what? 又如何?

当别人向你描述某事的来龙去脉,但并没有点出真正的意图,你可以用此表达让对方切入重点。

(40)What a waste! 真可惜!

对浪费行为的一种惋惜和感叹。

(41)This is amazing! 真了不起!

这是一个使用范围比较广泛的表达,只要表达赞叹和赞美都可以使用。

(42)See you around! 再见!

这句话也是分手时常用的表达,意为“再见,回头见”。延展记忆:See you later!

(43)I'll check it. 我去看看。

这里的“看看”不能简单地理解为 see 等仅用眼睛看看的意思,这个表达强调“核实、核查、查看”的意义。

(44)Don't bother! 别麻烦了!

希望对方不要为了自己而费事张罗时,可采用这句话。延展记忆:“你在烦什么? /What's bothering you?”,“没什么大不了的。/It's no bother.”等。

(45) Do you have time? 几点了?

向别人打听时间,除了 What time is it now? 以及 What's the time? 之外,还可以用这句话询问时间。

(46) That was explaining everything. 事情原来如此。

当别人向你讲清事情的原委时,你可用这个表达接话。

(47) I really hope you can make it! 我真诚希望你能成功!

预祝别人"马到成功!"时,这句话是最好的鼓励,或简单一点,"你能做到的。You can make it."。

(48) My treat. 我来付钱/我请客。

请客时常说的一句话,或可采用 It's on me! 一说。

(49) Your apology is accepted. 没什么。

这个表达十分正式,注意使用语境。

(50) That's the sense. 有道理。

对别人的分析、观点、建议等的肯定。延展记忆:"to make sense /有道理,言之有理","很有道理/to make a perfect sense"。

(51) After you. 你先请。

这是出于礼貌让别人先行、先做时常说的一句话。

(52) He is available. 他有空。

表示某人有空,有时间,这是一个使用较频繁的表达。

(53) I screwed it up. 我把它搞砸。

screw 也是一个在口语中常用的单词。勇于承认错误是有责任心的表现。

(54) Do I lose you? 你还在线吗?

两种情况使用该句:一、可能对方长时间没有应答,想确认一下对方是否在线上。二、现在手机普及,有时候对方手机处于信号不好的地方,你可采用此句话检查对方是否在线上。

(55) Suit yourself. 随你便。

让对方不要顾虑太多或随意一些的宽慰话。

(56) Heads or tails? 人头还是字?

众所周知,很多场合需要用"抛硬币"来进行公平的选择,那硬币的"正面"和"反面"怎么说呢? 可以用以下三种选择:"head"和"tail","obverse"和"reverse"或者"top"和"bottom"。

(57) How bad is it? 有多糟?

碰到不好的事情发生,用此句表达了解情况。

(58) Take care. 保重。

分手时常说的一句话,也是一种美好的祝愿。

(59) Who cares? 谁在乎呢? (管它呢?)

劝慰别人不要太在意某事。

(60) I got to run. 我得赶时间。

这是想要离开比较好的理由。

(61) This is not happening. 这不是真的。

当我们不愿相信所发生的事情时,可用这句话安慰自己。

(62) It means too much for me. 这对我来说太重要了。

在强调某事或某物的重要性时,这句话常被提起。

(63)What we're supposed to do? 我们应该做什么?

这是一种"重在参与"积极的态度。当你希望能做点什么时,可用这句话获知。

(64)This is not what you think. 这不是你想的那样。

消除别人的误解,这句话是不错的选择。

(65)That's enough about. 我说完了。

这个表达切忌与"That's enough!"混淆,因为后者表示"够了! 受够了!"的意思,含有厌烦的情绪。

(66)Time to go. 该走了。

在离开的时候,这句话常被用来作为不是理由的理由。

(67)Hang on for a second. 先等一下。

打电话时,让对方不要挂断电话时说的话。

(68)You watch your back. 你小心点。

劝告别人小心提防某人或某事。

(69)Pardon me. 不好意思。

在口语中,这个表达有时候可替换 excuse me 和 sorry。

(70)I'll take care of it. 我来搞定。

当你想要负责解决某个问题,可以有这样的豪言壮语。

(71)What's the hell? 到底怎么了?

这是在逼问对方究竟是怎么回事时常用的结构,表示不在乎、无可奈何、气恼、不耐烦。

(72)I'm sorry for your loss. 节哀顺变。

对别人遭遇人财损失时可用的句子。

(73)No offense. 恕我冒犯。

当你对即将说的话不知是否会冒犯别人,加上这个表达,会显得更加委婉。

(74)Don't you dare. 你敢!

这是一种不客气的说法,起到震慑对方的作用,威胁对方不要做某事。

(75)What's the occasion? 有什么大事(喜事)?

当你不了解事发状况用这句话进行询问。

(76)It doesn't concern you. 不关你事。

不希望别人插手某事,可以用此表达劝退。

(77)Believe in yourself! 相信自己!

这是传递正能量的句子,可以用这句话自己鼓劲。"I can because I think I can! /我行,因为我相信我行!"

(78)That's it. 就这样。

当我们想强调所有一切就是我们之前所说的,就可以加上一句"That's it."来强调没有别的了。

(79)How goes it? 情况如何?

这个表达一般是询问对方的事情进行得怎么样,对方的生活、情况等如何。

(80)I'll say. 没错;还用说。

对于对方所说的话,我们深感同意,但是我们认为对方的说辞太含蓄了应该要说出更有力的言词。

(81) You got me. 你问倒我了。

当别人问我们问题而我们回答不出来时,就可以用这句话来表示我们不清楚。也可只说 Got me. 或 Beats me.

(82) Oh, for Pete's sake. 哦,看在老天的份上。

恳请某人停止做某事。

(83) Search me. 我不知道。

Search me! 这句话从字面上来说,意是"搜我的身"。用 search me! 来回答对方,就表示"我不知道!"因为如果有人询问某事物在哪里,而说话者以这句话来回答就表示你来搜我的身,如果找不到就表示没有,也就是"我不知道"的意思,这句话俏皮意味十足,常用在朋友之间。

(84) What do you recommend? 你有什么好建议吗?

初到一家餐厅,常不清楚有什么时候好吃的,这时候你可以直接问服务生 What do you recommend? 或 What's your recommendation?。通常服务生会直接请你点当天的 special,如果你不喜欢"特餐",服务生还会告诉你:"The chef's recommendation is …/主厨推荐菜是……"

(85) What are you talking about? 你在说什么啊?

当别人说了一些无意义的话或者指控、责怪我们时,都是可以用这句话来作为表示清白的开场白,表示我们根本就不知道对方到底在说什么,又怎么可能做了什么。

(86) What do you say? 你说好不好?(你有什么意见?)

这种句子有两种用法:①引导或后接提议的句子希望征得同意或赞同。②表示问候,不需回答。"Let's not argue anymore. What do you say?/我们别再争论了。你说好不好?","Let's eat at a restaurant tonight. What do you say?/我们今晚去餐厅吃,你说好不好?"

(87) Whatever you say. 随便你;就照你的话做。

Whatever you say. 原意是"无论你说什么"。本句常用于下列两种情形:一种随你怎么说,就是"随便你。"的意思。另外,当畏惧或不得不听命行事时,说 Whatever you say. 则表示"你说了就算,就照你的话做。"

(88) Whatever. 无所谓。

"Whatever./随你便。"在听长辈、老师、上司训话时,人在心不在,对他们所说的毫不在意。一旦被对方询问:"听到了吗?"我们可以用这句话来表示满意我们的态度。这是相当没有礼貌的表达方式。当受到他人威胁,而我们并不在意时,也可以用这句话。

(89) You bet. 当然;一定;没问题

当你对某事用非常大的把握时,就用此表达搞定。

(90) You got it. 没问题。

这是一种相当口语的说法,it 是指对方请我们去做的事。相同的情况也可说:Sure, no problem, OK 来表示答应对方的要求。

(91) You said it, brother. 你说得对。

这是表示同意对方的一种说法。brother 指的就是我们说话的对象,这句话是指对方说的话完全正确,我们百分之百同意对方的说辞。

(92) Do you have everything? 都准备好了吗?

行动前的例行问句。

(93) If it will make you happy… 如果这样你会比较快乐的话……

当别人要求我们去做某些事,但我们并不愿意时,可说这句话,意思是告诉对方,我们会去做是因为对方的要求,不然我们是不会去做的。

(94) If you say so. 如果你这么认为的话。

这句话是形容"你自己都是这么说了,我也不好再说什么。"强调尊重并同意对方的做法,虽然自己本来有不同的看法,在听见对方刚才说的话之后,已不再坚持己见了。

(95) It always does. 一向如此。

当别人呈现担心、焦虑、害怕等情绪时,这句话可以帮助消除不良情绪。

(96) What gives? 怎么回事?

询问事情的原因的简洁说法。

(97) I sympathize. 我有同感。

sympathize 是动词,表"同情、怜悯"或是"同意;有同感;赞成"。说 I sympathize. 表示满意自己能理解并体会对方的心情,与单纯表示满意同意的 I agree. 并不相同,后面可接 with。

(98) It's now or never. 机不可失;好机会总是一闪而过;永不回头。

这里的 It's now or never. 就是巧妙地用了 now 和 never 来表示"要么马上把握,否则就永远错过"的意思。所以要劝人好把握眼前难得的大好机会,不妨这么说。

(99) Precisely my point. 我的意思正是如此。

当某人说了某些他认为可以反驳我们的话,但我们却认为他说的话正可以支持我们的论点,我们就可以用这句话来表示这就是我的意思。

(100) That'll be the day. 那是不可能的。

本句是取自一句习惯用语"That'll be the day when hell freezes over. /等到地狱结冰那天才会发生"。因为地狱不会结冰,所以那天就不会到来,也就是"不可能会有这一天"的意思是。类似中文的"太阳打西边出来",都是用来表示"绝对不会发生的,永远不可能的"。

(101) So far, so good. 到目前为止还好。

这个句子常用于别人问你近来身体,工作等如何时,你的正面回答。So far, so good."相当于 It's good till now.

(102) That figures. 有道理;合理;讲得通

figure 是指"计算",而 that 则是"所提到的事情"。这句话表示对某人所说的事情深有同感,有时可说"That's typical. /那是典型的。"

(103) You must be mad. 你一定是疯了。

当某人说了某些我们认为很疯狂的话,就可以这么说,表示我们不同意或拒绝对方所说的话。

(104) It could happen to anyone. 这种情况谁都可能遇到。

当别人遇到困难或不顺时,这句话可以使对方心理平衡些。还可以简化成 It happens to anybody. 或 That happens.

(105) Why don't we give this a try? 我们为何不试一下呢?

鼓励别人勇于尝试。

(106) You did it! 你做到了!

还可以说 You made it! 口语中要注意 make、do 等词的运用。

(107) nice fellow 一等的好人

说得更亲热点，一般使用 good guy。表示对别人人品的赞美，但通常是在对方提供帮忙之后。

(108) Forget it! 别提了！

提醒对方不要再提类似的话题。还可以用 Skip it! 和 I don't wanna talk about this any more. 等。

三、巩固练习

1. 熟读并背诵下列常用表达。

(1) Look! 听着！

(2) Bravo! 太棒了！

(3) Please! 拜托了！

(4) I quit! 我不干了！

(5) Sure thing! 当然！

(6) I'll fix it! 我去搞定！

(7) I'm on it. 我知道了。

(8) Poor thing! 真可怜！

(9) Anytime! 随时吩咐！

(10) Is that so? 是这样吗？

(11) Out of the way! 闪开！

(12) Be my guest! 请自便！

(13) Please be safe! 请保重！

(14) That's so sweet. 你真好。

(15) Bravo on him! 为他喝彩！

(16) Kick things off. 闲话少说。

(17) Don't be sorry. 不用道歉。

(18) It isn't working. 不起作用。

(19) Hang on a second. 等一会。

(20) I get the picture. 我明白了。

(21) Freeze! 别动！(Hold still!)

(22) Good for you! 你真不错/好！

(23) You got a second? 你有空吗？

(24) Don't badger me! 别纠缠我！

(25) I'm counting on it. 我静候佳音。

(26) So sorry for your loss! 请节哀！

(27) It's no big deal. 没什么大问题。

(28) Do whatever you want. 随便你。

(29) Two coffees to go. 两杯咖啡打包。

(30) You're being silly! 你别说傻话了。

(31) Cut a long story short. 简而言之。

(32) Leave me alone! 别管我! /别惹我!

(33) Present! /Here! 到! /有! (用于点名时)

(34) You are so cute. 你真好(真可爱)。

(35) Just follow my lead. 听我指挥好了。

(36) What was your mission? 有何贵干?

(37) Are you kidding me? 跟我开玩笑啊?

(38) Before you know. 在你明白之前(或:不等你回过神来)。

(39) Would you like to find out? 想知道吗?

(40) You are too modest. 你太客气了。

(41) I' m happy to oblige! 我乐意奉陪(效劳)!

(42) Where did that come from? 这话从何说起?

(43) Would you like hanging for a moment? 留一会好吗?

(44) We welcome you under our roof. 我们欢迎您的大驾光临。

(45) Actions speak louder than words! 行动胜于言语。

(46) I hear you. 我知道你要说什么。(我懂你的意思了。)

(47) Nothing to see here! 这里没什么好看的。(看什么看!)

(48) May God have mercy upon your soul. 愿主宽恕你的灵魂。

(49) I have no idea what are you talking about. 我真不知道你在说什么。

(50) Fantastic! 妙极了! (Great! /Gorgeous! /Impressive! /Incredible! /Perfect!)

(51) You must let me know if I can return the favor. 有什么需要我帮忙的尽管说。

(52) You have the right to remain silent. Anything you say can and will be used against you. 你有权保持沉默。你所说的一切都会用于呈堂证供。(You are not obliged to say anything unless you desire to do so, whatever you say will be taken down in writing and may be given in evidence against you upon trial. 你有权保持缄默,但你所说的一切将被记录在案,并有可能成为呈堂证物。)

2. 用本单元所学的知识造句。

(1) 考得差并不是问题的关键。关键在于你有没有用心学。

(2) 别问我关于他的事情,我和他已经分手了。

(3) 说来话长,我现在没有功夫告诉你来龙去脉。

(4) 感谢你的及时帮助。你真是太好了。

(5) 不要因为这样的小事而烦恼。

(6) 晚饭供应大约七点,甚至更晚。

(7) 您和我们的哪位理财顾问有预约吗?

(8) 你和那个新来的家伙是怎么回事?

(9) 如果运动让你快乐,你根本不用担心时间问题。

(10) 我已经被这样问过很多遍了。说实话,我不知道。

(11) 外面闹嚷嚷的,什么事呀?

(12) 我们必须要小心伤病,但是我们也必须要为比赛做准备。

(13)为了你自己,让过去的事情过去吧。
(14)他将会为此事做出反应,我不会。
(15)还有一件事,餐厅在哪里?
(16)别慌张!提前考虑很好,但对自己控制之外的事情烦恼是没有用的。
(17)照片里站在你旁边的是谁?
(18)用体罚学生的方式维持课堂秩序是不管用的,要与学生多交流。
(19)我明白了。你要我放学后立即回家。
(20)对于我来说,这一切似乎讲得通,我认为它是可读的。
(21)怎么搞的,这个聚会你到底来不来?
(22)我不是在指责你,不过说说罢了。
(23)非常感谢你能来。
(24)谢谢你们今晚光临。祝一路平安到家。
(25)你只要听我们的就可以得到很好的学习技巧。就这样。
(26)A:见到你很高兴,一切好吗?B:谢谢,一切都好。
(27)A:你想他接下来要做什么呢?B:你问倒我了。
(28)看在老天的份上,你别抽烟了行不行?
(29)你是说你想把这些打包回去吗?
(30)你非常大方,能把你的新车借给他们。
(31)他经常奉承我,使我感到受宠若惊。
(32)再见,祝您今天过得愉快。
(33)你得不到你想要的,这很平常。
(34)真没想到啊!什么风把你给吹来了?
(35)抱歉让你久等了。我没什么啦。
(36)但是延迟使那些谁觉得时间不多了的人感到沮丧。
(37)扔掉它多浪费啊!
(38)这些美国高中生能唱这首中文歌真是太神奇了。
(39)我会尽快核查的,这个星期内给你一个答复。
(40)再见,记得今天下午带来这本书。
(41)不用麻烦了。我自己来吧。
(42)我很高兴你们能这么明智,同时我相信你们都会成功。
(43)我还得感谢你的帮忙呢。走,我们一起去吃饭。我请客!
(44)接待处就在前面,请您先走。
(45)请稍等,我看看他现在有没有空,请坐。
(46)如果你不想来就别来。随便你。
(47)我昨天有个面试,但是被我弄砸了。
(48)我不能准确告诉你这到底有多糟。
(49)说实话,谁还在乎这事?
(50)我得走了,我得去图书馆还书。
(51)别再说了,这不是真的。
(52)谢谢你善意的提醒。对我来说太重要了。

(53)我们刚参加这个活动。我们应该做什么?
(54)妈妈,爸爸,不是你们想的那样。你们得相信我。
(55)请稍等片刻,不要挂掉,我去找经理并告诉他接你的电话。
(56)在这家公司你可要多加提防,否则你会发现你的有些同事想利用你。
(57)请原谅我没能早点来。
(58)我会亲自去解决这件事的。
(59)绝无冒犯之意,但我真的不在乎你在讲的事。
(60)不准你动他一根毫毛。
(61)怎么啦?你彩票中奖了吗?
(62)那与你无关。我会自己处理。
(63)报纸在哪儿呢?不知道,我没看见哦。
(64)你可以推荐给我一些学英文会话的书吗?
(65)我们听听音乐。你说好不好?
(66)你说了算,我太紧张了,无法思考。
(67)我们今晚吃中国菜还是印度菜?无所谓。
(68)你会告诉她吗?当然会。
(69)准备出发了吗?该拿的东西都准备好了吗?
(70)别担心,很快就会过去的,一向如此。
(71)怎么回事,有三辆警车停在外面。
(72)要么现在干,要么永远也不干,我们碰碰运气好吗?
(73)你一定是疯了,干出这样的事来。

3. 你的英语口头禅是什么?请找到更多英语常用表达,并与大家分享。

Chapter 12 Spirit-lifting Sentences
提劲话语

一、思路讲解

"正能量"是一个充满阳光的单词。人生是一条漫长的路,有时在高峰,有时处于低谷。当我们处于"人生得意"之时,一路高歌,狂飙突进,"尽欢"人生。但请想想,当我们处于低谷时,是谁,是什么帮我们从低谷中走出来,攀上另一个高峰?是朋友!是家人!是他们一次次的鼓励,一次次的加油,一次次的宽慰,一次次的呐喊,让我们振作起来,"良言一句三冬暖"。"正能量"的话语在心烦意乱时给我们带来心灵的平静,在受到伤害时抚慰我们的心灵,在遇到困难时救我们于水深火热之中,在孤独无助时是我们最忠实的伴侣,在迷茫时为我们拨开迷雾,在无助时向我们伸出援助之手,在沮丧时激励我们的斗志。"正能量"的话语是人生经验,让我们少走弯路;是生活方法,为我们指点迷津;是人性之美,容我们感悟生命。

再从英语学习的角度来说,"正能量"的话语首先是现成的好句,掌握好他们,可以让我们"出口成章"。其次,这些句子充满着各式各样的美:用词之美、结构之美、修辞之美、内容之美,不仅可以让我们获得人生睿智,也能提高语言知识。再者,这些句子的优美结构可以帮助我们进行第二次改写,从一个句子衍生出无数的表达。最后,对这些经典的背诵,可以为我们的语言活动——课堂辩论、英语演讲、论文写作等提供充足的语料,形成语言学习的良性循环。

我们将以下的"正能量"语句分为两大类,一类是较长的段落型句群,供大家欣赏;另一类是较短的句子,供大家背诵。不管是哪一种形式,都是很好的语料,可供大家在需要时查阅。

二、佳句欣赏

(1) A strong man stands up for himself. And a stronger man stands up for the others. 强壮的人为自己而战。强大的人为他人而战。

这里的中文译文比英文更出彩。"强壮"是指身体,而"强大"是指能力,可能英文的本义也是如此。

(2) The people you know best are the ones most capable of surprising you. 你最熟悉的人是最能给你惊喜的人。

只有最熟悉你的人才会知道什么能带给你惊喜。

(3) People get carried away. They make rush decisions based on their excitement. 人们往往一时冲动就做了鲁莽的决定。

"冲动是魔鬼",做决定,尤其是重大决定,一定要冷静。

(4) It goes by so quickly. In a flash, the life we knew is gone forever. And we're left to ask ourselves. When did my beauty start to fade? Why has my friend changed? Was I the best mother I could have been? 时光的脚步如此匆匆,转眼间,我们熟悉的生活便永远消失。我们只能扪心

自问:我的美丽的容颜是几时开始衰退的? 我的朋友怎么会改变的呢? 我是否有尽力去做一个最好的母亲了呢?

时间飞逝,岁月如梭。当不停追问自己这些问题时,人已近中年。三个排比加强语气,感叹人生。

(5) Women only have five seconds to be young and beautiful. And then it's gone. 女人年轻漂亮的时间不过一瞬间,之后就人老珠黄了。

虽然不知道为什么用"five seconds"来形容时光短暂,但把道理说得很清楚,女人不要太注重外表,那都是浮云。

(6) Because feeling good on the inside is all about looking good on the outside. 内在感觉良好取决于外在视觉美观。

这种"由内而外"或"由外而内"的感觉是辩证的。

(7) What one has not been given by birth one may acquire through efforts. 先天若不足,后天可补足。

正所谓"先天不足后天弥补"或"天道酬勤"!

(8) Sometimes you chain yourself to the tree, and sometimes you go after the guy with the saw. 有时候要按兵不动,有时候要主动出击。

"saw"是"大锯"的意思。用"树"和"大锯"来表达这个意思,很形象。

(9) In this never-ending drama we call life, everyone has a part to play. 所谓人生是场永不落幕的戏剧,每个人都有角色要扮演。

这就是人生,每个人都有自己的人生位置,每个人都有自己的作用:"天生我才必有用"说的大致就是这意思。

(10) Everyone steps over the line now and then let's all make an effort not to. 每个人总有做错事的时候。我们不妨来个有则改之无则加勉。

每个人都会犯错,不要因为这样就不敢尝试。这句话鼓励大家勇于冒险,但有错也要勇于承担改正。

(11) Some lie to keep from losing what they love. Some lash out because they fear the future. Some put up walls because they have regrets. 有人编造谎言,以留住心中挚爱。有人恶言相向,因为他们惧怕未来。有人紧锁心门,因为他们存有遗憾。

人生经验共分享。

(12) Looking at what has been taken from us is a bad way to go through life. 回顾不堪回首的往事并非继续生活的明智之举。

不管过去是美好的还是痛苦的,都已经过去了,人生还要继续向前。

(13) That's why it's important to search for the meaning of living. We find it in our daughters' smile, in the warmth of our friends or the comfort of our faith. Then there are those who make their lives meaningful by making a great sacrifice. 因此,找到活着的意义至关重要。我们能在女儿们的微笑,朋友们的温暖和信仰的笃定中找到。然后还有一些人为此做出巨大的牺牲。

生活中美好的事物是我们人生的重要支撑。

(14) We can put a stop to this awful cycle, and reach some sort of closure. 让这个恶性循环就此打住,尽弃前嫌。

这才是一种积极的人生态度。

(15) And a wise man once said that to begin the journey of change we must pull on the boots of self - awareness. 曾经有一个先哲说过要想开启改变之旅我们必须具备中肯的自我认识。

想改变除了勇气之外,还应该有底气。

(16) In the stressful world we can all be forgiven for having a few weaknesses. 如今压力无处不在,有些许弱点,大可宽恕原谅。

(17) There's always drinking when it's work. (We're golfing with a client——beer. We're hammering out a deal——wine. We make a deal——champagne.) 每逢公事,总免不了喝酒。

这不是工作中的"酒文化"又是什么呢?

(18) As much as death takes from us it also gives. It teaches us what's truly important. 死亡夺走我们许多东西,它也给予,它教会我们什么才是真正重要的。

珍惜眼前人,珍惜你所拥有的一切,不要等到失去了才觉得追悔莫及,这是"死亡"对我们的给予。

(19) Nothing lifted her spirits like a good workout of her credit. 没有什么比挥霍一下信用卡更能让她振作的了。

女人都是天生的"shopping animal",是女人获得人生乐趣的方法之一。

(20) There is a saying: "You know you've hit middle age when your memories become more important to you than your dreams." 常言道:"人到中年,回忆比梦想更珍贵。"

这绝对是经验之谈。

(21) Don't ever forget: Always remember how much you wanted to be loved. 请不要忘记:永远记住你曾经多么需要爱。

人人都需要爱。

(22) Everything seems so golden, one minute, then turns to ashes, the next. 前一秒还笙歌鼎沸,下一秒就曲终人散了。

人生无常啊!

(23) Everybody is praised for his response to our national crisis. 国难当头,每个人的表现都值得表扬。

正所谓"国家兴亡,匹夫有责"。

(24) Keeping their spirits up is an important part of the cure. 使他们振奋精神的是疗养过程中很重要的一环。

想要帮助情绪沮丧的人走出心灵的阴霾,调节精神状态是首要环节。

(25) If you wish to understand things, you must come out from behind your prejudice and listen. 如果你想了解什么,你得先摒弃自己的偏见并学会倾听别人。

"兼听则明,偏听则暗"。

(26) You are nervous because you are intelligent. Only stupid people are foolhardy. 你紧张是因为你聪明,只有笨蛋才莽撞无畏。

对感到紧张的人的一种安慰。

(27) But when you fall off a horse, you need a bit of time to get back in the saddle. 如果你摔了一跤,爬起来是需要一些时间的。

字面意思是"如果你从马上摔下来,需要花点时间才能重新坐上马鞍。"

(28) When work is a pleasure, life is joy! When work is duty, life is slavery. 若工作是乐趣

时,生活便是享受!若工作是义务时,生活则成苦役。

所以态度很重要。

(29) Although the world is full of suffering, it is also full of the overcoming of it. 虽然世界多苦难,但也充满了战胜苦难的方法。

这就是万物相生相克的道理。

(30) Why waste precious time dreaming when waking life is so much better? 醒着的生活如此美好,干嘛要把时间浪费在做梦上呢?

这是对"醉生梦死"者的劝告。

(31) Didn't the war teach you never to make a promise? 战争没教会你永远不要许下承诺吗?

战争的发动往往以撕毁条约或承诺开始。

(32) Maybe you're in the middle of a storm, you know, and the waves are crashing over your tiny little boat there, and maybe you did what you had to do to get out. Maybe you become a psychologist. 你也许身陷暴风雨之中,巨浪滔天,冲击你的小船。你也许不惜一切,力图脱险。也许你因此才成为心理学家。

"经一事,长一智。"

(33) "We were near starvation all the time," she told a friend. "I could not go to school. I haunted the recording studios, singing songs for pennies just to survive." "我们当时无时无刻不在忍饥挨饿,"她对一位朋友说,"我没法上学,经常都待在录音室里,唱歌只是为了赚几文钱活下去!"

正能量也通过事例传递,这句话来自美国电影《风雨哈佛路》Homeless to Harvard,讲述一个家境恶劣的女孩完全通过自己的努力进入哈佛大学学习的感人故事。

(34) A woman of my age can face reality far better than most men. 我这个年纪的女人可比大多数男性的承受力强多了。

经历人生大风大浪的老年人,他们的心理承受能力不可低估。

(35) When tragedies strike, we try to find someone to blame. In absence of a suitable candidate, we usually blame ourselves. 当悲剧降临,我们总想把责任归咎于人。如果无人可指责,我们往往会责备自己。

"怨天尤人"虽然可以让情绪得到一定的疏解,但终究不是好办法。

(36) When the going gets tough, the tough gets going. 艰难之路唯勇者行。

字面意思为"形势愈来愈糟,强者也变得更坚强",正所谓遇强则强,遇更强则更强的意思。

(37) Your wish is my command. 我一定会实现你的愿望。

这句话原本是天方夜谭中神灯里的精灵所说的名句,因无论主人要求什么,他也会照着都会使它实现。用在一般生活中,是强调实现对方的承诺,只要对方高兴,自己就会拼命照办。可译为"我一定会实现你的愿望"。

三、佳句背诵

(1) Life can change with every breath we take. 人生每秒都会发生变化。

注意这儿“每秒”生动且深刻地使用了“every breath /每一次呼吸”。

(2) You can't count on anyone. 你别依靠任何人。

人始终是要长大的,始终是要独立的,“靠自己,硬道理”。

(3) No victory comes without price. 胜利必须付出代价。

注意这里的双重否定“no…without…”表示强调,“没有胜利是不付出代价的”。不要只看到胜利的喜悦,更应该明白为夺得胜利所付出的代价。

(4) You'll never be happy if you spend all your time goofing off. 你如果一天四处游荡,将永远不会快乐。

goof off 是“混日子,游手好闲”的意思。“吊儿郎当,无所事事”是心灵空虚的表现,内心不充实,怎会快乐?

(5) Let the past be past. 过去了的就过去吧。

这是劝慰别人不要纠结于过去的痛苦和失败的“国际通用句子”,过去的就让它过去吧,一切向前看,没有迈步过的坎,翻不过的坡。

(6) Home is where your history begins. 家是我们的根。

中国人把“家”看得很重,“落叶归根”是最具代表性的,没想到英国人的想法与中国人如出一辙。这句话规劝大家重视家庭。

(7) There is no a life in this room that you have not touched. 这里没一人不曾受您的影响。

这是对德高望重的人的一种褒奖。

(8) You should feel good about what you have done. 你应为自己所做的感到自豪。

这句话用于表扬别人的成绩,肯定别人的所作所为。

(9) Men are made, not born. 男子汉是练就的,不是天生的。

这句话用于鼓励男孩要学会吃苦,不要做温室里的花朵,明白“宝剑锋自磨砺出”的道理。

(10) You don't jump to the conclusion before you know the situation. 不知道情况就不要妄下结论。

强调实事求是,在弄清情况之后再下结论,这样才能做到不吓自己,也不冤枉别人。

(11) It isn't important who wins or loses. 输赢不重要。

劝诫不要把输赢看得太重,“胜败乃兵家常事”,否则就是“庸人自扰”。

(12) There is no “I” in a team. 团队中没有个人。

强调团队精神,在一个团队中“大家好才是真的好”,不要把自己看得太重。

(13) No good parents like to see their children go without. 父母都希望自己儿女得到更多啊。

“可怜天下父母心。”可父母对子女的这种良苦用心经常遭遇孩子反感,希望孩子们理解“理解万岁”一说!

(14) Put those rumors to rest once and for all. 让这些谣言永远消失吧。

“谣言止于智者”。劝诫大家“不信谣、不传谣”。

(15) The truth always comes out. 真相终将大白于天下。

被人冤枉时,这句话是安慰;想要说谎时,这句话是警告。

(16) We should be on the same side. 我们应团结一致。

“人心齐,泰山移”,“团结就是力量”,加油鼓劲时必备之佳句。

(17) I wish you would continuously find your expectation. 希望你常常心想事成。

这是送给别人的美好祝福。

(18) There are consequences to everything. 事事都有因果报应。

规劝别人多做善事,别起歹念。

(19) I'm gonna use every weapon at my disposal. 我会尽我所能。

at one's disposal 是"任由人支配"的意思,这里的 weapon 用得很生动,似应该引申理解为"手段、方式"等。

(20) Marriage is a big step. 婚姻是人生的一件大事。

a big step 应该理解为"一个大的跨越",意味着长大成人,意味着责任的承担。

(21) Silence is as deep as eternity. Speech is as shallow as time. 沉默如永恒般深厚,言语如光阴般肤浅。

中国人讲"沉默是金","此时无声胜有声",有时候,沉默真能胜过千言万语,言语尤显肤浅、苍白无力。

(22) When they were little and they'd act out. 他们年幼时常常任性。

act out 是"表现出来"的意思。年轻人想到什么就做什么,"初生牛犊不怕虎","年少轻狂"就是这样来的。

(23) If it wears a skirt, it's off-limits. 凡穿裙子的就打不得。

这是对小男生的教育。

(24) Everything I gain comes at some horrible price. 我所得到的一切都付出了可怕的代价。

"天下没有白吃的午餐",任何事情都要付出代价。

(25) We needed to wipe the slate clean. 我们要把旧账一笔勾销重新开始。

wipe the slate clean 意为"勾销往事"。这是双方抛弃前嫌,重归于好的信号。

(26) Don't cramp the boy's style. 别束缚孩子的行为。

别让孩子的行为都是 mother style 或 father style,务必使他们能充分发挥个性和创造性。

(27) Desire——it's an emotion designed to lead us astray. 欲望这样东西总是会让我们误入歧途。

"欲望"会将人变成贪得无厌的魔鬼,误入歧途是迟早的事。

(28) Everything is not all cut and dry. 凡事没有绝对的。

cut and dry 是"事先准备好的,内定的"的意思。这句话让大家明白做任何事都要掌握好灵活性。

(29) There is first time for everything. 万事总有第一次。

"万事开头难",这是对做事畏手畏脚者的极大鼓励。

(30) I get by with a little help from my friends. 人生路上朋友助我前行。

"朋友一生一起走",朋友的相互支持是我们走得更高更远的动力。

(31) Old habits die hard. 江山易改,本性难移。

明白这个前提,我们就一定不要让坏习惯"生根发芽",一定要将它消灭在萌芽状态。

(32) What is it you care for most in the world? 这个世界上你最宝贵的东西是什么?

经常问问这个问题,会让我们学会珍惜。

(33) A small advantage makes them overbearing. 他们略占优势便会傲慢十足。

这样的句子是从反面的角度提醒我们注意待人接物的态度。

(34) The slightest adversity makes them despondent. 稍遇小灾小祸,他们就绝望起来。

despondent 是“沮丧的,失望的”的意思。这是一面镜子,反映了一些人怕困难,意志力薄弱的缺点,希望大家不要成为这样的人。

(35) Happy marriage is devoutly something to be wished for. 幸福的婚姻可遇不可求。

劝告未婚人士不要为自己的幸福设定规则和条款。

(36) Women are variable. 女人善变。

有些人认为这句话有性别歧视,但我等更愿意将这句话理解为女人更具灵活性。

(37) The good seem to suffer and the wicked to prosper. 好人要受罪,坏人却逍遥。

我们更愿意从宗教的角度来理解这句话:佛教说“吃亏是福”,基督教说“我不入地狱谁入地狱?”。

(38) All art is a lie. 所有的艺术都遮盖真相。

有些年轻人由于生活经验不足,容易被“来源于生活而高于生活”的艺术形式所欺骗,而忽视了现实生活的真相。这句话倒可以让年轻人清醒。

(39) What doesn't kill us makes us stronger. 愈挫愈勇。

这句话有助于培养年轻人百折不挠的精神。

(40) For without knowledge, life is not worth having. 人若胸无点墨,生命便毫无意义。

“活到老,学到老”。

(41) Things can change at a blink of an eye. 事情会在一眨眼间发生改变。

形容变化大,变化迅速。也可用在提醒注意安全方面。

(42) No excellence can be acquired without constant practice. 熟能生巧。

这是用反向思路强调这个道理。

(43) The worst is behind us. 最坏的已经过去了。

这是比较有用的宽心话。

(44) Why do you need to label everything? 为什么你要给任何事情下定义?

善意提醒对方灵活性不够。

(45) Time is a killer. 时间是无情的。

地球人都有体会。

(46) Small strokes fell great oaks. 水滴石穿。

stroke 是“敲打、击打”的意思,原意是“慢慢地击打会砍倒一颗橡树。”

(47) Small steps, we'll get there. 不积跬步无以至千里。

劝诫年轻人一步一个脚印,踏实努力。

(48) People are people. 人性不堪。

这句话的另一理解是“人终归是人”,都有局限性,都会犯错误。

(49) Popularity has its price. 人气高也要付出代价的。

这是告诉追星族或梦想成名成星的人冷静理智对待名气的好建议。

(50) Wealth corrupts us all. 财富使人堕落。

虽说“富贵不能淫,贫贱不能移”,但又有几人能做到,反倒是财富带来了无尽的烦恼。

(51) The only way to deal with the world is to fight fire with fire. 以其人之道还治其人之身。

我们虽不提倡这种做法,但偶尔为之,至少对“欺软怕硬”的人能产生一定的威慑力。

(52) Ugly is something that goes up inside you. 只有内心不健康才叫丑。

“心灵美”比“外在美”更重要。

(53) A man accepts responsibility for his actions. 男人就应该为自己的行为负责。

这是区别男人和男孩的标准。

(54) It's never too late to change your life. 任何时候都可以改变你的生活。

鼓励别人去做新尝试的经典句型。

(55) Leaving is never easy. 告别从来不易。

"相见时难别亦难","难分难舍"。

(56) Anything that's worth doing is hard. 值得做的事情总是很难。

"樱桃好吃树难栽"。

(57) Looking for what we can give to others is far better. 向有需要的人伸出援手才更有意义。

"帮助别人是快乐之源","大家好才是真的好","只要人人都付出一点爱,世界将会变成美好的人间"。

(58) All your efforts had paid off. 你们的辛苦终于换来回报。

有努力就有收获,不管大小。"一分耕耘一分收获"。

(59) A good deed comes straight from the heart. 做好事是发乎真心。

如果做好事不是出于真心而是其他目的,这是对善心的玷污。

(60) Sometimes good deeds have bad consequences. 但有时好事却招致恶果。

这是"好心办坏事"或"好心讨不到好报"的另一种解释。

(61) Money saved for the rainy day. 存钱以备不时之需。

"月光族"需牢记这句话。

(62) She may amount to something one day. 她说不定哪天会有所作为的。

"天生我才必有用","每个人心中都有小宇宙"。

(63) Isolating yourself is only gonna make matters worse. 封闭自己只会使情况越来越糟。

"自闭症"、"忧郁症"就是"封闭自己"的糟糕后果。

(64) Repressing your feelings is not healthy. 压抑情感会憋出内伤。

糟糕的情绪需要宣泄:运动、嗨歌、聊天、喝茶等都是不错的选择。

(65) You still mean a world to me. 对我来讲,你仍是最重要的。

记着一定要对自己爱的人大声说出这句话。

(66) When it comes to being a mother, you can run but you can never hide. 做了母亲,你可以逃避但永远不可能清净。

中国人说"养儿一百岁常忧九十九",异曲同工之妙。

(67) Do not compare yourself to me! 别拿我跟你相提并论。

常言道:"人比人,气死人"。这句话道理是对的,可语气可以稍缓和一下。

(68) Beauty is suffering. 美丽是很辛苦的。

整容、化妆、捯饬等,哪样不辛苦? 哪样不付出代价?

(69) Never forget that it takes a lot of love to make a house a home. 请记住,要倾注大量的爱才能拥有真正的家。

一个温馨幸福的家庭的建立是不容易的。

(70) We live by certain standards. 我们凡事都有个规矩。

"没有规矩不成方圆"。

(71) I must do what conscience tells me. 做事得对得起我的良心。

有时候“良心”比“规矩、法律”更管用,是我们言行的指引。

(72) We all have chapters we would rather keep unpublished. 谁都有不愿为人知的过去。

劝慰别人时,这种“有难同当”的方式或“踩自己”的手段都是很有效的。

(73) No one hits the bull's eye with the first arrow. 多少人能一击就中?

开始不顺,这句话或多或少能帮助我们减轻压力。

(74) What would be the point of living if we didn't let life change us? 要是一成不变,人生还有什么意义?

人生要勇于尝新,不怕失败。不要因循守旧,墨守成规。

(75) It's always sad when you love someone who doesn't love you back. 单恋总是件让人痛苦的事儿。

“天涯何处无芳草,何必单恋一棵树”。

(76) Better safe than sorry. 宁可事先谨慎有余,不要事后后悔莫及。(凡事需谨慎。)

“小心驶得万年船”。

(77) I'd love to help but it's not within my power. 我乐意效劳,但只怕有心无力。

想帮忙,又怕自己做不好,先给对方打打“预防针”。

(78) And I'd rather face it than dodge it. 宁愿直面现实,也不愿逃避。

逃避不能解决任何问题。

(79) Appearances can be cruelly deceptive. 外表可能极具欺骗性。

“透过现象看本质”是非常重要的。

(80) It just happens and we should live it. 世事无常,我们要随遇而安。

人要活得开心幸福,心态很重要。

(81) A light heart lives long. 豁达者长寿。

“事从容则有余味,人从容则有余年”;“心里头能撑船,健康快乐活百年”。

(82) Genius only means hard-working all one's life. 天才只意味着终身不懈的努力。

“天才”尚且如此,平凡人呢?

(83) A friend is easier lost than found. 得朋友难,失朋友易。

“路遥知马力,日久见人心”,“患难见真情”,要想得一知己,确实不容易。但毁掉友谊却是“分分钟”的事情。

(84) Time is money, but money is not time. 时间是金钱,但金钱买不来时间。

时间的重要性由此得以凸显。

(85) Sooner or later, the truth comes to light. 真相迟早会大白。

一是安慰被冤枉的人;二是警告要做坏事的人。

(86) Patience is bitter, but its fruit is sweet. 忍耐是痛苦的,但其果实是甜蜜的。

“小不忍则乱大谋”;“忍一时风平浪静,退一步海阔天空”。

(87) I am a slow walker, but I never walk backwards. 我走得很慢,但是我从来不会后退。

坚持就是胜利。

(88) Wisdom in the mind is better than money in hand. 脑中有知识,胜过手中有金钱。

知识就是力量,智慧就是资源。

(89) The devil is in the details. 细节决定成败。

小事成就大事,细节成就完美。

(90)There are many varieties of happy marriage. 幸福的婚姻并非千篇一律。

与托尔斯泰的“幸福的家庭都是相似的”有出入,但个人比较赞成这种说法。

(91)Let's try to be positive. 凡事往好处想。

这就是乐观者的标签。

(92)Being tested only makes you stronger. 磨难使人成长。

“宝剑锋自磨砺出”,不要害怕磨难,它的出现可看成是帮助我们成长的机会。

(93)All God's creatures have their troubles. 每个人都有各自的烦心事。

“家家有本难念的经”,坦然面对麻烦,冷静处理困扰。

(94)It's always an idea to be prepared. 未雨绸缪总是好的。

“有备而来”,“不打无准备之仗”。

(95)I do think a woman's place is eventually in the home. 我的确认为女人的最终归宿是家庭。

“家”不仅对女人重要,对男人同样重要。幸福的生活和成功的事业都离不开温馨而稳定的家庭生活。

四、巩固练习

1. 经典背诵。

(1)The past is past. 往事如烟。

(2)I think for I am. 我思故我在。

(3)Love conquers all. 爱无坚不摧。

(4)This is a good sign. 这是个好兆头。

(5)Nothing in life is sure. 天有不测风云。

(6)Memory is subjective. 记忆是主观的。

(7)Our lives are brief. 人的一生如此短暂。

(8)All for one, one for all. 人人为我,我为人人。

(9)Let bygones be bygones. 过去的就让它过去吧!

(10)It's far too early to say that. 现在说还为时太早。

(11)The human life is unpredictable! 人生变化无常。

(12)Everyone deserves a chance. 人人都该有个机会。

(13)There is no shame in hard work. 努力工作不可耻。

(14)All time is no time when it is past. 光阴一去不复返。

(15)Honesty is the best policy. 坦白从宽是最好的方法。

(16)Evil to him who evil thinks. 居心叵测者,必自取其辱。

(17)Old friends and old wine are best. 陈酒味醇,老友情深。

(18)A fool and his money are soon parted. 傻子守不住自家财。

(19)Life can be terribly unfair, can't it? 人生有时真是不公是吧?

(20)You have to keep moving, don't you? 人总的向前看,不是吗?

(21)The young are all so calm about change. 年轻人倒是处变不惊。

(22)We need to move past the past. 我们得将过去的纠葛一笔勾销。

(23)A lot of water is running under that bridge. 太多事都已成过去了。

(24)The brightest stars burn out the fastest. 最亮的星星也会最先熄灭。

(25)Better without gold than without friends. 宁可没有金钱,不可没有朋友。

(26)Will wonders never cease? 奇迹永远不会停止。(太阳打西边出来了啊?)

(27)Women have choices, men have responsibilities. 女性有选择,男人有责任。

(28)Opportunities like this don't keep falling from the sky. 天上不会掉下来馅饼。

(29)It has been said that change doesn't happen overnight. 俗话说,改变需要时间。

(30)Nothing makes you hungrier or more tired than grief. 化悲痛为食欲,化糨糊为力气。

(31)It's funny the way works out sometimes, isn't it? 生活有时就是这么戏剧性,对吧?

(32)We're all seeking control over something in our lives. 我们都寻求各自生活的主宰权。

(33)Man gives woman accepts. This is biological rule. 男人挣钱女人花,这是天经地义的。

(34)All work and no play makes Jack a dull boy and Jill a dull girl. 只工作不玩耍,聪明的孩子也变傻。

(35)I know it sounds kinda lame, but it's a stepping - stone. 我知道听起来很差劲,但是得一步一步来。

(36)We both know what it means to commit a crime for the greater good. 你我都懂得舍小我成全大我。

(37)Any good general knows you never let your soldiers see you sweat. 所有英明的将军都知道,在士兵面前要面不改色。

(38)I just have to get past this rough patch and then the money will be rolling in. 我只需要挺过这段困难时期之后就能财源广进了。

2. 你最喜欢的正能量句子是什么?请你再找些正能量的句子与大家分享。

3. 请利用正能量的句子帮助处于以下情境中的朋友。

(1)Mary 在四级考试中失败了,这几天挺郁闷的……

(2)Mike 最近要选第二专业,不知该从就业的角度还是自己喜好的角度选择。

(3)Tom 的女朋友最近与他分手了,他很难过。

(4)William 找了份兼职工作,虽然找了些钱,减轻了父母的经济负担,但对他的学习造成了不小的影响,他很矛盾,不知是否应该放弃这份兼职工作。

(5)John 被同寝室的室友误会为偷钱的人,十分委屈。

Chapter 13 Famous Quotations
名正言顺

一、思路讲解

在口语交流中,前面章节已经介绍了迅速组织语料和找到思路的方法,这一章我们将就名人名言给我们口语交流带来的帮助,通过丰富的案例向大家做具体分析,姑且把篇名叫做“名正言顺”吧。

“名人名言”,指那些从小事中悟出的大道理,为人类发展做出贡献的,富有知识的名人所说能够让人懂得道理的一句较为出名的话。“名人名言”涉及理想、勤奋、读书、志向、劳动、事业、志趣、爱情、婚姻、友谊、幸福、诚信、生命、爱国、励志、奉献、人生等。阅读背诵“名人名言”的好处很多:第一,虽然不提倡“名人效应”,但话语系出“名门”,或多或少有些号召力和影响力。歌德说:“读一本好书,就如同和一个高尚的人交谈。”那读这么多的名人名言,就如同和无数的高尚的人在交谈,让人增长知识,开阔眼界,使人的境界更高一层。第二,语句中所反映的睿智,如醍醐灌顶。陆游曾讲过:“书到用时方恨少,事非经过不知难。”人的一生是短暂的,不可能事事亲历,但用较短的时间获取最大量的经验,这不是人生幸事吗? 不是一种人生智慧吗? 第三,名人名言是语言中的历史文化精华,是非常宝贵的人文资源,充分展示了语言的魅力,更体现了语言的力量,多接触优美的语句会提高我们的审美能力,陶冶情趣。从提高口语的角度来讲,多看、多读、多背名人名言,可以积累广泛语料,了解知识背景,熟悉经典结构,跟学精辟用词,吸收人生智慧。另外,通过反复咀嚼体会,可对这些语句的修辞、句式、语气等进行改写、仿写,提高我们的表达水平。

这些只言片语总能带来无言的感动,帮助我们吸取教训,丰富经验,主宰命运,衡量生命,掌控未来;在语言表达上,用优美的词汇,经典的结构,多变的修辞,深刻的含义为我们提供了典范,助推我们在口语表达中更上一层楼。

下面对名人名言的案例分析和模仿练习都是抛砖引玉,希望大家通过学习,能找到更多的语料和探索出更多的使用方法。

二、佳句背诵

(1) Home is the place where, when you have to go there, it has to take you in. (Frost Robert, American Poet) 无论何时何地,家永远是向游子敞开大门的地方。(美国诗人 罗伯特·F)

家就是避风港,家就是永远的依靠。

(2) If you want your children to keep their feet on the ground, put some responsibility on their shoulders. (John Bryan British Essayist) 你若希望自己的孩子总是脚踏实地,就要让他们负些责任。(英国散文家 约翰·班扬)

责任的力量。

(3) The house of everyone is to him as his castle and fortress. (E. Coke, British Jurist) 每个人的家对他自己都像是城堡和要塞。(英国法学家　科克·E)

城堡和要塞就是起保护作用的建筑,所以家就是最安全的地方。

(4) The sooner you treat your son as a man, the sooner he will be one. (William John Locke, British Novelist) 越早把你的儿子当成男人,他就越早成为男人。(英国小说家　洛克·W·J)

培养孩子的经验之谈。

(5) Every man's work, whether it is literature or music or pictures or architecture or anything else, is always a portrait of himself. (Samuel Butler, American Educator) 每个人的工作,不管是文学、音乐、美术、建筑还是其他工作,都是自己的一幅画像。(美国教育家　勃特勒·S)

任何一份工作都能体现个人的特点。

(6) Growth and change are the law of all life. Yesterday's answers are inadequate for today's problems——just as the solutions of today will not fill the needs of tomorrow. (Franklin Roosevelt, American President) 生长与变化是一切生命的法则。昨日的答案不适用于今日的问题——正如今天的方法不能解决明天的需求。(美国总统　罗斯福·F)

不能刻舟求剑,要与时俱进。

(7) Happiness, I have discovered, is nearly always a rebound from hard work. (David Grayson, American Journalist) 我发现,辛勤工作的报酬几乎总是幸福。(美国记者　格雷森·D)

这就是人类辛勤工作的动力。

(8) It is no use doing what you like; you have got to like what you do. (Winston Churchill, British Prime Minister) 不能爱哪行才干哪行,要干哪行爱哪行。(英国首相　丘吉尔·W)

人生不如意十有八九,工作也是如此。干一行爱一行才能真正从工作中获得满足和幸福。

(9) My philosophy of life is work. (Thomas Alva Edison, American Inventor) 我的人生哲学就是工作。(美国发明家　爱迪生·T·A)

"工作狂"到家了。

(10) To youth I have three words of counsel——work, work and work. (Otto Bismarck, German Statesman) 对于青年,我的忠告只有三个词——工作,工作,工作。(德国政治家　俾斯麦·O)

"少壮不努力,老大徒伤悲"。

(11) Work banishes those three great evils: boredom, vice, and poverty. (Voltaire, French Philosopher) 工作撵跑三个魔鬼:无聊、堕落和贫穷。(法国哲学家　伏尔泰)

"一勤生百巧,一懒生百病"。

(12) Work is the grand cure for all the maladies and miseries that ever beset mankind. (Thomas Carlyle, British Historian) 工作是良药,能医治一切困扰人的疾苦。(英国历史学家　卡莱尔·T)

"勤劳一日,可得一夜安眠;勤劳一生,可得幸福长眠"。

(13) All splendor in the world is not worth a good friend. (Voltaire, French Thinker) 人世间所有的荣华富贵不如一个好朋友。(法国思想家　伏尔泰)

朋友就是最大的财富。

(14) If you would know the value of money, go and try to borrow some. (Benjamin Franklin, American President) 要想知道钱的价值,就去借钱试试。(美国总统　富兰克林·B)

“借钱给一个朋友,你会失去他;借钱给一个敌人,你会俘获他。”人与人之间如果有了金钱因素,就很难再像从前一样维持良好的关系。

(15)Money is a good servant and a bad master.(Francis Bacon, British Philosopher)金钱是善仆,也是恶主。(英国哲学家　培根 · F)

把金钱的双重性说得很透彻。

(16)No country, however rich, can afford the waste of its human resources.(Franklin Roosevelt , American President)再富裕的国家都浪费不起人力资源。(美国总统　罗斯富 · F)

人才可是世上最稀缺的资源。

(17)Sometimes one pays most for the things one gets for nothing.(Albert Einstein, American scientist)有时人为不花钱得到的东西付出最高昂的代价。(美国科学家　爱因斯坦 · A)

“天下没有白吃的午餐”。人情债难还。

(18)Do you love life? Then do not squander time; for that's the stuff life is made of.(Benjamin Franklin , American President)你热爱生命吗?那么就别浪费时间,因为生命是由时间组成的。(美国总统　富兰克林 · B)

时间就是生命。

(19)If you want to understand today, you have to search yesterday.(Pearl Buck, American female Writer)想要懂得今天,就必须研究昨天。(美国女作家　赛珍珠)

前车之鉴,后事之师。

(20)Never leave that until tomorrow, which you can do today.(Benjamin Franklin, American President)今天的事不要拖到明天。(美国总统　富兰克林 · B)

今日事,今日毕。

(21)Ordinary people merely think how they shall spend their time; a man of talent tries to use it.(Arthur Schopenhauer, German Philosopher)普通人只想到如何度过时间,有才能的人设法利用时间。(德国哲学家　叔本华 · A)

人与人之间的差别咋就这么大呢!

(22)To choose time is to save time.(Francis Bacon, British philosopher)合理安排时间就是节约时间。(英国哲学家　培根 · F)

运筹学原理。时间利用率高了就是节约时间。

(23)We always have time enough, if we will but use it aright.(Johan Wolfgang von Goethe, German Poet)只要我们能善用时间,就永远不愁时间不够用。(德国诗人　歌德 · J · W)

与上一句比较,真是“英雄所见略同”。

(24)I succeeded because I willed it; I never hesitated.(Bonaparte Napoleon, French Emperor)我成功是因为我有决心,从不踌躇。(法国皇帝　拿破仑 · B)

要成功就不能犹豫,要抱着必胜的信念,采取果断的行动。

(25)Success covers a multitude of blunders.(George Bernard Shaw, British Dramatist)成功由大量的失败铸就。(英国剧作家　萧伯纳 · G)

“失败是成功之母”的另一个版本。

(26)You have to believe in yourself. That's the secret of success.(Charles Chaplin, American Actor)人必须相信自己,这是成功的秘诀。(美国演员　卓别林 · C)

如果自信都没有了,什么都别谈了。

(27) If you don't learn to think when you are young, you may never learn. (Thomas Edison, American Inventor) 如果你年轻时就没有学会思考,那么就永远学不会思考。(美国发明家　爱迪生·T)

强调了培养年轻人创造性思维的重要性。

(28) Natural abilities are like natural plants that need pruning by study. (Francis Bacon, British Philosopher) 天生的才干如同天生的植物一样,需要靠学习来修剪。(英国哲学家　培根·F)

"玉不琢不成器"。

(29) Something attempted, something done. (Henry Wadsworth Longfellow, American Poet) 有所尝试,即有所作为。(美国诗人　朗费罗·H)

尝试是迈向成功的第一步。

(30) Victory won't come to me unless I go to it. (M. Moore, American Poet) 胜利是不会向我走来的,我必须自己走向胜利。(美国诗人　穆尔·M.)

胜利是靠自己争取的。

(31) A great man is always willing to be little. (R. W. Emerson, American Thinker) 伟大的人物总是愿意当小人物的。(美国思想家　爱默生·W·R)

看来低调能成就未来。

(32) Dare and the world always yields. If it beats you sometimes, dare it again and again and it will succumb. (W. M. Thackeray, British Writer) 大胆挑战,世界总会让步。如果有时候你被它打败了,不断地挑战,它总会屈服的。(英国作家　萨克雷·M·W)

顽强的意志成就最后的辉煌。

(33) The sum of behavior is to retain a man's own dignity, without intruding upon the liberty of others. (Francis Bacon, British Philosopher) 人的行为准则是,维护自己的尊严,不妨碍他人的自由。(英国哲学家　培根·F)

做人的道理。

(34) One may overcome a thousand men in battle, but he who conquers himself is the greatest victor. (Jawaharlal Nehru, Indian Premier) 一个人能在战场上制胜千军,但只有战胜自己才是最伟大的胜利者。(印度总理尼赫鲁·J)

战胜自己才是最难的。

(35) Education is a progressive discovery of our own ignorance. (W. Durant, American Writer) 教育是一个逐步发现自己无知的过程。(美国作家　杜兰特·W)

知识越多越觉得自己浅陋。

(36) In education we are striving not to teach youth to make a living, but to make a life. (W. A. White, American Journalist) 教育不是为了教会青年人谋生,而是教会他们创造生活。(美国记者　怀特·A·W)

我们的教育要强调实用性和谋生技能的培养,更要强调综合人文素养的培养。

(37) Time is a bird for ever on the wing. (T. W. Robertson, British Dramatist) 时间是一只永远在飞翔的鸟。(英国剧作家　罗伯逊·W·T)

这跟"光阴似箭"、"时光如流水"等是一个道理。

(38) Poor, and content is rich and rich enough. (William Shakespeare, British Dramatist) 安

贫就是富有。(英国剧作家　莎士比亚·W)

“知足者常乐”。

(39)That all happy families are alike, but every unhappy family is unhappy in its own way. (Leo Tolstoy, Russian Writer) 幸福的家庭都是相似的,但不幸的家庭各有各的不幸。(俄罗斯作家　列夫托尔斯泰)

尽管现在有人认为这句话说反了,但并不影响其知名度。愿大家都拥有幸福的家庭。

(40)We are not going in circles. We are going upward. The path is a spiral. (Siddhartha Gautama, Indian Prince) 我们的人生并非是原地打转,而是不断向上。前路是曲折向上的。(印度王子　乔达摩·悉达多)

道路是曲折的,前途是光明的。

(41)The man who has made up his mind to win will never say “impossible”. (Bonaparte Napoleon, French emperor) 凡是决心取得胜利的人,从来不说“不可能的”。(法国皇帝　拿破仑·B)

霸气!

(42)Every man is the master of his own fortune. (Richard Steele, British Writer) 每个人都主宰自己的命运。(英国作家　斯梯尔·R)

“我的地盘我做主,我的命运我掌控。”

(43)All that you do, do with your might; things done by halves are never done right. (R. H. Stoddard, American Poct) 做一切事都应尽力而为,半途而废永远不行。(美国诗人　斯托达德·H·R)

咬紧牙关拼到最后的人才是胜利者,半途而废的人永远看不到胜利的彩虹。

(44)Few things are impossible in themselves; and it is often for want of will, rather than of means, that man fails to succeed. (La Rocheforcauld, French Writer) 事情很少有根本做不成的;其所以做不成,与其说是条件不够,不如说是由于决心不够。(法国作家　罗切福考尔德·L)

怨天尤人,不如找找自己的原因。

(45)The proper function of man is to live, not to exist. (Jake London, American Writer) 人应该生活,而不是单纯为了生存。(美国作家　杰克·伦敦)

高质量和低水平的人生差异。

(46)As soon as you trust yourself, you will know how to live. (Johann Wolfgang von Goethe, German Writer) 只要你相信自己,你就会懂得如何生活。(德国作家　歌德·W·J)

活出自己的精彩!

(47)Almost any situation——good or bad——is affected by the attitude we bring to. (Lucius Annaus Seneca, Ancient Roman Philosopher) 差不多任何一种处境——无论好坏——都受到我们对待处境态度的影响。(古罗马哲学家　西尼加·L·A)

心态很重要。

(48)There is no absolute success in the world, only constant progress. (Jonathan Swift, British Writer) 世界上的事没有绝对成功,只有不断地进步。(英国作家　斯威夫特·J)

奋斗是永远的进行时。

(49)Every person has two educations, one which he receives from others, and one, more important, which he gives himself. (Edward Gibbon, British Writer) 每个人都受两种教育,一种来

自别人,另一种更重要的是来自自己。(英国作家　吉朋·E.)

这是对自学和自省的充分肯定。

(50)No man is happy who does not think himself so.(Publilius Syrus, Ancient Roman Writer) 认为自己不幸福的人就不会幸福。(古罗马作家　西鲁斯·P)

幸福是一种态度。

(51)Too intimate friendship is liable to turn to the negative side against people' s wishes at last.(Guozhen Wang, Chinese Poet) 过于亲密的友情,最终很容易走向双方愿望的反面。(中国诗人　汪国真)

"君子交淡如水,小人之交甘如醴"。

(52)To make a lasting marriage we have to overcome self-centeredness.(George Gordon Byron, British Poet)　要使婚姻长久,就需克服自我中心意识。(英国诗人　拜伦·G)

"爱情保鲜"的秘诀。

(53)Young men make great mistakes in life; for one thing, they idealize love too much.(John Ray, American Scientist) 年轻人一生中常犯大错误,其中之一就是把爱情太理想化了。(美国科学家　雷伊·J)

"犯错"是年轻人的特权。

(54)If you fight for yourself, only you can win; when you fight for your marriage, you both win.(Pearsall Paul, American Philosopher)　如果你只为自己奋斗,只有你一个人是赢家;若为婚姻奋斗,夫妻两人都是赢家。(美国哲学家　保罗·P)

家庭靠两个人共同营造。

(55)Treat other people as you hope they will treat you.(Aesop, Ancient Greek Fable Writer) 你希望别人如何对待你,你就如何对待别人。(古希腊寓言家　伊索)

善待别人就是善待自己。

(56)One never notices what has been done; one can only see what remains to be done.(Marie Curie, French Scientist) 切不要注意已经做了哪些,而只能去考虑还有哪些有待去做。(法国科学家　居里夫人·M)

躺着功劳簿上就别指望有更大进步。

(57)So long as there is a beginning, there will be no end.(Kun Chen, Chinese Actor) 行走,只要开始,就不会结束。(中国演员　陈坤)

人在路上。

(58)Truth needs no color; beauty, no pencil.(William Shakespeare, British Dramatist) 真理不需色彩,美丽无需涂饰。(英国剧作家　莎士比亚·W)

完美不需要装饰。

(59)Don't waste life in doubts and fears.(Ralph Waldo Emerson, American Thinker) 不要把生命浪费于怀疑与恐惧中。(美国思想家　爱默生·W·R)

让有意义的事情充实我们的生命。

(60)Nothing in life is to be feared. It is only to be understood.(Marie Curie, French Scientist) 生活中没有什么可怕的东西,只有需要理解的东西。(法国科学家　居里夫人·M)

无知才是最恐怖的事情。

(61)A man can succeed at almost anything for which he has unlimited enthusiasm.(C. M.

Schwab, American Industrialist）只要有无限的热情，一个人几乎可以在任何事情上取得成功。（美国实业家　施瓦布·M·C）

热情是做好一切事情的助推器。

（62）The important thing in life is to have a great aim, and the determination to attain it.（Johann Wolfgang von Goethe, German Writer）人生重要的在于确立一个伟大的目标，并有决心使其实现。（德国作家　歌德）

远大的目标+强烈的决心=巨大的成功

（63）To live is to function. That is all there is in living.（O. W. Holmes, American Writer）活着就要发挥作用，这就是生活的全部内容。（美国作家　霍姆斯O·W）

这就是活着的意义。

（64）Better be unborn than untaught, for ignorance is the root of misfortune.（Plato, Ancient Greek Philosopher）与其不受教育，不如不生，因为无知是不幸的根源。（古希腊哲学家　柏拉图）

不妨体会教育的重要性。

（65）When the fight begins within oneself, a man's worth something.（R. Browning, British Poet）当一个人内心开始斗争时，他就有了价值。（英国诗人　布朗宁·R）

"我思故我在"。

（66）We must accept finite disappointment, but we must never lose infinite hope.（Martin Luther King, Jr., American Civil Rights Leader）我们必须接受失望，因为它是有限的，但千万不可失去希望，因为它是无穷的。（美国民权运动领袖　马丁·路德·金）

希望在，成功在。

（67）Better to light one candle than to curse the darkness.（A. L. Strong, American Journalist）与其诅咒黑暗，不如燃起蜡烛。（美国记者　斯特朗·L·A）

"与其临渊羡鱼，不如退而结网"。

（68）A man can fail many times, but he isn't a failure until he begins to blame somebody else.（J. Burroughs, American Writer）一个人可以失败许多次，但是只要他没有开始责怪别人，他还不是一个失败者。（美国作家　巴勒斯·J）

"怨天尤人"是失败者的标志之一。

（69）And gladly would learn, and gladly teach.（Chaucer, British Poet）勤于学习的人才能乐意施教。（英国诗人　乔叟）

就跟有钱人喜欢做慈善一样。

（70）Happiness is a butterfly, which, when pursued, is always just beyond your grasp, but which, if you will sit down quietly, may alight upon you.（N. Hawthorn, American Writer）幸福是一只蝴蝶，你要追逐它的时候，总是追不到；但是如果你悄悄地坐下来，它也许会飞落到你身上。（美国作家　霍桑·N）

幸福就喜欢跟人"捉迷藏"。

三、佳句欣赏

（1）As a modern parent, I know that it's not how much you give children those count, it's the love and attention you shower on them. A caring attitude can not only save you a small fortune, but also even make you feel good about being tight-fisted and offering more care than presents. (O. Noel, American Writer) 作为一个现代的父母,我很清楚重要的不是你给了孩子们多少物质的东西,而是你倾注在他们身上的关心和爱。关心的态度不仅能帮你省下一笔可观的钱,而且甚至能使你感到一份欣慰,因为你花钱不多却给予了胜过礼物的关怀。(美国作家　诺埃尔·O)

结构:It' s not…it' s…;not only…but also…;好词:the love and attention you shower on them; tight-fisted 等。

(2)Happy are the families where the government of parents is the reign of affection, and obedience of the children the submission to love. (Francis Bacon, British Philosopher) 幸福的家庭,父母靠慈爱当家,孩子也是出于对父母的爱而顺从大人。(英国哲学家　培根·F)

好词:the government of parents, the reign of…, affection, obedience 等。

(3)It was the policy of the good old gentlemen to make his children feel that home was the happiest place in the world; and I value this delicious home——feeling as one of the choicest gifts a parent can bestow. (Irving Washington, Father of Literature of the United States.) 让孩子感到家庭是世界上最幸福的地方,这是以往有涵养的大人明智的做法。这种美妙的家庭情感,在我看来,和大人赠给孩子们的那些最精致的礼物一样珍贵。(美国文学之父　华盛顿·I)

结构:It was the policy of sb. to do…, and I value…,好词:delicious home, the choicest gift, bestow 等。

(4)My father had always said that there are four things a child needs: plenty of love, nourishing food, regular sleep, and lots of soap and water——and after those, what he needs most is some intelligent neglect. (Ivy Baker Priest, American Officer of Government) 我父亲总是说,一个孩子需要四样东西——充分的爱、富于营养的食物、有规律的睡眠、大量的肥皂和水——这些完了呢,他最需要的是一些明智的放任。(美国政府官员　普里斯特·I·B)

结构:sb. says that there are some things sb. needs:…——and after those, what he needs most is …;好词:intelligent neglect 等。

(5)Why should work be such a significant source of human satisfaction? A good share of the answer rests in the kind of pride that is stimulated by the job, by the activity of accomplishing. (Leonard R. Sayles, British Writer) 为什么工作竟然是人们获得满足的如此重要的源泉呢?最主要的答案就在于,工作和通过工作所取得的成就,能激起一种自豪感。(英国作家　塞尔斯·L·R)

结构:Why should … be such a significant source of…?;A good share of the answer rests in…;好词:stimulate, accomplish 等。

(6)The people who get on in this world are the people who get up and look for circumstances they want, and if they cannot find them. They make them. (George Bernard Shaw, British Dramatist) 在这个世界上,取得成功的人是那些努力寻找他们想要机会的人。如果找不到机会,他们就去创造机会。(英国剧作家　萧伯纳·G)

结构:The people who…are the people who…;好词:get on in this world, look for circumstances 等。

(7)Histories make men wise; poems witty; the mathematics subtle; natural philosophy deep; moral grave; logic and rhetoric able to contend. (Francis Bacon, British Philosopher) 历史使人明智;诗词使人灵秀;数学使人周密;自然哲学使人深刻;伦理使人庄重;逻辑修辞学使人善辩。

(英国哲学家　培根·F)

经典不需要解释,只需欣赏和背诵。

(8)We should so live and labor in our time that what came to us as seed may go to the next generation as blossom, and what came to us as blossom may go to them as fruit. This is what we mean by progress. (H. W. Beecher, American Orator, Priest) 我们一生应该这样地生活和劳动,使给予我们的种子能在下一代开花,使给予我们的花朵能在下一代结果,这就是我们所说的进步的意义。(美国演讲家、牧师　比彻 H·W)

结构:We should so live and labor in our time that what came to us may…, and what came to us …. This is what we mean…

(9)There is no royal road to science, and only those who do not dread the fatiguing climb can gain its numinous summits. (Karl Marx, German Revolutionary) 在科学上没有平坦的大道,只有不畏劳苦沿着其崎岖之路攀登的人,才有希望达到它光辉的顶点。(德国革命家　马克思·K)

结构:There is no …to …, and only those who… can do…;好词:royal road,fatiguing climb,numinous summit 等。

(10)As selfishness and complaint cloud the mind, so love with its joy clears and sharpens the vision. (Helen Keller, American Writer) 自私和抱怨是心灵的阴暗,愉快的爱则使视野明朗开阔。(美国作家　海伦·凯勒)

结构:As…and … do…, so … does…;好词:cloud the mind,clear and sharpen the vision 等。

(11)We have no more right to consume happiness without producing it than to consume wealth without producing it. (George Bernard Shaw, British Dramatist) 不创造幸福的人无权享用幸福,正如不创造财富的人无权享用财富一样。(英国剧作家　萧伯纳 B·G)

结构:We have no more right to do …than to do…;好词:consume happiness & consume wealth 等。

(12)My fellow Americans, ask not what your country can do for you; ask what you can do for your country. My fellow citizens of the world, ask not what America will do for you, but what together we can do for the freedom of man. (John Kennedy, American President) 美国同胞们,不要问国家能为你们做些什么,而要问你们能为国家做些什么。全世界的公民们,不要问美国将为你们做些什么,而要问我们共同能为人类的自由做些什么。(美国总统　肯尼迪·J)

结构:两个并列排比;好词:fellow Americans,fellow citizens 等。

(13)The world can be changed by man's endeavor, and that this endeavor can lead to something new and better. No man can sever the bonds that unite him to his society simply by averting his eyes. He must ever be receptive and sensitive to the new; and have sufficient courage and skill to novel facts and to deal with them. (Franklin Roosevelt, American President) 人经过努力可以改变世界,这种努力可以使人类达到新的、更美好的境界。没有人仅凭闭目、不看社会现实就能割断自己与社会的联系。他必须敏感,随时准备接受新鲜事物;他必须有勇气与能力去面对新的事实,解决新问题。(美国总统　罗斯福·F)

结构:用"endeavor"首尾相接;好词:unite sb. to sth. ,avert one's eyes,be receptive and sensitive,novel facts 等。

(14)Ideal is the beacon. Without ideal, there is no secure direction; without direction, there is no life.(Leo Tolstoy, Russian Writer)理想是指路明灯。没有理想,就没有坚定的方向;没有方向,就没有生活。(俄国作家　托尔斯泰·L)

结构:两个并列的“without… without…”;好词:secure direction 等。

(15)It is at our mother's knee that we acquire our noblest and truest and highest, but there is seldom any money in them.(Mark Twain, American Writer)就是在我们母亲的膝上,我们获得了我们的最高尚、最真诚和最远大的理想,但是里面很少有任何金钱。(美国作家　马克·吐温)

结构:强调句结构“It is …that…”。

(16)Experience proves that most time is wasted, not in hours, but in minutes. A bucket with a small hole in the bottom gets just as empty as a bucket that is deliberately kicked over.(Paul Meyer, French Linguist)经验证明,大部分时间都是被一分钟一分钟地而不是一小时一小时地浪费掉的。一只底部有个小洞的桶和一只故意踢翻的桶同样会流空。(法国语言学家　梅尔·P)

结构:not in…but in…;as…as…。

(17)Time cures sorrows and squabbles because we all change, and are no longer the same persons. Neither the offender nor the offended is the same.(Blaise Pascal, French Mathematician and Philosopher)时间可以去除忧虑和争吵,因为我们大家都在改变,不再与从前一样。触犯者和被触犯者都已不是从前的那个人了。(法国数学家、哲学家　帕斯卡尔·B)

结构:neither…nor…;好词:squabble,the offender 等。

四、佳句模仿

(1)A mother is not a person to lean on but a person to make leaning unnecessary.(D. C. Fisher, American female novelist)母亲不是赖以依靠的人,而是使依靠成为不必要的人。(美国女小说家　菲席尔·D·C)

(A teacher is not a person to lean on but a person to make leaning unnecessary.)

(A friend is a person to lean on…)

(2)He is the happiest, be he King or peasant, who finds peace in his home.(Johann Wolfgang von Goethe, German Dramatist and Poet)无论是国王还是农夫,家庭和睦是最幸福的。(德国剧作家、诗人　歌德·J·W)

(He is the smartest, who finds methods solving this difficult problem.)

(He is the most energetic, who finds fun in all sports.)

(3)We never know the love of the parents until we become parents ourselves.(Henry Ward Beecher, American Clergyman and Orator)不养儿不知父母恩。(美国牧师、演说家　比沏·H·W)

(We never know the truth until we investigate it.)

(We never know how simple it is until we try it.)

(4)The best preparation for good work tomorrow is to do good work today.(Elbert Hubbard, British Writer)为把明天的工作做好,最好的准备是把今天的工作做好。(英国作家　哈伯德·E)

(The best preparation for good performance in exams is to brush through all points.)

(The best preparation for tomorrow is to do good work today.)

(5) Work is more than a necessary for most human beings; it is the focus of their lives, the source of their identity and creativity. (Leonard R. Sayles, British Writer) 对大多数人来说,工作不仅仅是一种必需,它还是人们生活的焦点,是他们的个性和创造性的源泉。(英国作家　塞尔斯 · L · R)

(Health is more than a necessary for most elder people, it is the focus of their lives.)

(Housing is more than a necessary for most young people, it is the focus of their lives.)

(6) If you wish to succeed, you should use persistence as your good friend, experience as your reference, prudence as your brother and hope as your sentry. (Thomas Edison, American Inventor) 如果你希望成功,当以恒心为良友、以经验为参谋、以谨慎为兄弟、以希望为哨兵。(美国发明家　爱迪生 · T)

(If you wish to make friends, you should use sincerity as your company, experience as your reference, and kindness as your sister.)

(If you wish to speak English well, you should use persistence as your good friend, others' experience as your reference, practice as your brother and confidence as your support.)

(7) Only those who have the patience to do simple things perfectly ever acquire the skill to do difficult things easily. (Friedrich Schiller, German Dramatist and Poet) 只有有耐心圆满完成简单工作的人,才能够轻而易举地完成困难的事。(德国剧作家、诗人　席勒 · F)

(Only those who have good preparation ever acquire the confidence to get success.)

(Only those who have health ever acquire the qualification for the challenge.)

(8) To sensible men, every day is a day of reckoning. (J. W. Gardner, American Educator) 对聪明人来说,每一天的时间都是要精打细算的。(美国教育家　加德纳 · J · W)

(To sensible men, every day is a day of new start.)

(To sensible men, every failure is a good harvest.)

(9) If winter comes, can spring be far behind? (Percy Bysshe Shelley, British Poet) 冬天来了,春天还会远吗?(英国诗人　雪莱 · B · P)

(If New Year's Day comes, can Spring Festival be far behind?)

(If courage comes, can success be far behind?)

(10) Do not, for one repulse, give up the purpose that you resolved to effect. (William Shakespeare, British Dramatist) 不要只因一次挫败,就放弃你原来决心想达到的目的。(英国剧作家　莎士比亚 · W)

(Do not, for one failure, give up the purpose that you resolved to effect.)

(Do not, for one success, give up constant effort.)

(11) Our destiny offers not only the cup of despair, but the chalice of opportunity. (Richard Nixon, American President) 命运给予我们的不是失望之酒,而是机会之杯。(美国总统　尼克松 · R)

(Our destiny offers not only tears, but laughers.)

(This competition offers us not only the chance to practice, but the opportunity to observe out rivals.)

(12) Patience is bitter, but its fruit is sweet. (Jean Jacques Rousseau, French Thinker) 忍耐

是痛苦的，但其果实是甜蜜的。（法国思想家　卢梭·J·J）

(The course is bitter, but its fruit is sweet.)

(The preparation is bitter, but old students' reunion is sweet.)

(13) When peace has been broken anywhere, the peace of all countries everywhere is in danger. (Franklin Roosevelt, American President) 无论哪个地区的和平遭到破坏，世界各国的和平都会受到威胁。（美国总统　罗斯福·F）

(When the environment of Antarctic has been broken, the environment of all countries everywhere is in danger.)

(When the eco-system of one area has been broken, the eco – system of many countries is in danger.)

(14) Everything can be taken from a man but one thing: the freedom to choose his attitude in any given set of circumstances. (Leonhard Frand, German Novelist) 我可以拿走人的任何东西，但有一样东西不行，这就是在特定环境下选择自己的生活态度的自由。（德国小说家　弗兰克·L）

(Everything can be taken from a man but one thing: wisdom.)

(Everything can be taken from a man but one thing: knowledge.)

(15) Life is measured by thought and action, not by time. (J. Lubbock, British Biologist) 衡量生命的尺度是思想和行为，而不是时间。（英国生物学家　卢伯克·J）

(Happy life is created by hands and sweat, not by talking around.)

(A person is measured by his kindness and generosity, not by his appearance.)

(16) The emperor treats talent as tools, using their strong point to his advantage. (Shimin Li, Chinese Emperor) 君子用人如器，各取所长。（中国皇帝　李世民）

(We treat English as a tool, using its strong point to our advantage.)

(We treat Computers as effective tools, using their strong point to our advantage.)

(17) The secret of being miserable is to have leisure to bother about whether you are happy or not. (George Bernard Shaw, British Dramatist) 痛苦的秘密在于有闲功夫担心自己是否幸福。（英国剧作家　萧伯纳·B·G）

(The secret of being happy is to know how to share with the others.)

(The secret of being healthy is to have balanced diet.)

(18) To really understand a man we must judge him in misfortune. (Bonapart Napoleon, French Emperor) 要真正了解一个人，需在不幸中考察他。（法国皇帝　拿破仑·B）

(To really understand a man we must judge him in unexpected situation.)

(To really love a person we must cultivate him not spoil him.)

Chapter 14 Language Taboo

禁忌忌讳

一、思路讲解

虽说口语的特点是简单、轻松、随意,但也存在言语上的禁忌,什么场合说什么话? 什么该说? 什么不该说? 都必须引起我们的关注,否则就可能因缺乏修养和教养的"粗口"引起不必要的麻烦和损失。另外,随着社会的发展、语言的演变以及交流情境的需要,我们也提出"半禁忌"和"全禁忌"两个概念。"半禁忌"意指在亲密朋友、兄弟姐妹以及闺蜜等关系很亲密的人之间可以讲但在公开场合需谨慎的说法。"全禁忌"是指在公开场合和私人场合都应小心避免的表达。

首先我们说说"半禁忌"的表达,主要指在生气、烦恼、痛苦等情绪不佳状态下所使用的语气难听,让听者心情十分不爽的单词和句子,这类句子主要以祈使句和反问句为主。比如:"Don't bother me! /别烦我!","Don't play possum! /别装蒜!","It's none of your business! /关你屁事!"。这些表达虽然在私下对关系亲密的人说说,别人也能理解,但这种不客气的,伤人的话还是尽量少说,当然用这种话开玩笑,那就另当别论。

我们再来讲讲"全禁忌"的表达。

在许多语言里都忌讳诅咒、骂人的脏话,英语也不例外。有些骂人的话过于粗俗、难听,所以受到社会十分严格的限制。英语中的 Jesus Christ, Holy Mary, son of a bitch 就是这种话;而 damn, damn it, hell 这样的话在语气上就稍微轻一些。提醒一下,在英语中,大部分诅咒、骂人的话与基督教的词语和名称有关,千万不要把它们和宗教用词混淆。另外,诅咒、骂人的话受到年龄、性别、职业的限制,也受到环境和场合的限制:在公开发言、课堂教学或和长辈在一起时,人们就不大会说诅咒、骂人的话,但在家里、在劳动场合、在办公室、在公共汽车上、球场上或市场上,说的人就比较多。应该指出,人们对诅咒、骂人的话反应并不都一样,比如:有些年轻人将"粗话"当成"口头禅"或"语句填充语",只是说起来顺口,并无实质意义,这样的话听得多了,也就不那么刺耳,不过,对英语学习者和非本族人,由于"轻重拿捏不准",单词背景不清楚,还是少讲粗话为妙。

关于隐私的禁忌。讲英语的人很重视 privacy(隐私),所以不愿别人过问个人的事,privacy 这个词含有"秘密"、"隐私"、"私下"、"隐退"、"独处"、"不愿别人干涉"、"不希望别人过问"等义。"个人的事"包括"个人事务"(private business)、"私事"(private affairs)、"个人所关切的事"(private concerns)等。在英语中有句谚语:"A man's home is his castle. /一个人的家就是他的城堡。"意思是:一个人的家是神圣不可侵犯的,未经许可,不得入内。个人的事也是这样,不必让别人知道,更不愿别人干预。对大多数英国人和美国人来说,打听陌生人或不大熟悉的人的年龄、收入、婚姻、家庭、政治倾向、宗教信仰等都是失礼的,尽管中国人不认为这样做有什么不妥。一提上列问题就会被认为是在打听别人的私事,即用另一种方式侵犯了别人的"城堡"。另外,隐私禁忌还涉及性行为、怀孕、人的私处以及排泄等话题的表达。在英语中，涉及隐私话题时，一般采用含糊其辞和拐弯抹角这两种方式。比如：当别人说“I' m going out.”时，你就不要再追问别人的去向。再看看：如果走在郊外，有女性说I want to pick flowers.（我想去摘花。）实际上就是想去“方便”的意思。

关于性别歧视语言。性别歧视语言主要指轻视妇女的语言。从英语历史来看，英语是以男子为中心的语言，偏袒男性，贬低女性，最明显的例子莫过于“人类”一词用 mankind，不用 womankind。不论说话还是写文章，提到性别不明的人时，一律用 he 而不用 she。如果男孩子或男人有女相，就称之为略带贬义的 sissy（女孩子气的男孩子，女人气的男人），如果女孩子或姑娘的行为举止像男孩子或小伙子，就称之为带有褒义的 tomboy（男孩子，小伙子似的顽皮姑娘）。在交流中，要想避免性别歧视语言，应尽量采用中性单词，无性别歧视的单词，单词的复数形式，第二人称形式，被动语态等方式回避性别歧视语言的使用。

关于种族歧视语言。种族主义认为，有些人种天生低劣，素质不如其他人种，种族歧视语言就是显示对某些种族带有偏见的词语和说法。在英语中，由于历史原因，多数这类词语显示对黑人有种族偏见。比如：“白”表示“清白”、“纯洁”、“干净”、“慈善”等，这些都是有积极含义的褒义词，而“黑”则与“邪恶”、“罪孽”、“肮脏”等有关，如：blackguard（恶棍）、blacklist（黑名单）、black mark（污点）等。全家引以为耻的“败家子”叫 black sheep，不叫 white sheep。无恶意的谎言叫 white lie，不像 ordinary lie（一般的谎言）或 black lie（用心险恶的谎言）那么坏。另外，用 nigger、boy 之类的词来称呼成年黑人男子有明显的轻蔑意味。不仅黑人有蔑称，某些其他国家或种族的人也有蔑称。如把意大利人叫作 dagos，把犹太人叫作 kikes，把波兰人叫作 Polacks，把中国人叫作 chinks，把日本人叫作 Japs 等。这些都是带有诬蔑性的名称，反映强烈的种族偏见。尽管我们不说这些词语，但在英语学习过程中和语料收集的时候，会听到带有污辱性的有种族歧视意味的谈论，所以我们要了解这方面的知识，学会辨别。

作为英语学习者，一定要注意语言使用的场合。清楚了解禁忌语，可以减少交流障碍，避免不必要的错误，不让自己处于交流中被动的境地，化解交流矛盾。

二、案例学习

1.“半禁忌”表达

(1) Out! 滚!

(2) Piss off! 滚开!

(3) Badass! 坏蛋!

(4) Bullshit! 胡说!

(5) Damn! 该死的!

(6) That spinster! 那个老处女!

(7) Bite me! 你管我!

(8) Stay out! 滚出去!

(9) Up yours! 去你的!

(10) You old bag! 你这丑老婆子!

(11) Crap on things! 该死!

(12) Who wants? 谁稀罕?

(13) Cut the crap！别废话！

(14) Big mouth！多嘴！

(15) Nuts！呸；胡说；混蛋

(16) Losers walk！输家滚蛋！

(17) Oh, crap！浑蛋！你骗人！

(18) Knock it off. 少来这一套。

(19) You are dirty. 你真下流。

(20) You deserved that！你活该！

(21) Bloody hell！天啊！该死的！

(22) Bottle it！闭嘴！Zip it！闭嘴！

(23) Watch your mouth. 嘴巴干净点。（说话文明点。）

(24) His is but a stupid-ass reason. 他那理由就是狗屁不是！

(25) How dumb are you? 你到底有多蠢？

(26) Mind your own business！少管闲事！

(27) It's a pain in the ass. 真伤脑筋。

(28) You clumsy little fool. 你这个笨手笨脚的蠢蛋。

(29) Look at your monkey suit！瞧你那身猴装！（对男子西装的轻蔑说法）

(30) The sad sack was a moron. 那个糊涂蛋就是个二货。

(31) Quit making an ass out of yourself. 你别表现得跟笨蛋一样！

(32) To hell！去死吧！Drop dead！去死吧！Screw you！去死吧！

2."全禁忌"表达

(1)案例分析

①"cock"在美式英语中指"男性生殖器"，所以在美式英语中"公鸡"最好用"rooster"表示，比如："I was born in the year of rooster. /我是鸡年出生的。"

②"rubber"在口语中有"避孕套"的意思，看看这句话，"He always carries a rubber just in case. /他总是随身携带避孕套以防万一"。

③女性怀孕，也很少直接用"pregnant"这个词，一般都绕着弯子说，比如："She is expecting. /她在待产中。"，"She is in a delicate condition. /她正怀孕中。"，"She is well-along. /她心满意足。"，"She is about to have a blessed event. /她不久会有喜事。"，"She is about to be in a family way. /她不久就要走向家庭之路。"。但如果是少女"未婚先孕"，这个句子就应该这样说"She is in trouble."。

④中国人避讳说"死"，英美人同样如此。一般不会直接说"He died."，改为说"He went to his rewards. /他去领奖了。"，"He passed away. /他离去了。"，"He breathed his last. /他咽下了最后一口气。"如果士兵在战场上牺牲，就用"He fell in battle. /他为国捐躯。"。

⑤"强奸"也是一个很敏感的词，一般不说"She was raped."，而采用"She was betrayed."，"She was attacked."，"She is the victim of felonious assault."等句子代替。

(2)案例列举

①Mrs. Flow 月经

②shtup 鬼混，性交

③a fallen woman 妓女
④a business girl 妓女
⑤peeping Tom 窥视狂
⑥a working girl 应招女郎
⑦nature calls 想上厕所
⑧a wild body 惹火的身材
⑨one-night stand 一夜情
⑩training bra 少女的胸罩
⑪do one's business 排便
⑫do No.1（小孩）小便
⑬do No.2（小孩）大便
⑭flip the bird 伸中指(以示侮辱)
⑮a whoremonger 拉皮条者,嫖客
⑯S. O. B = son of the bitch 混蛋
⑰button-on-a-fur-coat kind of guys 小鸡鸡的男人

三、巩固练习

1.请看看下面的句子,你能看出其中的禁忌表达吗?

(1) She is in labor! 她要生了。
(2) He's a John. 他是小白脸。
(3) I am with child. 我怀孕了。
(4) I got my period. 我来月经了。
(5) You are full term? 你快要生了?
(6) He is shooting blank. 他阳痿。
(7) He is full of shit. 他满口谎言。
(8) She is a B-girl. 她是个酒吧女。
(9) Her water broke. 她的羊水破了。
(10) I want to go to John. 我想去厕所。
(11) I want to wash my hand. 我想上厕所。
(12) She flipped him to the bird. 她对那人比中指。
(13) I have missed my bleeding. 我的经期推迟了。
(14) You've started menopause. 你的更年期开始了。
(15) Guys need to blow off steam. 男人得发泄发泄的。
(16) What team are you playing for? 你的性取向到底是什么呢?
(17) This is the kind of thing that chaps my ass. 这种事最让我头疼。
(18) Quit making an ass out of yourself, and put your pants on. We're in public. 别像个白痴一样,冷静点。我们是在大庭广众之下。
(19) Where's the rest room? (男生)休息室(厕所)在哪里? Where's the powder room?

（女生）化妆室（厕所）在哪里？

（20）Listen, you old bag, hand over the pocket book now and no one will get hurt. 丑老太婆给我听着，马上把你的手提包交出来就不会受伤。

2. 同英美人士交流时，应尽力避免如下问题：

（1）How old are you?（你多大年纪？）

（2）What's your age?（你多大年纪？）

（3）How much do you make?（你挣多少钱？）

（4）What's your income?（你的收入是多少？）

（5）How much did that dress cost you?（你的连衣裙花多少钱买的？）

（6）How much did you pay for that car?（你那车花了多少钱？）

（7）Are you married or single?（你结婚了吗？）

（8）How come you're still single?（你怎么还没结婚呢？）

（9）So you're divorced. What was the reason? Couldn't you two get along?（唉，你离婚了。什么原因呢？两人合不来吗？）

（10）Are you a Republican or a Democrat?（你是共和党人，还是民主党人？）

（11）Why did you vote for…?（你为什么投……的票？）

（12）Do you go to church?（你信教吗？）

（13）What's your religion?（你信什么教？）

（14）Are you Catholic?（你信天主教吗？）

References
参 考 文 献

[1] Della Thompson. 牛津简明英语词典[M]. 北京:外语教学与研究出版社,2001.

[2] 李国南. 汉语比喻在西方的可接受度[J]. 四川外语学院学报,1996(3):7-10.

[3] 刘晓晖. 试论文学作品中基本颜色词的翻译方法[J]. 陕西师范大学学报,2001(9):311-315.

[4] 平洪,张国杨. 英语习语与英美文化[M]. 北京:外语教育与研究出版社,2001.

[5] 王治奎. 大学英汉翻译教程[M]. 济南:山东大学出版社,1999.

[6] 温洪瑞. 英汉谚语文化涵义对比研究[J]. 山东大学学报,2004(4):10-13.

[7] 吴月珍,柴春花. 汉语修辞学研究和应用[M]. 郑州:河南人民出版社,1997.

[8] 中国社会科学院语言研究所词典编辑室. 现代汉语词典[M]. 5 版. 北京:商务印书馆,2005.

普通高等学校规划教材

看看再说

Read Before You Speak

当代非英语专业口语教程

Oral English for Non-English Majors

张周易　曹顺发　主　编

人民交通出版社股份有限公司
China Communications Press Co.,Ltd.

CONTENTS

Chapter 1　Cultural Similarities
文化相通

1. 从文化相通的角度说说下面中文词组或句子的英语表达。

(1) as proud as a peacock
(2) as faithful as a dog
(3) paper tiger
(4) to lose one's face
(5) Stop talking in circle.
(6) honesty conversation
(7) Many dishes, many diseases.
(8) Many men, many minds.
(9) as solid as a rock
(10) a bed of thorns
(11) one foot in the grave
(12) hang by a hair
(13) (as) light as a feather
(14) add fuel to the flames
(15) in black and white
(16) a lady's choice and a gentleman's agreement
(17) Money is tight.
(18) at lightning speed
(19) to give sb. green light
(20) to go to the green wood
(21) a wolf in sheep's clothing
(22) to be red with anger
(23) Money makes the man.
(24) a thunder of applause
(25) Consider it an investment in good karma.
(26) I shut my ear for that.
(27) Bad news travels fast.
(28) hang up his name
(29) bring people back to health, back to life
(30) anyone with information
(31) A woman's heart is like the needle in the haystacks. (A woman's heart is a deep ocean of secret.)

2. 从文化相通的角度说说下面英文词组或句子的中文表达。

(1)纪念日、喜庆日子
(2)点灯熬油
(3)体力与脑力
(4)他是条蛇。(有阴险小人之意)
(5)敬酒
(6)你很难读懂。
(7)眼见为实。
(8)走高端路线
(9)拥有权力的位置
(10)一时糊涂
(11)深刻的交谈
(12)聪明一世糊涂一时。
(13)贫穷是非多。
(14)欲速不达。
(15)无苦即无乐。
(16)来得容易去得快。
(17)有其父必有其子。
(18)江山易改,本性难移。
(19)饥不择食。(乞丐是没有选择权利的人)
(20)过街老鼠,人人喊打。
(21)滚石不生苔。
(22)滴水穿石。
(23)笔伐胜过刀枪。
(24)人性不堪。/人无完人。(人终归是人。局限性/错误)
(25)果真是饱汉不知饿汉饥。
(26)养不教父之过。
(27)祸不单行。(厄运从不单独到来)
(28)积少成多。
(29)知足常乐。
(30)吃一堑,长一智。
(31)爱叫的狗很少咬人。

4. 用本单元所学的知识造句。

(1)Her plans for a movie career had all been a pipe dream.
(2)I got an eye for human behavior.
(3)You read my mind.
(4)I am not a mind reader.
(5)He'll do anything for her —she's got him eating out of her hands.

(6) He got the bag for stealing money from the till.

(7) I think it was really a bad decision of them and it's going to eat their own bitter fruit.

(8) He always seems to be of two minds about everything.

(9) To be an effective communicator, the first thing you need to do is to learn how to break the ice.

(10) You don't have to win every argument, agree to disagree.

(11) Of those polled, nine out of ten said they preferred the new product.

(12) Do we want torun away from the embarrassing problem with our tail between our legs, like a beaten dog?

(13) Before you start you're a comprehensive cover-all-the-bases English review, step back and think about what you really need to study.

(14) We have to cut through all of the red tape to quickly attain a goal.

(15) Beginner's luck! Everything was going well with me.

(16) We bite off more than we can chew. It's time to get some help.

(17) I have turned over a new leaf.

(18) Tell me the truth; don't beat around (about) the bush, man!

(19) You were mistaken. You shouldnt hold your ground.

(20) She is selectively deaf to my repeated warnings.

(21) Tomorrow is our first meeting with the new client, so let's try not get off on the wrong foot.

(22) Temporary lapse is not a dead end street.

(23) In order to be a good salesman, you need to develop a thick skin.

(24) Now how to deal with or utilize the city renewable resources has been a burning question in China.

(25) Don't shoot the messenger, and you are supposed to find the initiator.

Chapter 2 Cultural Differences
文化差异

1. 从文化差异的角度说说下面中文词组或句子的英语表达。

(1) be (caught) in a catch-22 (situation); be (caught) in a dilemma

(2) He loves to pull a stranger's leg.

(3) make blood boil

(4) I never had beef with George.

(5) see red

(6) Nothing could stay hidden forever.

(7) talk to a wall

(8) I suggested she leave the lane for a while.

(9) resolved the issue

(10) old-fashioned progressive dinner

(11) I meant every word.

(12) fight fire with fire

(13) Mr. Lah-di-dah (Mr. La-di-da) (Lah-di-dah 故作上流人士姿态的;故充高雅的 a. 装模作样的人 n.)

(14) has sb. wrapped in silk and feathers

(15) I'll cross that bridge when I come to it.

(16) I'm not quite on top of this.

(17) Every Tom, Dick and Harry is looking for work these days.

(18) follow the sheep

(19) false hope

(20) talk until one is blue in the face

(21) frank and salty question

(22) I know we sound like parrots.

(23) Uncle Tom Cobley (是英式英语中用于表示"一干人等"的幽默说法)

(24) I feel kind of blue today.

(25) Literally he has to fall flat 平卧在地,(面朝下)跌倒 on his face.

(26) You head is spinning.

(27) pick a fight

(28) yo-yo (墙头草)

(29) You have a lot of gall. (胆汁)

(30) bar mitzvah (满 13 岁开始负有宗教义务的犹太受戒龄少年 n. 给男孩行受戒礼 v.)

(31) greasy-haired (油头的) little boy

(32) Thank god and hallelujah!
(33) look for a few bucks
(34) hangover cure
(35) drive a wedge between friends (wedge 楔形物;导致分裂的东西)
(36) sleepover
(37) And you have set the bar so high on that name. (设高婚姻门槛 Set the marriage bar high)
(38) We're more than evenly matched.
(39) lucky charm
(40) employ sb for a job he can't do
(41) There are two properties I have my eye on.
(42) Why do you care people say?
(43) They won't hear a word from me.
(44) You are grounded for two weeks.
(45) But don't say anything to alarm him.
(46) They're royalty. We're peasants.
(47) He is a cupcake.

2. 从文化差异的角度说说下面英文词组或句子的中文表达。

(1) 对牛弹琴
(2) 山中无老虎,猴子称霸王。
(3) 挂羊头卖狗肉
(4) 胆小如鼠
(5) 一箭之遥
(6) 水中捞月
(7) 蠢得像猪
(8) 守口如瓶
(9) 害群之马;败家子;不孝子女
(10) 重回某处
(11) 自已有弱点就不要说别人的坏处。
(12) 躲得了初一躲不过十五。
(13) 留意你说的话
(14) 不可能
(15) 为什么你要给任何事情下定义?
(16) 结论就显而易见了。
(17) 以其人之道还治其人之身。
(18) 羊群效应; 从众心理;群体效应
(19) 否认事情有时会越描越黑。(paraffin 石蜡)
(20) 谁叫她羊入虎口来着。
(21) 这吓人的东西还是敬而远之好。

(22)拆了东墙补西墙

(23)我不希望你哭丧着脸,终日劳神伤心。

(24)我什么都不懂。

(25)真是漫长啊!

(26)不要揽事太多。(同事有很多重要的事情要做 Tom always has many irons in the fire. 汤姆总是日理万机。)

(27)辅导员(中英这个单词在内涵上还是有差异的,英语的意思是"咨询顾问;指为学校工作的人向学生提供就业和个人问题建议。"在中国,辅导员的工作大家都清楚,勿用赘言。)

(28)有时她会为了大局着想而牺牲她所爱。

(29)让某人坐冷板凳

(30)拼字大赛

(31)你觉得对号,那就入座呗。

(32)我在恋爱。

(33)胎死腹中。

(34)救命稻草

(35)嘘声(性)(嘲笑的不满的嘘声)

(36)忙得不可开交

(37)一幅心事重重的样子

4.用本单元所学的知识造句。

(1)Perhaps you should tell your son about the birds and the bees.

(2)Ask him to do it—he is an eager beaver.

(3)He is a real blue blood.

(4)When we make contradiction with others, we'll take off the gloves or turn hostility into friendship.

(5)As the sole breadwinner for his family of four, he could not remain idle for long.

(6)My neighbor is a cold fish.

(7)The last three years there has been a lot of sensitization about this issue so governments are now beginning to realize they cannot sweep it under the carpet.

(8)We shall sleep more soundly in our beds when this violent criminal has been put behind bars.

(9)Dont jump the gun by making a statement about what caused the explosion before the investigation is completed.

(10)All that is now just water under the bridge.

(11)Just because you may get rejected once, that doesn't mean you have to throw the towel.

(12)The two stars who play the father and mother are good in the lead roles but this young man who plays the son steals the thunder.

(13)He was the black sheep of the family.

(14)As the students,I think it is not necessary for us to sing the blues about homework.

(15)The bell had rang and we were all eager to leave, but the teacher asked us to hold our

horses until he had finished.

(16) A person who is in the habit of talking big often has to eat crow in the end.

(17) He is working so hard that he is as busy as a beaver. (海狸)(bee)

(18) If you don't learn how to keep your nose clean, you're going to end up in trouble.

(19) The rich old lady really put the cat among the pigeons. She told her sons and daughters that she would leave everything to her gardener and nothing to them.

(20) Sorry for my voice. I've got a frog in my throat.

(21) Her room is always at sixes and sevens, even without room to swing a cat in.

(22) They actually know nothing about what fashion is. They're only following others like sheep.

(23) He has lost more than 60 million dollars. If you invest more, you are throwing good money after bad.

(24) The boss criticized him at the meeting, but it was just like water off a duck's back.

(25) Ann really is a good egg. If only she didn't have such a short fuse.

(26) I've apologized till I'm blue in the face.

(27) It's true that he makes a lot of mistakes, but don't be too hard on him. He's just not dry behind the ears yet.

(28) We have to put a bold front (勇敢面对现实) and confront this situation. It's no use burying our heads in the sand. (缩头乌龟)

(29) Buying an apartment in Beijing will cost you an arm and a leg.

(30) The cheese here can't hold a candle to the cheese in France.

(31) All right, now that we have covered the social amenities, let's talk turkey about what really happened.

(32) The truth is that Mr. Peabody is resigning as chairman, and I heard that from the horse's mouth, Mr. Peabody himself.

(33) I'll come for you when the coast is clear.

(34) Tom was suspended from school after he called the principal an old goat.

(35) You just have to get on her god side. She's really just a pussycat.

(36) Ten thousand dollars! That is highway robbery!

(37) Tom has to face the music for his rash behavior.

(38) I've studied Chinese for a long time, but it's still Greek to me.

(39) You won again! You have the luck of the Irish.

(40) His business has been in a bad state, so his hope of living high on the hog is shattered.

(41) The road hog won't pull over and let me pass.

(42) Tom always ticks us pink.

(43) Speak of the devil! Hi, Mark! We were just taking about you.

(44) Because she is so independent, she always says that marriage is for the birds.

(45) He was so cocksure that she would call him first.

(46) He likes to wet his whistle on the way home from work in the evening.

(47) I'm not sure whether John will win the election or not. It's a toss-up.

(48) I think she's just a really good egg.

(49) We just scraped some students together for the school basketball team. Our success was simply the luck of the draw.

(50) My grandfather looks like he's sixty but he's really eighty years old and fit as a fiddle: he still has his own teeth, doesn't need glasses, and walks four miles every day.

Chapter 3 Idioms & Slangs

习语俗语

1. 请翻译和理解以下谚语。

(1)旁观者清,当局者迷。
(2)不要自砸饭碗。
(3)一个巴掌拍不响。
(4)美酒一下肚,话匣关不住。
(5)好聚好散。
(6)欲尽得,必尽失。
(7)痛快一时,痛苦一世。
(8)少说为佳。
(9)傻子有傻福。
(10)男人盖房,女人持家。
(11)既往不咎。多一事不如少一事。
(12)兼听则明,偏听则暗。
(13)树大招风。
(14)要取得经验,须付出代价。
(15)谎言终究要败露。
(16)学的快,忘得快。
(17)人急造反,狗急跳墙。
(18)众人的事儿没人管。
(19)英雄所见略同。

4. 请用本单元所学的知识造句。

(1)The dispute about inheriting estate formed an apple of discord between them.
(2)His voluntary offer to help may be a Greek gift.
(3)Profit tends to play second fiddle to revenue in many entrepreneurs' plans.
(4)I often like to think aloud.
(5)Hisresignation came out of the blue.
(6)You get a chance like this once in a blue moon.
(7)It can be easy to fall into a fast food rut on the road.
(8)No wonder they met their Waterloo in this match. They hadn't been trained for months.
(9)Dont forget to clock in, otherwise you wont get paid.
(10)Dont play games with me, Jane. I'm on to your tricks and manipulations.
(11)He thinks nothing of a twenty-mile walk.

(12)No big talk with me,I have your number.

(13)Mark found it easy to eat with chopsticks, once he got the hang of it.

(14)We were the end of rope.

(15)I just assumed you had your hands full.

(16)I am in the middle of something. Could you call back later?

(17)Tom seems to be in high cotton. He has made a lot of money.

(18)I get hot under the collar every time i think about it.

(19) Joe got fired from that big company because they thought he was too much of a free-wheeler.

(20)Choices, choices! How can I pick a college when there are so many to go to?

(21)I think he must be a policeman, he keeps fishing for information.

(22)I' ve heard enough of your line of lies. Leave me alone.

(23)Not for anything in the world willI ever sell my friend down the river.

(24)You are the very milk of human kindness.

(25)As the saying goes "One good turn deserves another. " I' m sure you will be rewarded.

(26)She made a meal of that job—— it took her five hours!

(27)Why don' t we play it by ear?

(28)How could he fall asleep at the switch?

(29)Ted didn' t go to school because he was under the weather.

(30)I can promise you that the products we send you will be of A-1 quality.

5. 借助词典理解下列习语并造句。

(1)正积极进行,达到高潮

The opponents' campaign efforts were already in full swing when the new candidate decided to run for election. 那位新的候选人决定参加竞选时,竞争对手的竞选活动均已达到高潮。

(2)合适

A Rolls Royce is simply too expensive for my blood. 劳斯莱斯轿车对我而言太贵了。

(3)(指不幸事等)应由某人承受;罪有应得

He failed his examination. It served him right because he had not studied. 他考试不及格活该,因为他没有学习。例:A:I got soaked in the rain. B:It serves you right——I told you to take an umbrella. A:我让雨浇坏了。B:活该—— 我早就告诉你带伞。

(4)淡忘(这个短语一般用于否定句中,表示以某种生活方式忘记他过去的难堪、丑闻、罪行、耻辱等,改过自新,重新做人)

Beaten by the worst team in the league? They'll never live it down! 让联赛中最差的劲队打败了? 这是永远也忘不了的事!

(5)大笑,大笑不止,捧腹大笑

The movie was so funny that we were all in stitches. 这部电影很有趣,我们全都前仰后合。

(6)忽视某人/某事;对某人/某事置之不理

He was supposed to pay today, but he blew it off. 他今天应该付款的,可是他还是对它置之不理。

(7)意见完全一致

I suppose one good reason for them to get married is that they see eye to eye on just about everything. 我猜想,他们结婚的理由是,因为他们的对每件事都有相同的看法。

(8)极稀少

My mother always told me that good men were few and far between. 我母亲常告诉我,好人很少。

(9)别再挂念这件事。

Don't give it another thought. Everything will be OK. 别再挂念这件事。一切都会好的。

Chapter 4 Reverse Thinking

逆向思考

1. 从逆向思考的角度说说下面词组的英语表达。

(1) a society without much culture
(2) move one's stuff out
(3) keep the details
(4) big mass
(5) magic words
(6) Mind your own business.
(7) disturb peace
(8) It's the half time
(9) clear your mind
(10) be under control
(11) strong word
(12) get some ideals (ideal 想象中的事物;设想)
(13) share one's problem with sb
(14) message received
(15) promote sb
(16) high-powered career
(17) full house
(18) perfect couple
(19) delightful surprise
(20) stand on one's pride
(21) penny side
(22) nursing house (home)
(23) pass-through (人可以通过) rear seat
(24) matching hats
(25) leave sb alone
(26) have an early night (比较 the night is young)
(27) choose your words carefully
(28) make sure you stick around

2. 从逆向思考的角度说说下面句子的英语表达。

(1) The boy is not cooperative.
(2) This is off-limits.

(3) I know how to deal with it.
(4) She is a woman of considerable culture.
(5) I accept your offer.
(6) I'm just born that way.
(7) I don't have time to stop.
(8) They seemed all right.
(9) How desperate am I!
(10) I think it's best that we just forget about it.
(11) I've got nothing against him.
(12) sb's heart belongs to sb.
(13) You must've crossed paths.
(14) I'll take you through it.
(15) There won't be a dry eye in the house.
(16) They're locked.
(17) That marriage has already be on repair.
(18) You can't be serious.
(19) She is under tremendous time pressure.
(20) I stay out of it.
(21) You don't know what you are talking about.
(22) except one more thing
(23) stay away from sth
(24) Stay out of it!
(25) Keep your mouth shut.
(26) Hold that thought!
(27) Don't feel bad.
(28) Let's stay on topic.
(29) Save your breath.
(30) Don't make yourself ridiculous.
(31) You look very dashing. dash 猛冲
(32) I've only made a few enquiries.
(33) I've started on it.(已经开始了,就要咬牙坚持下去)
(34) I'll get straight to the point.
(35) If we were you I'd keep out of it.
(36) He's not minor.
(37) keep sth to oneself 别到处说。Keep it to yourself.
(38) I'm past help.
(39) It cant be helped.
(40) It cant be less interesting.
(41) You can say that again!

3. 用本单元所学的知识造句。

(1) The problem is that his elder brother doesn't get the stomach for cats, so she couldn't keep the cat at home.

(2) Not every child is the piano type of person. Don't push her.

(3) The best way to avoid accidents is doing it by the book.

(4) Oh, my! I searched every inch of my house but I couldn't find my keys.

(5) He must be kept by the traffic jam.

(6) I couldn't get the beautiful music off my head.

(7) His heroic deeds strike her.

(8) But I am OK with boxed lunch.

(9) I am uncomfortable with getting up early on the cold morning.

(10) I hate to be given the silent treatment.

(11) Get a full night sleep every night.

(12) He is a good judge of art.

(13) I'll come to attend the class on time, you have my word.

(14) She looks really sad. Let me steel her nerves with encouragement.

(15) Crying won't change anything, and work hard for your next test.

(16) It is important to learn how to turn the page when you are in the hot water.

(17) Don't make me started. I'm afraid I can't tell you.

(18) The elder should positively take part in community activities. Don't be housebound.

(19) Actually, going shopping is the very last thing I want to do!

Chapter 5　Connotative Understanding
内涵相助

1. 利用“内涵相助”的方法说说下面中文词组的英语表达。

(1) police business
(2) lunch rush
(3) return the favor
(4) average citizens
(5) regular chores
(6) second-guessing
(7) high-leveled meeting
(8) criminal record
(9) skip the school
(10) state dinner
(11) serious buyer
(12) play dirty
(13) dirty-dance
(14) a little more human
(15) not good for him
(16) matching clothes
(17) heartfelt letter (heartfelt adj. 衷心的;真诚的;真心真意的)
(18) be scratched
(19) disposal camera
(20) at a bit of a disadvantage
(21) appreciated glance
(22) the first rule of competition
(23) late fee/late charge
(24) security deposit
(25) full refund
(26) positively glowing
(27) standard procedures
(28) straight answer
(29) dreaming job
(30) a difficult transition
(31) reality show
(32) attack sb

(33) old married couple
(34) another break-down
(35) establishment of intimacy
(36) one dayout of nowhere
(37) soul mates
(38) comfortably handsome
(39) dream man
(40) It's mind-boggling
(41) drive sb away
(42) No games! (别玩花样)
(43) aggressive question
(44) seal the deal
(45) a sense of timing
(46) specify the context
(47) explore your mind
(48) refuse to acknowledge
(49) some tricks of the trade
(50) hidden meaning song
(51) take a wild guess
(52) word person
(53) second glasses
(54) persistent son (坚持不懈的;执着的)

2. 利用“内涵相助”的方法说说下面中文句子的英语表达。

(1) That's trade-off.
(2) It's confusing.
(3) It's so embarrassing!
(4) She is in her appointment.
(5) He is my hero.
(6) Are you making an offer?
(7) I'm getting dumped.
(8) He can't handle it.
(9) Put that back where it is belonging.
(10) I'm not comfortable about this.
(11) I painted my hair.
(12) What's done has done.
(13) My duty is to my heart.
(14) You are this close from being suspended.
(15) I'm the citizen of the world.
(16) I can't abandon my friends.

(17) I've got splitting headache.
(18) It's all in your head.
(19) Are you out of you mind?
(20) She's awfully attached.
(21) I know the drill. ([英国口语]常规,正确方法;规定程序)
(22) She has the same size with me.
(23) We should take the plunge.
(24) Do you think it just happened overnight?
(25) He is the most popular guy in school.
(26) There is no place for you to go.
(27) What's the big occasion here?
(28) Do you have to put on such an exhibition?

4. 用本单元所学的知识造句。

(1) Here are a few things that help me when I'm feeling a little down in the dumps.

(2) I love this song! Let's boogie.

(3) How many regrets do you have? How many times have you wished that you would have had the courage to do something?

(4) The judge dedicated his life to fighting corruption.

(5) Would you think less of me if I didn't go to your wedding ceremony?

(6) Why would she cover for someone who was trying to kill her?

(7) Harry took me to a fancy restaurant for our anniversary.

(8) Just give me the lowdown, and you'll be fine.

(9) On second thought, he deserves a decent meal.

(10) The idea of going back to school is tempting, and why not?

(11) "Loving the new and hating the old" is a normal attribute of human behavior.

(12) I'm going to sweet-talk my mom into giving me a new car.

(13) We just have so much baggage.

(14) He complained about being blindsided by the decision.

(15) Dont bargain for an instant cure.

(16) Overcoming suffering and finding happiness are in the blood of all human beings.

(17) We have an opinion in the paper on how to do moral education.

(18) You'd better hold your peace, or you'll ask for trouble.

(19) He has been a bit high-strung lately, because he's been under a lot of pressure at work.

(20) That plan has been cooking for a week.

Chapter 6　Gelivable Affixes (Roots)
词根/词缀给力

1. 请根据词缀或词根提示完成下列词和词组的英语表达。

(1) misspend
(2) undergrounded
(3) well-adjusted person
(4) deportation
(5) citizenship
(6) disgrace
(7) unaccompanied minors
(8) nderdog(斗败了的狗)
(9) self-righteous
(10) sublet
(11) inseparable
(12) insufferable
(13) low-keyed (卑劣的人、下层阶级的人、来历不明的人 lowlife)
(14) chatty
(15) footy
(16) tricky
(17) inexcusable
(18) entangle
(19) for some unknown reason (区别句子 I don't know why)
(20) infamous (notorious)
(21) share-holder
(22) muscular man
(23) disassemble sb
(24) unconditionally
(25) cranky
(26) rebrand oneself
(27) disinvite sb
(28) cosign
(29) midlife crisis
(30) mysteriously missing
(31) ungrateful (忘恩负义的人 ingrate)

(32) to behave in reckless ways
(33) nasty gesture
(34) reputable
(35) publicity
(36) rematch
(37) educative
(38) prophet
(39) flatterer
(40) bystander
(41) overexerted
(42) event planner
(43) sportsmanship
(44) engagement ring
(45) overlook your upbringing
(46) World No-Tobacco Day
(47) unnatural thoughts
(48) under – covered cop
(49) judgmental tone
(50) in all seriousness
(51) a stricken friend
(52) disciplinarian
(53) nonrefundable
(54) malfunction
(55) laughable
(56) dispiriting
(57) threatening note
(58) homicide division

2. 请根据词缀或词根提示完成下列句子的英语表达。

(1) She was powerless.
(2) This blanket is spotless.
(3) I undervalued all of you.
(4) It's unnatural.
(5) I am not heartless.
(6) We have unshakable bond.
(7) You take your life and throw it around just like it is worthless.
(8) No good deed goes unpunished.
(9) It does make you pause and rethinking your parenting.
(10) You are unfeeling.
(11) Are you distrusting my sense of style?

(12) People might view it as a sign of , um, disrespect.

(13) MaybeI misread some signals.

4. 用本单元所学的知识造句。

(1) Kids find *Harry Porter* is areadable book.

(2) The importance of education cannot be overemphasized.

(3) They don't have the time or the energy for meaningless crap.

(4) People can be so self-involved.

(5) His superior grades at high school enabled him to be enrolled at the tuition-free college in New York.

(6) It's not an outrageous question.

(7) I am sorry that I can't attend your lecture due to the pre - arranged appointment.

(8) Although the work of rural teachers is unknown and unappreciated, their dedication is great.

(9) The bank carried out a lot of business to drawcustomers, including inflation - proof interests.

(10) Please don't be so harsh on kids. You are so hypercritical.

(11) I'm coming for your advertisement for a trainee salesperson.

(12) Two-timers always end up in bad situation.

(13) The course is free but you have to provide your own books.

(14) Dads have long been celebrated for their role as breadwinner in the family.

(15) Believe it or not, hot - headed stock investors make better decisions.

(16) Body language is a kind of non - verbal communication.

(17) It is such willful and unreasonable behavior leads to her failure of marriage.

(18) Manyherbal teas use catchy names and packaging to enhance their appeal.

(19) I'm often amazed at how resourceful people are in the poorest families and neighborhoods.

(20) He awoke feeling completely refreshed.

(21) It was now his turn to misjudge his opponent.

Chapter 7　Common Collocations

固定搭配

1. 从固定搭配的角度说说下面中文词组或句子的英语表达。

(1) raise money
(2) dote on
(3) make a wish
(4) be on board
(5) visual aid
(6) and such like
(7) put to the test
(8) cut off all contact(断绝同某人的关系,同某人绝交 throw sb over)
(9) shut sb. out
(10) be in overall charge
(11) for good or ill
(12) take the afternoon off
(13) accept the consequence
(14) make a mess
(15) a sense of humor
(16) sneak out
(17) bump into sb.
(18) win sth. over
(19) pick A over B
(20) have the guts to do
(21) bust up one's family
(22) stick up for sb.
(23) get about
(24) keep an eye on situation
(25) in the hands of fate
(26) be preoccupied with
(27) I am on the way.
(28) Don't count on me!
(29) Don't let me down!
(30) I want to turn myself in.
(31) We're never gonna get along.

(32) Don't ever let me get in the way, please!
(33) Are you by yourself?
(34) I'm trying to figure out.
(35) Let you to catch up.
(36) What are you intended to do with us?
(37) I am running out of fake polite here.
(38) Can't you see I'm enjoying myself?
(39) It is considered somewhat tacky to pass out resumes at a party.
(40) I'm afraid I'm not much good at family history.
(41) The math was so wonderful that he was totally carried away.

2. 从固定搭配角度说说下面英文词组或句子的中文表达。

(1)表决
(2)使震惊,使不安
(3)压力太大了
(4)做个约定
(5)装样子
(6)发号施令;操纵
(7)发情的兔子
(8)背叛某人
(9)最后出现在这儿
(10)努力做好自己分内的工作
(11)不出声,沉默;别费口舌
(12)对……太挑剔
(13)写了一份简历
(14)目空一切
(15)跑腿
(16)直接闯入
(17)在愤怒中冲动行事(act out 把……付诸行动)
(18)与朋友吵架
(19)妄下断论
(20)借题发挥
(21)让某人良心发现(prevail on 劝说)
(22)大费周章
(23)产生负面影响;造成损失
(24)我天生喜欢旅行。
(25)你让我不知所措。
(26)她的婚姻处处碰壁。
(27)她扭头就走。(pull out 撤离现场)
(28)他替我顶罪。

(29)当然还需要更进一步的研究来加以证实。

(30)不过,一些老师已经开始着手了解美国的教育模式。

(31)我对人们总是觉得杯子里还有一半水(指乐观地看问题)已经厌烦透了。

4.用本单元所学的固定搭配造句。

(1)As her teacher,I was very happy for her and hoped that she could hold on her belief, grow healthily and fulfill her dream.

(2)When it is out of control, the anger can quickly turn into a nightmare.

(3)Don't worry, you'll get your figure back in no time.

(4)If you would keep your secret from an enemy, tell it not to a friend.

(5)In case of fire, keep a level head and phone the Fire Department.

(6)He angrily asserted that he had been set up.

(7)Sometimes being willing to play rough is the only way to stop a bully.

(8)I get a cold and I freak out because I know it's going to be there for three weeks.

(9)She passed out when she heard the bad news.

(10)People have told me to my face that my working style is unbearable.

(11)The idea has been around for ages without catching on.

(12)You seemed pretty caught up talking with someone.

(13)So it may sort itself out.

(14)When you've chosen what looks like the best solution, take another couple of minutes to think it through.

(15)For an hour I was walking around in a daze.

(16)A philosopher once said, man can't set foot in two rivers at the same time.

(17)You can get your customers around if you go the right way about it.

(18)We will see to it that every child in the nation (get) good education.

(19)I was about to take the last cake, but he beat me to it.

(20)The only way we'll meet the schedule is to buckle down and get on with the job.

(21)He hel ped patch up Mary's relationship with her mother.

(22)Never has he wrapped up his idea.

(23)Both of them have to settle in their new married life.

(24)Drop a line to a friend if you haven't heard from them for a while, a text or an email.

(25)You'd better brush up on your English since you decide to study in the U. S. A.

(26)I don't want to spoil their fun.

(27)If you lead a stressful life, try to chill out by relaxing with friends after work.

(28)Then why do you shove me away? (push me away)

(29)I tried to make a farewell address to my mother, but I could not breathe a word.

(30)I felt as if I was the only one in the room who didnt have a clue.

(31)Linda asked about you when I met her yesterday.

(32)He came up against a series of problems.

Chapter 8　Free Transition
词性转换

1. 从词性转换的角度说说下面中文词组或句子的英语表达。

(1) outburst n.
(2) getaway n.
(3) upstanding a.
(4) mock – up n.
(5) make amends for (amend v. – n.)
(6) topiece together something
(7) apartment hunting
(8) to take your pick
(9) to trash sb
(10) international pursuit
(11) to frame sb. (试图嫁祸某人 try to frame sb)
(12) to make us suffer
(13) skinny(n. 机密情报;小道消息)
(14) to face the reality
(15) a call to arms
(16) be part of them
(17) to trumpet one' s own praises
(18) to weigh pros and cons(权衡选择 weight sb' s option)
(19) a little communication
(20) to make an exception
(21) to sidebar (v. n. [美国英语]补充新闻报道或特写)
(22) tasting dignity
(23) to keep close watching
(24) to steel oneself to do something
(25) to spy the woman
(26) to fish in troubled waters
(27) a man who is emotionally distraught (distraught adj. 发狂的;心烦意乱的)
(28) be good to one another
(29) I' m furious.
(30) to fire a feeling of interesting
(31) to bridge the gap with sb

(32) Isn't such a good idea?
(33) I just need some air.
(34) You're natural.
(35) I have no doubt.
(36) They've stopped his visitors.
(37) The strong tend to bully the weak.
(38) You're a catch.（catch 值得追求的人）
(39) There was quite brouhaha.（[法] n. brouhaha 骚乱；喧嚷）
(40) It's a hard language.
(41) I'm fooling myself.
(42) I will cup water for you.
(43) Somebody is a frustrated man.
(44) He's got depressed.
(45) No more screw - ups.
(46) Dont disorder my papers.
(47) to distance sb from
(48) If you don't end this...
(49) I am a man of faith.
(50) He buses to work every day.
(51) Stop over for some coffee some time.
(52) Don't wolf down your food.
(53) Sb.'s health took a turn for the worse.
(54) He drafted a draft proposal for the boss to review.
(55) He has had to shoulder the responsibility of supporting family.

2. 从词性转换的角度说说下面英文词组或句子的中文表达。

(1) 报复（n.）
(2) 醇厚，浓郁的
(3) 为运动员送水送毛巾的人
(4) 劝某人谨慎
(5) 聚会
(6) 备用计划（备用的 backup）
(7) 哭穷
(8) 庆祝之夜
(9) 削苹果
(10) 描眉
(11) 替我当班
(12) 自毁前途
(13) 利益冲突
(14) 值第一班

(15)利润分成
(16)立即生效
(17)把指关节弄得吱吱作响
(18)什么东西的吸引力
(19)完全康复
(20)与某人交换地位
(21)示爱
(22)翻阅字典
(23)不小心闯祸
(24)落实一些原则
(25)盘问（v. cross - examine）
(26)换张餐巾
(27)我们走运了。
(28)我很讲道理。
(29)动手吧！
(30)你真投入。
(31)你决定。
(32)给他个惊喜。
(33)我能载你一程吗？
(34)他气得满脸通红。
(35)她讨厌听。
(36)别娇惯你的孩子。
(37)这是个好的结束。
(38)这是你闯的祸。
(39)你骗不了我。
(40)我们感到孤立无援。
(41)我辅修舞蹈课。
(42)父亲的头发开始变白了
(43)我可以给你的牛奶加点糖吗？
(44)你必须得强迫他去做。
(45)你会署真名吗？
(46)他已经用煤灰把脸抹黑了。
(47)他出去给那些植物浇点水。
(48)他们从人群中挤了过去。
(49)这孩子两只眼睛一直盯着巧克力蛋糕。
(50)史密斯先生写了一本关于艾滋病的书。
(51)我可以换个地方换个心情。
(52)你想他带着这种仇恨。
(53)我并不想麻烦你。
(54)你不要跟我唱反调。

4. 用本单元所学的知识造句。

(1) I second his motion that we should set up a special board to examine the problem.

(2) Even if someone mistreats you, your life will not be hard on you.

(3) We first met in library, if memory serves.

(4) She likes to boss her kids around.

(5) I can't produce a meal at such short notice!

(6) The soldier was honorably discharged.

(7) He must man up and tell the truth about what happened.

(8) All of these things dance around the essential truth: we want to be happy.

(9) This question cornered me.

(10) Playing rock music is a good outlet for his energy.

(11) They booted him out of the company for not working.

(12) He trumpeted his son's high intelligence quotient.

(13) I am an optimistic, confident, steel and self-motivated person.

(14) To sustain love, we need to continually fuel whatever inspires us on the deepest level.

(15) Can you free up some time for physical exercise?

(16) They were all dolled up for the party.

(17) All they wanted to make bad blood between them and fish in troubled waters.

(18) We must map out program step by step.

(19) At acafé, the emphasis is not on food and beverages but relaxing in the company of people.

(20) Steven went back into the kitchen to dish up.

(21) All the students in the college rooted for the plan of the new president.

(22) Stop beefing about the price increase.

(23) Peter cannot stomach the violence in that movie.

(24) But when the tempers start to flare, step back and take a breather.

(25) The starving man wolfed down the food.

Chapter 9 Brief Expressions
简洁表达

1. 从简洁表达的角度说说下面中文词组的英语表达。

(1) point taking
(2) no need for that
(3) be good (感觉一切尽在不言中。)
(4) one – man show
(5) second chance
(6) in due time
(7) too much talking
(8) perfect being
(9) make it quick
(10) newbie
(11) stop eating stop sleeping
(12) embezzle money(embezzle 盗用;挪用)
(13) holding company
(14) a terrible connection
(15) for what it's worth
(16) good note
(17) watch your mouth
(18) get one thing straight
(19) happy to oblige
(20) fair enough
(21) declining health
(22) home coming party
(23) public record

2. 从简洁表达的角度说说下面中文句子的英语表达,尤其注意画线部分。

(1) Why ask? (为什么这样问啊?)
(2) Don't be hurt.
(3) Don't stir!
(4) Don't smirk! (smirk 得意的笑)
(5) Save your strength.
(6) No cuts!

(7) I deserved that! (注意语境“你应得的”。)

(8) Is that clear?

(9) You missed.

(10) Back in a moment!

(11) I'm done.

(12) He is family.

(13) That's too much.

(14) Is it done?

(15) Just say the word.

(16) No return.

(17) Sounds like a plan.

(18) Don't make it little.

(19) Treat you on hotpot.

(20) He flatters me.

(21) Anything the matter?

(22) Who's there?

(23) That's none of our concern.

(24) Feel free to watch.

(25) Something means a lot.

(26) Can't wait!

(27) My hopes are up.

(28) Play-offs are on.

(29) It's all set up.

(30) Lunch is served!

(31) Watch your tone.

(32) I owe all it to you.

(33) I ended with her.

(34) That's incredible touching.

(35) Baby's coming soon.

(36) I don't want to be here.

(37) It changed nothing.

(38) Let's get him.

(39) It's too awful (sad) for any words.

(40) Saved.

(41) Be silent this instant, sir!

(42) I'm on a reality to show.

(43) I don't deserve this.

(44) You and I know each other very well.

(45) I will stay single forever.

(46) We have needs.

(47) You're on trial for murder.

(48) Let him now declare.

(49) Didn't you do it with her once?

(50) We can finally be together.

(51) It's too late to turn back now.

(52) I know my place was here.

(53) Are you sure she is trustworthy?

(54) He has big muscles.

(55) Her parents had a lot of dreams on her.

(56) Do you think this girl for me?

(57) You left him? We left each other.

(58) She had no way of knowing the secret.

4.用本单元所学的知识造句。

(1) Nothing personal, but I never socialize with clients.

(2) Relaxed! It's just a quiz.

(3) The rescue is off due to the pass of golden 72 hours.

(4) Don't give up! Look how much you've done already! You're almost there.

(5) Stop blabbering! You are so chatty.

(6) Being a parent is her first priority.

(7) We can count on him. He won't fail us.

(8) Hold your tongue before an elder.

(9) I want to quit this demanding job.

(10) Don't be disappointed if you don't get your way emotionally.

(11) Sources say the royal newlyweds are currently in the Seychelles for a 10 – day trip.

(12) He bought those stocks for a song.

(13) Put the comprehensive capabilities ahead of the performance in exam.

(14) But flexibility comes at a price.

(15) He is a man of few words, but we all like him.

(16) Be specific about where you are and what you can see.

(17) Research suggests that children whose parents split up are more likely to drop out of high school.

(18) We caution readers not to make too much of these findings.

(19) That may not seem fair at the individual level, but it is what it is.

(20) It could be anything really: going out and meeting new people, learning a new language, or even going bungee jumping.

(21) Sarcasm and demeaning remarks have no place in parenting.

(22) Rarely did he raise his voice to anyone.

(23) They will try to catch you out, so have all your answers well prepared.

(24) Don't drink too much wine. Much more and you'll hurt yourself.

(25) He is in a fix to decide which the best answer is.

Chapter 10 Dramatized Expressions
生动表达

1. 下面这些词组表达生动有趣,请试着说出其中文意思。

(1)驾车兜风
(2)手机放在裤子后兜不小心拨了电话
(3)旋风腿
(4)到达(“被风吹进来;偶然来访”。类似的表达还有“drop by”。)
(5)眼光放长远点
(6)好事的人,多管闲事的人
(7)粗人(史前石器时代的)穴居人;野人
(8)大懒虫,贪睡者
(9)怯场
(10)天生当领导的料
(11)轻易得来的钱,投机赚的钱
(12)抗议纸条
(13)大话王
(14)烂尾楼(原)鬼镇;废弃的城市
(15)闺蜜时间
(16)在我看来
(17)承担费用
(18)下班(on the clock 上班)
(19)众目睽睽之下;显而易见;一览无遗
(20)加快速度
(21)侥幸逃脱
(22)前科
(23)特大新闻,即时新闻
(24)繁忙时间表
(25)浅薄之人
(26)头号人选
(27)翻白眼
(28)人气先生
(29)饱受折磨的
(30)不健全的制度(broken English)
(31)内部预映(先睹为快 sneak peek)sneak v. 暗中进行,偷偷做

(32)老花镜、阅读用的放大镜、近视眼镜

(33)保持头脑清醒

(34)长“圆”了(胖)(委婉且生动)

(35)干预

(36)谢幕

(37)意见箱

(38)通力合作

(39)前景美妙的开局

(40)上市

(41)扫兴

(42)随便猜猜

(43)模范员工

(44)摆脱困难,走出深渊

(45)恐高症

(46)会哄小孩的人

(47)全能天才

(48)双人盥洗室

(49)来得正好

(50)枉费心机

(51)通晓历史的

(52)外界传言

(53)板着个脸(雷公脸)

(54)背井离乡

(55)丧气话

(56)各个击破

(57)筋疲力尽(“dead”形容词,“无生气的,呆滞的”。该词组的字面意思是“像死人一样站在那里,了无生气”,形容人“筋疲力尽”的样子。)

(58)临时决定

(59)周围治安不好

(60)色狼

(61)在你偏执的想法里

(62)中了魔法

(63)听得进去意见

(64)被软禁

(65)不计较某人的某事

(66)私房话(wife & husband talk)

(67)小题大做

(68)应大家的要求

(69)尽力表现好

(70)守身如玉

(71)唤回良知
(72)大力推荐
(73)很黏人;麻烦缠身(像强力胶一样老黏着某人,形容某人很黏人或麻烦缠身。)
(74)经过深思熟虑
(75)归根结底……
(76)意义深远
(77)东躲西藏的日子
(78)提及
(79)把事情弄清楚
(80)大为成功("come off/计划、方案等成功";"colors /旗帜","flying colors/胜利的旗帜"。)
(81)缓解某些人之间的紧张关系"thaw/融化";"chilly/寒冷"
(82)热恋中的人
(83)勤工俭学

2. 试体会下面句子中画线部分的生动表达,并说出句子的中文意思。

(1)这是我的强项。
(2)她很漂亮。
(3)你应得的。
(4)你们孤立我。
(5)向某人说清楚。
(6)我放下架子。
(7)你耍我。(你放我的鸽子。)
(8)这下你可倒霉了。
(9)加油!
(10)我不相信爱情。
(11)你瘦了。
(12)你真是守口如瓶。
(13)这是命运神的眷顾。
(14)所有事情都是捏造的。
(15)他总是循规蹈矩。
(16)我是废人一个。
(17)我说了算。
(18)你看透了我。
(19)你是我心中的至宝。
(20)我可不会照着你的规矩来。
(21)就会往积极的方面想。
(22)真是个美好的惊喜!
(23)我的耐心有限。
(24)我确实没时间。(抽空做什么 spare time for sth.)

(25)你没有尽力。

(26)你让我过得生不如死。

(27)但我觉得他是有大麻烦了。

(28)他从未对我敞开心扉。

(29)今晚的事够人们议论的了。(feed off 以……为食物的来源;从……获得供应)

(30)也许你还娶错了老婆。

(31)那我们只好得拐弯抹角了。

(32)你们对圣经有自己的理解。

(33)现在,手机可是年轻人的命根子啊。

(34)男人对你趋之若鹜。

(35)你不是给他下逐客令了吗?(marching orders 被逐离场)

(36)大家都很想见她的新男友。("dying to 急于",这个短语表示急于做某事,急得快要死了。)

(37)你要是对老师撒谎就会有麻烦。(be in the hot seat 遇到麻烦)

(38)我弟弟脾气暴躁,常惹是生非。(stir up trouble 惹是生非)

(39)她很擅长对上司溜须拍马。(dance attendance upon someone 奉承某人,向某人献殷勤)

(40)山姆决定不去上课,下午到湖里游泳。(cut class 逃课、旷课)

(41)在莉莎搬进新居不久,就与邻居交上了朋友。("in no time 非常迅速地";"no time"就是说"没费时间",比喻行动非常迅速。)

(42)他先是发生不幸的事情;然后又破产了;他进来真是倒霉透了。(down on one's luck 倒霉)

4.用本单元所学的知识造句。

(1)He is outgoing and making friends is like taking candy from a baby.

(2)We searched high and low for a better place to live, but in the end, we stayed in our old house.

(3)A wife may hit the ceiling because her husband forgot their wedding anniversary.

(4)I can't remember anyone of that name; and yet somehow it seems to ring a bell.

(5)Don't worry. He has Three Rules for living high on a shoestring budget.

(6)Dont push the panic button. Time is enough.

(7)The computers in the accounting department are always on the blink and the bills don't get paid on time.

(8)Attending meetings like this drives me all up a wall.

(9)Many things had changed a lot. You'd better wake up and smell the coffee.

(10)Many people have an itch for excitement.

(11)She is still in the dark and doesn't know about it at all.

(12)We've no time to waste, so let's get cracking.

(13)The company has been on the rocks since the Internet bubble was exploded.

(14)Don't ask for his ideas. He is a yes—man.

(15) Since she only has a temporary job. She has to live from hand to mouth.

(16) I want you out of here—kit and caboodle—by noon.

(17) She is so shy and sensitive you have to handle her with kid gloves.

(18) Jack is a motor—mouth. I can never get a word in.

(19) Our holiday got off to a flying start because the weather was good and the trains were on time.

(20) So you're only supposed to use fatal force when you run out options.

(21) He always has to have the last word in any argument.

(22) The suffering and failures of the past year are put behind us.

(23) Were you always confident that you had a rock solid case?

Chapter 11 Regular Expressions
常用表达

2. 用本单元所学的知识造句。

(1) Poor performance in exam is not the point. The point is you didn't put your focus on it.

(2) Don't ask me anything about him. I'm done with him.

(3) It's a long story, I don't have time to tell you the details now.

(4) Thank you for your timely help. You are so sweet.

(5) Don't trouble yourself with such a trifle.

(6) Dinner is served around 7 pm or even later.

(7) Do you have an appointment with any of your financial advisors?

(8) So what's up with you and the new guy?

(9) You won't worry about the time as much if you are enjoying yourself in sports.

(10) I've been asked this questions so many times, and to be honest, I have no idea.

(11) What's all that noise about outside?

(12) We have to be careful about injuries but we have to prepare for that game.

(13) For your own sake, let go of the past.

(14) He will respond to that, not me.

(15) One more thing, where is your restaurant?

(16) Don't panic! It's good to think ahead, but it is useless to worry about things beyond your control.

(17) Who's that in the picture with you?

(18) This can't work——to keep the class order by physical punishment. You should have more communication with students.

(19) I got it. You want me to come home right after school.

(20) To me, this all just seems to make sense and I think it's readable.

(21) What's the deal? Are you coming to the party or not?

(22) I'm not blaming you. I'm just saying.

(23) I very appreciate you have come.

(24) Thank you for coming tonight and have a safe drive home.

(25) You get good learning skills for just listening to us. That's it.

(26) A: Nice to see you . How goes it? B: Thanks, everything's ok.

(27) A: What do you think he is going to do? B: You got me.

(28) For Pete's sake, stop smoking, will you?

(29) Do you mean that you want to pack them back?

(30) It is very generous of you to lend your new car to them.

(31) He often apple—polishes me and I' m flattered.

(32) Goodbye, and have a nice day.

(33) You don't get what you deserve. This is normal.

(34) What a surprise! What brings you here?

(35) I' m sorry to keep you waiting so long. That' s fine to me.

(36) But the delay has frustrated those who feel time is running out.

(37) What a waste to throw it away!

(38) This is amazing. These American high school students can sing this Chinese song.

(39) I' ll check it soon, and give you an answer within the week.

(40) See you around. Remember to bring the book this afternoon.

(41) Dont bother. I can help myself.

(42) I am so glad to see that you can be so wise and I believe you can make it!

(43) I' d like to thank you for your help. Let' s go get dinner together. My treat!

(44) The reception desk is straight ahead. After you, please.

(45) Just a moment. Ill see if he is available. Please take a seat.

(46) If you dont want to come, dont come. Suit yourself.

(47) I got an interview yesterday, but I screwed it up.

(48) I couldnt tell you exactly how bad it is yet.

(49) To be honest, who cares?

(50) I got to run, my books are due in the library.

(51) Please, don' t mention that. This is not happening.

(52) Thank you for your sensible advice. It means too much for me.

(53) We' re newcomers in this activity. What we' re supposed to do?

(54) Mom, dad, this is not what you think. You have to believe me.

(55) Please hang on a second; I' ll look for the manager and tell him you are on the phone for him.

(56) If you don' t watch your back in this company, you' ll find your colleagues taking advantage of you.

(57) Please pardon me for not arriving soon.

(58) I' ll take care of it personally.

(59) No offense, but I really dont care about what you are saying.

(60) Don' t you dare do him the slightest harm!

(61) What' the occasion? You won the lottery?

(62) That doesnt concern you. I' ll handle it myself.

(63) Where' s the newspaper? Search me, I havent seen it.

(64) Can your recommend some books on English conversation for me?

(65) Let' s listen to some music. What do you day?

(66) Whatever you say. I' m too nervous to think.

(67) Are we going to eat Chinese dishes or Indian dishes? Whatever.

(68) Will you tell her? <u>You bet</u> (I will).

(69) Are you ready to go? <u>Do you have everything</u>?

(70) Don't worry about it. It'll pass soon. <u>It always does.</u>

(71) <u>What gives</u>? There are three police cars parked outsides.

(72) <u>It's now or never</u>. Shall we chance it?

(73) <u>You must be mad</u> to do such a thing.